WHERE THE END BEGINS

a new story emerges

Stephanie C. Vang

Windgarden
Books

Message from the Author

Dear Readers,

Thank you for embarking on this deeply personal journey with me. After enduring 20 years in a toxic and abusive marriage, I found myself divorced, never anticipating that I would find love again. I had never known unconditional love until I met my husband, Logan. He restored my belief in true, everlasting love. Losing him so unexpectedly and early in life brought about the deepest pain I have ever experienced.

I'm not one to openly share my feelings, not even with those closest to me, especially when it comes to sorrow. My husband was the only person I confided in wholeheartedly; he was the keeper of all my secrets, fears, happiness, and dreams. After losing him, I began documenting all my memories, fearing I would forget them. As I wrote, I realized that revisiting our memories was like stepping through a portal, bringing me back to him and helping me grieve. Additionally, unexplainable things started happening, which I also captured in my writing. Somehow, every memory and experience transformed into this book.

"Where the End Begins" is more than a memoir; it's a testament to the resilience of the human spirit and the enduring power of love that transcends realms, proving that love never dies. Within these pages, I delve into the depths of grief, the heights of healing, and the transformative nature of loss.

Through every word, I reveal layers of my vulnerability. I

invite you to witness not only the profound emotions of falling deeply in love with my twin flame—from happiness, hopes, and pleasure to the intensity of our bond—but also the raw and excruciating pain of losing him.

This book is a tribute to my beloved husband, whose memory and ethereal presence continue to inspire me every day. I hope that by sharing my story, I can offer solace and courage to those navigating their paths of loss, healing, or spiritual awakening. May you find moments of reflection, inspiration, and ultimately, a renewed sense of hope within these pages.

Perhaps one day, in another life, my husband and I will stumble upon this book in an old-fashioned bookstore somewhere and simply know—this was our story, once again.

With love and gratitude,

Stephanie C Vang

Meet me where the end begins, in echoes,
Where your world is me, and my world is you.

- Author unknown

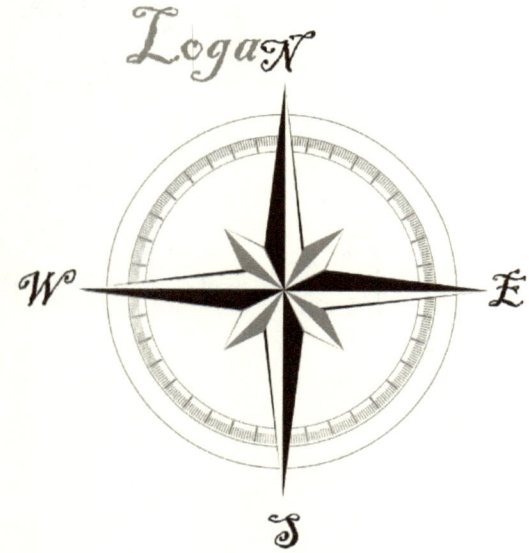

For my dearest husband, Logan,

Thank you for your unwavering
authenticity and boundless love,
And for the precious gift of self-love
that you have bestowed upon me.
Through seven lifetimes, I have cherished you,
And I vow to continue loving you through countless more.
With eternal gratitude and devotion.

Until we're home again.

PROLOGUE: *Unraveled*

MY HUSBAND WAS LIKE MY FAVORITE oversized knitted sweater— warm, safe, bold, and comforting, and he was unequivocally mine. As an empath, I feel the weight of the world differently, sensing every emotion around me, sometimes all at once. There have been times when the flood of emotions becomes overwhelming, and I feel it engulfs me entirely.

On my toughest days, he'd drop everything to wrap his arms around me with care and love. I knew everything was alright because he was my sanctuary, a haven where all my worries dissipated. I'd let down my guard and let all the emotions I had been holding unravel. He'd hold me for as long as I needed, without rushing, because he just knew. The stress and weight I had carried melted away effortlessly.

When my tears dried, he would ask in a low caring voice if I felt better and if I wanted to talk about it, never making me feel diminished. He was always patient and gentle, yet undeniably strong. He understood me in a way no one else did, as if my soul was an extension of his own. It was as though God had crafted him solely for me.

His passing began as a snag on my favorite sweater, and grieving felt like the unraveling of torn yarn—irreparable, no matter how diligently I tried to mend or undo it.

I'd see steak at the grocery store, and my heart would clench as tears welled up in my eyes—his favorite meal came to mind. The roads we have traveled on hold so many of our memories like a recorder. Every time I drive through them, our memories are replayed back to me, and I can hear our conversations, his jokes, and laughter—the ones that fill my heart with contentment and love; the yarn of my favorite sweater unravels further.

My tears continued as I carefully planned his funeral, selecting his last outfit and attending to every detail that reminded me of what he loved most. Closing his accounts, dissolving our shared businesses, and organizing his belongings—his car, his garage, his tools, putting them away one last time—the yarn unraveled even more. Each act tugged at the fabric of my existence, and it was painful to witness the gradual loss of my favorite sweater, piece by piece.

As I watched his casket close and my favorite person lowered into the earth, my heart shattered into pieces beyond what I could have imagined possible. My once perfect and beautiful favorite sweater had transformed into a tangled mess of yarn—knotted with grief, love, and the lingering memories he left behind. It was no longer the same comforting sweater it once was. I could no longer wrap it around me to find solace or reassure myself that everything was okay.

While those who knew him mourned in their own ways, this favorite sweater of mine held a uniquely profound significance. No one wore it like I did, and no one could see it or feel it like I did. This is the essence of grieving—intensely personal and often solitary. Though the world may offer its sympathy and attempt to understand what I'm going through, the truth is no one can fully grasp the depth of my pain. So, if you see me lost in my tears, understand that there are no words that can ease or mend this grief. Simply give me the space to cry for as long as my heart needs.

CONTENTS

INTRODUCTION

TWO DAYS AFTER MY HUSBAND'S TRAGIC PASSING, I found myself seated at our kitchen table, staring at a crumpled hand towel before me. Sleep had eluded me for days, leaving my eyes tired and swollen, my mind cloaked in a foggy haze of exhaustion. I felt mentally besieged, grappling with the harsh reality of what had unfolded. The moment I received the call that shattered my world played over and over in my mind, haunting me in traumatic depths. The pain in my heart was palpable, almost physical, as if a heavy brick had been forcefully lodged into my chest. Its jagged edges scraped against my wounded heart with each breath, making it difficult to even inhale. How my heart continued to beat under such weight, I couldn't fathom.

A sudden panic overcame me as I strained to remember our last moments together, a cherished memory that felt as if it was slipping like sand through my fingers. *What had we said to each other? Was there a parting kiss? Did I walk him to his car, or had I been too engrossed in work, merely watching his departure from the detached view of my upstairs office window?* I asked myself as more questions swirled through my mind.

Desperate for clarity, I searched my memory, but the details wouldn't materialize. It had only been two days since I received the harrowing news of his passing, and only three days since I last saw him. *How could my mind betray me? Was this my new reality? Had I truly lost the love of my life to an abyss so vast it seemed cruel?* Countless questions ran through my mind. It felt like a nightmare, too unbearable to face, and if this was indeed my new reality, I cannot lose my memories of him as well.

Holding my breath, I closed my eyes and immersed myself in the depths of my recollections of him. Gradually, his smile began to emerge in the darkness of my mind, his laughter and voice gently breaking through the silence. I yearned to reach out, to feel his reassuring embrace just once more. Tears cascaded down my cheeks as the floodgates of memory flung open, unleashing a torrent of emotions.

We were supposed to share a lifetime together, yet fate had allotted us only less than five years. Determined not to let a single cherished moment fade into the escaping grains of time, I hurried upstairs to my office and positioned myself at my desk.

With determined fingers, I began to chronicle every nuanced detail of our final moments together on the screen of my computer. My intent was clear: to preserve this memory with such vividness and emotion that decades from now, even as I navigated the twilight of my years, I could revisit it as if it had unfolded just yesterday. Like a portal, it would take me back to him through my recounted memories.

In the wake of profound loss, we are transformed, forever altered by the love that once touched us. As I tenderly immortalized each cherished memory, I discovered that the love I feared lost was quietly weaving its way back into my heart, mending the fractures with gentle persistence. He had not truly left me, for the love he bestowed upon me continued to glow—a cherished ember that warmed the cold nights.

How to Read This Book: To maintain an uninterrupted and engaging narrative flow, I have included footnotes throughout this memoir. These footnotes serve a dual purpose: they provide precise dates for the events described and timestamps for the photos taken. Additionally, they offer explanations of specific terms, events, and individuals pivotal to understanding the broader context. I encourage you to refer to these notes as you read through my journey to gain deeper insight into my experiences.

CHAPTER 1

Goodbye California

*I*T WAS THE SUMMER OF 2019 AND IT SUDDENLY DAWNED ON ME that there were only two weeks left before the end of July and my impending move to Minnesota. What seemed so certain two months ago when I was on the phone with my dad had now been laden with fear and panic and I realized I wasn't ready to make this move.

A few of my close friends and cousins had gathered at my place to share a meal with me and celebrate this new chapter I'd be embarking on. Up until just a few minutes ago, I was sure of my decision. Little did I know that while reminiscing about life since high school, my cousin Rachel's casual quip about not being able to keep up with my addresses or phone numbers anymore would trigger a panic attack. It forced me to retreat, fearing this move would just be another empty endeavor amidst my uncertainties. I didn't want them to witness my emotional breakdown, especially after maintaining a strong facade for so long.

Politely excusing myself from my company, I retreated to the bathroom and locked the door behind me. Leaning over the sink, my hands trembled as I grasped a handful of water and splashed it onto my face. The cool droplets offered a fleeting sense of relief against my flushed skin. I rinsed my mouth and spat out the water, watching it cascade down the drain, mirroring the rush of thoughts swirling through my mind.

Breathing became a struggle, each inhalation feeling like a battle against an invisible force constricting my chest. My heart raced, its erratic beats pounding as if seeking an escape from the overwhelming tide of emotions crashing over me.

This was the second time in my life I found myself in the grip of a panic attack, a relentless storm brewing within the confines of my own body. The first instance occurred during my early career days when I was tasked with giving an impromptu presentation to high-level executives, caught off guard and unprepared. Yet, that moment of anxiety paled in comparison to the sheer intensity of the emotions I was grappling with now. It felt as though every fear, doubt, and worry I had ever harbored had converged into a storm, threatening to engulf me completely.

As water droplets continued to fall off my face, I felt the weight of impending change pressing down on me. I couldn't help but question every decision that had led me to this moment. My move to Minnesota loomed over me like a daunting challenge. *What had I been thinking? Was this new chapter of my life truly a step forward, or a leap into a raging ocean where I couldn't see beneath the dark abyss?*

The bathroom, once a place of mundane routines, had now become a sanctuary for my spiraling thoughts. I sank to the cool tiles and covered my face. My warm tears mingled with the coolness of the water droplets, created a bittersweet sensation against my skin.

It wasn't just about the physical act of moving—it was about leaving behind a life that, despite its flaws, had become familiar. I felt like a fugitive from my own existence, fleeing from a past that had lost its luster and meaning. Yet, in my quest for a fresh start, I found myself on a path filled with unpredictability and ambiguity, each step forward tinged with trepidation.

After two decades in a marriage that had soured well before its official end, I found myself divorced. It had been a long time coming, marked by toxicity that left permanent scars, both visible and hidden. Yet, despite the clear signs to let go, I clung to the wreckage for all the wrong reasons: my children, my fear of being alone, my parents' reputation, and the small glimmer of hope that if I continue loving him long enough, enduring his abuse, he might just notice my unselfish love and change.

In the three years since my divorce, I dipped my toes into the murky waters of dating. It was a foreign experience for me, as my ex-husband was my first love and only relationship, and then I married him. This new landscape was clouded and riddled with emotional landmines I was not expecting. My empathic nature, a double-edged sword, allowed me to sense deeply and feel the nuances of every interaction, but it also made me prone to overanalysis and intense emotional responses that I could never express due to years of conditioning. As a child, I was told not to say things if they "weren't pretty" or "tsis zoo nkauj.[1]" As an adult, my ex-husband would meet me with his fist before his words if he sensed any displeasure in my conduct.

The men I've dated were successful and accomplished, each in their own right, with their own strengths and charms. On the surface, they seemed like a good fit, but beneath the veneer of compatibility, there was a fundamental disconnect. They couldn't grasp the depth of my emotions or the intensity with which I experienced the world. This left me to believe that I was too much, too complicated, too sensitive, that I

---

[1] A Hmong phrase, "tsis zoo nkauj" or "tsis zoo mloog," which often means that if it isn't pleasant to the ears, then it shouldn't be said.

thought too much, or that I was not enough at all. I was never fully comfortable around any of them to truly be myself in my vulnerability.

It wasn't that they lacked empathy or kindness; it was simply that they couldn't comprehend how deeply my feelings ran. It was something I didn't know how to explain to them because I don't quite understand it myself when my emotions fall apart. As each relationship fizzled out, I came to a poignant realization: *perhaps relationships, at least in the traditional sense, weren't my forte.*

I concluded that even if I were to spend the rest of my days in solitude, navigating life's twists and turns alone—with the exception of my children—I would still find contentment in my own company.

However, at the age of 40, a profound sense of self-doubt settled over me like a dense fog, obscuring the future I had once envisioned. The life I had imagined, complete with milestones and accomplishments, now seemed elusive. I lost my drive, which takes me back to two months ago.

In a moment of raw vulnerability, with tears streaming down my cheeks, I called my dad, who had always been a wise lighthouse in my harbor during storms. I poured out my heart, confessing my overwhelming desire to reset my life entirely—to wipe the slate clean and embark on a new journey. One where I wasn't bound by the constraints of the life I had built, where everything I once thought I wanted began to gradually come undone after my divorce.

My dad listened patiently to my emotional outpouring. His words offered gentle reassurance, urging me not to despair. "Don't cry," he comforted me. "Why don't you consider moving to Minnesota? Your mom, your stepmom, and I are all here for you. There's still so much ahead for you. It might be the ideal place for you to gather your thoughts and rediscover who you are outside of the roles that have defined you."

As I hung up the phone, his words echoed in my mind, planting the seed of a new beginning—perhaps a *change of scenery* could be the catalyst for *inner exploration* and *self-discovery*. This time, my journey wouldn't be driven by career aspirations or familial responsibilities, but by a quest to reconnect with the essence of who I am, beyond the titles of wife, mother, or career professional. I yearned to rediscover the person who once thrived on life's adventures, found joy in music, art, and cultural exploration, and felt a deep-seated desire to positively impact my community.

For too long, I had felt tethered to the expectations and obligations that came with marriage, career, and parenthood. These roles had dictated the course of my life, shaped my decisions, and overshadowed my own desires. But in that pivotal moment, I craved *liberation*—a chance to *relinquish* control and let the *winds of change carry me toward uncharted territories*.

You might think that after 15 different addresses over the last 20 years, scattered across the country, I'd be used to moving by now. But it seems the more I move, the less I understand what "home" really means, and that was the *root of my panic*. I grew up in Fresno, and in my yearning to find "home," I thought returning to Fresno would fulfill that need. Yet, less than a year later, I find myself moving again, unsure if I'm going somewhere or running away from some place. All this moving around feels like I'm just chasing the ghost of a home that doesn't really exist for me—a perpetual quest for a *sense of belonging* that continues to elude me.

July is disappearing too quickly.

So here I am, despite the allure of a fresh start, torn between the familiarity of the past and the tentativeness of the future. My tears continue to mingle with doubt on the bathroom floor, in a silent battle raging between the comfort of staying put and the fear of embracing the unknown.

After what felt like an eternity in my own confinement, I regained my composure and stepped out of the bathroom. The evening sky had already crept up on us through the window, and some of my friends were still in the kitchen cleaning up.

As soon as I stepped back into the kitchen, Janet joked, "Did you fall into the toilet?" Her laughter rang out. "Blame it on Mary," she added playfully. "That coconut curry noodle broth was spicy." Laughter burst out, filling the room as Janet clarified her teasing and commented that the food was indeed very good. Mary, who used to work in a Thai restaurant, makes, in my opinion, the finest Thai curry noodles. Despite my reluctance for a farewell gathering, I relented under one condition—Mary's Thai curry noodles had to be on the menu. She was the only person I knew who made it the way I liked it, with extra coconut cream.

"Minnesota would be so lucky to have you. You've done so much here in California. I just know that whatever you do there, you'll make waves of success," Mary said with a smile.

"Quite honestly, I'm tired. I just want to be a hermit," I responded.

"Go get yourself a Minnesota man and be happy!" Janet exclaimed, having the biggest grin on her face.

"Yeah, I'll just snag myself a five-foot-eight Minnesota man," I responded sarcastically, forcing a false laugh.

None of the men I'd been in relationships with were taller than 5'3", not that I care much about it—I'm only 5'0". But if I were to conjure the man of my dreams, I'd envision someone taller, someone whose height would allow me to look up into his deep, soulful eyes even when I wore heels. Then again, it really doesn't matter anyway. I'm done with relationships for the foreseeable future.

Before the evening was over, I took out my phone and captured one last photo of us sitting around my kitchen table.[2] A token to remind me that no matter where or how far I travel, I can always come back to visit

---

[2] Photo timestamped at 8:23 p.m. on Saturday, July 20th, 2019.

those who love me and hold dear to my heart.

After all my guests had departed, I stood in the midst of my nearly empty home and exhaled a somber sigh. The space now held only the bare essentials, the items I still needed until our move. My oldest daughter Charlotte would dispose of everything afterward. The nomadic rhythm of my life over the past two decades, dictated by career demands, had instilled in me a certain detachment from materialistic objects. With each move, I shed possessions like old skin, leaving behind a trail of memories and a sense of liberation from the weight of worldly goods.

This time was no different; we bid farewell to our furniture and household items, parting with them through sales or donations. The items we wanted to hold onto, such as clothing and a collection of sentimental treasures attached to stories and emotions that made them priceless to me, had already been shipped to my dad's address in Minnesota.

It was time to say good-bye to California. *Again.*

CHAPTER 2

HELLO MINNESOTA

*W*EDNESDAY MORNING ARRIVED, [3] and it marked the beginning of a new chapter as Charlotte, dropped off my son, Keith, and me at the airport.

"Thank you for dropping us off," I said to Charlotte, holding her tightly in one last embrace before our departure.

"Anytime, Mom. Just let me know when you've landed in Minnesota," she replied. She turned to Keith, embracing him tightly, then carefully helped us unload our two carry-ons from the trunk of her car. As we made our way to the airport entrance, she kept her eyes on us, waving one last time until we vanished from her sight. Then she climbed back into her car and drove off.

We were living in San Diego five years ago when Charlotte graduated from high school. She hasn't lived with me since. Immediately after graduating, she moved to Fresno for school and work because her

---

[3] Wednesday, July 31, 2019 at 9:30 a.m.

boyfriend and best friends lived there. Just last year, she and her boyfriend got engaged and moved in together. Although parting with her in California tugged at my heart, I found reassurance in knowing she is very capable. My future son-in-law is an exceptional young man, and I am confident they will take great care of each other in my absence.

As we navigated through the airport, a subtle shift in my emotions took hold—a sense of hope amidst the sea of doubt and discomfort that had engulfed me just two weeks prior when I was crying on the bathroom floor. I've come to recognize that when my heart is set on something, everything else seems to align without wavering. It's usually when my mind is the decision-maker that I tend to talk myself out of things when faced with distress.

Making our way through airport security brought an unexpected encounter. Keith was faced with questioning from a TSA agent probing into his age and details of his schooling. He was taller than the average teenager, and she was in disbelief that he was only 12. The agent's tone and demeanor were borderline intrusive. She asked Keith, "If you're really 12, then why do you have facial hair?" It was a moment that caught us off guard, leaving Keith visibly uncomfortable and unsure how to respond.

In that moment, I felt a surge of protectiveness, addressing the agent, "I understand your need to be diligent, but I assure you he's a minor and my son. You're making him uncomfortable." I asserted, reminding her of the sensitivity required when interacting with young travelers.

Fortunately, a TSA manager intervened, diffusing the situation, and allowing us to proceed through security without further hindrance.

As I settled into my seat and fastened the seatbelt, the familiar routine of air travel sank in. The engine hummed to life, and I watched through the window as the world outside transformed from stationary to a blur of motion. The plane ascended, carrying with it a mix of emotions that stirred within me like a gentle whirlwind.

Looking out at the passing scenery below, I couldn't help but reflect on the significance of this move. Leaving California, the state that had been my home for most of my life, evoked a bittersweet mix of emotions. It was anticipation tinged with nostalgia dancing in my heart, weaving a tapestry of memories and hopes for the future.

As our flight neared Minneapolis, it was a quarter after three in the afternoon. The landscape below unfolded like a patchwork quilt, with shimmering bodies of water dotting the terrain. From above, it truly was the land of ten thousand lakes—an emerald city regarded by many as the land of opportunity for the Hmong American dream. The Twin Cities held the largest Hmong population in the country, and I was about to immerse myself in it.

One particular lake caught my eye.[4] From my angle, its shape resembled a heart etched into the earth's canvas. It appeared like a precious gem, a testament to the natural beauty that graced this state. In that moment, as the plane descended closely over the heart-shaped lake, a sense of serenity washed over me. It was a silent acknowledgment, a whispered reassurance from the universe that I was on the right path. Despite the uncertainties that lay ahead, the sight of that heart-shaped lake affirmed that this could be home. I took out my phone and captured a photo of the lake for memory.[5]

The moment I stepped out of the airport, the Minnesota air greeted me with a freshness I hadn't felt in years. My Dad met us outside baggage claim and loaded our luggage into the back of his car. He expressed how happy he was that we were finally in Minnesota. After my parents' divorce ten years ago, he has since remarried and relocated

---

[4] Lake Bde Maka Ska in Minneapolis, Minnesota.

[5] Photo timestamped at 3:44 p.m. on Wednesday, July 31, 2019

to Minnesota from Colorado to be closer to my uncles and his new in-laws. As we drove toward his house, his enthusiasm for the surrounding area was infectious. He pointed out hiking trails and parks with such excitement that I couldn't help but feel a spark of thrill myself.

The view outside the car window unfolded into a lush scene of vibrant trees and shrubs, a stark departure from the golden dryness of California that I often teased as why it's called the "Golden State." Now, surrounded by this flourishing foliage, I couldn't help but be captivated by the charm of this unfamiliar landscape. The natural splendor of the area was undeniable, and as we continued to drive on, my initial doubts about relocating here began to dissipate.

Arriving at my dad's house, I was shown to my room. Though small, it was a sanctuary of my own on the first floor. Adjacent to my room was a private bathroom with a jetted tub that my dad and stepmom had recently installed, and I imagined myself soaking away the daily tensions. The boxes I had shipped ahead of time were neatly stacked against the wall, waiting to be unpacked and turned into familiar comforts.

As I settled onto the bed, looking up at the ceiling, a sense of peace was starting to settle within me.

"Minnesota, I guess you're my home now," I murmured to myself, releasing a sigh of acceptance as the reality of my decision began to sink in.

The doubts and worries that had clouded my mind prior to moving seemed trivial now, replaced by a growing curiosity and interest in this new chapter of my life.

Perhaps I should have made this move sooner, I thought.

Suddenly, realizing that I hadn't spoken to Charlotte since our arrival, I swiftly dialed her number. Within two rings, she answered.

"Hi, Mom," she greeted. "I already miss you and Keith."

"I miss you too," I replied. "Just wanted to let you know we've landed. Grandpa picked us up, and now I'm contemplating whether to unpack right away or save it for another day.

"How are you liking Minnesota?" she inquired.

"It's actually quite lovely," I shared. "Green and beautiful, and so many parks and trails. Makes me think I could grow to love this place and call it home."

Our conversation continued for another 10 minutes before I reluctantly said I had to go. My dad and stepmom had prepared dinner ahead of our arrival, and I didn't want to seem rude by lingering in my room.

"Love you, Mom," Charlotte said. I quickly echoed the sentiment before ending the call.

Entering the kitchen, the inviting smell of a homecooked meal filled the room with a sense of nostalgia. Despite having been away for over two decades, the familiar scents and sounds of my dad's cooking immediately brought back a sense of my childhood.

Growing up, my parents often mentioned that we didn't have much, yet I never truly felt the effects of scarcity. Everything they provided always seemed sufficient, and I never yearned for more or less. Our family of eight siblings, with me being the oldest, would gather around the dining table with our parents for meals, and there would always be lively chatters as my mom reminded us to eat and not talk so much because the food was getting cold. Whether it was a simple dish like ramen noodles and eggs or something more elaborate, it always felt like the best meal, especially when my bowl of ramen was accompanied by a scoop of rice—something I still enjoy now and then as an adult.

My job had taken me all over the world, and though I enjoyed immersing myself in different cultural cuisines, the rarity of a home-cooked meal was truly missed. Being here in my dad's home and sharing the simple pleasures of a meal together with my son feels like circling back again to simpler days.

CHAPTER 3

THOSE EYES

I WOKE UP EARLY SUNDAY MORNING.[6] It had been four days since our arrival in Minneapolis, and I found myself in a contemplative state, still adjusting to the idea of this new beginning. Despite the passing days, I hadn't reached out to anyone in town to share my arrival, nor had I made any concrete plans. I needed this time to navigate the unfamiliarity and establish my priorities.

One certainty in this transition was a new client I had secured in Golden Valley, a pharmaceutical company. It was only a 15-minute drive from my dad's place, conveniently close, offering a new professional chapter. For the past five years since starting my consulting firm to provide IT integrations and management consultation for highly regulated industries, I've been working remotely and traveling 80% of the time to clients' sites, including locations as far as Japan. Moving here and reducing my work to predominantly remote meant not having to

---

[6] August 4, 2019

travel anymore, which was a much-needed change from my burnt-out lifestyle of living out of suitcases. Starting work with this new client in a week gave me a refreshing focal point despite the distractions of my current precariousness.

Reflecting on my past, I recalled a time when Minnesota was the last place I would have imagined calling home. Living in Denver at the time,[7] I had an opportunity to move to Minnesota after graduating from college. I was given two job offers: one in Minneapolis and the other in San Diego. Both were equally competitive, offering enticing opportunities and generous benefits. However, choosing sunny beaches over the snowy tundra was an easy decision.

Yet here I was, embracing uncharted territories. The only time I had ever been to Minnesota was a year ago when I was invited to speak at an event on emerging technologies. Before settling on moving here, I had considered other states but then realized that I would end up in the same boat as when I was living in San Diego and Long Beach—stranded in a beautiful paradise but depressed with no family around.

My thoughts drifted to my twin daughters and siblings in Denver, and the idea of being closer to them. Then there was the allure of Seattle, my favorite city, which also lingered in the back of my mind—a place I thought I would one day retire to. There was something about the rain there that always seemed to clear the hazy fog from my mind and infuse it with creativity—something I craved.

However, I was determined to give Minnesota a fair chance—a year or two, perhaps—before reconsidering my options. After my panic attack, I resolved that life was never meant to be spent in one place, as it always had a way of surprising us. I was ready to see where this unexpected journey would lead me.

---

[7] Late spring of 2004

After spending half a day delving into the task of unboxing my belongings, my phone chimed, displaying Jasmine's name. She was my brother's ex-girlfriend, with whom I had maintained a cordial relationship even after their breakup a few months prior.

"Hey, are you in town yet?" Jasmine's voice floated through the phone.

"Yeah, I've been here for a few days, just sorting through boxes," I replied, glancing at the remaining boxes still waiting for my attention.

"Great! Would you be up for a little trip? I need to pick up my brother. He was discharged from the hospital a few days ago and needs a ride to a friend's house. If you have some time to spare, I'll pick you up," Jasmine's request was subtly urgent.

I hesitated momentarily, eyeing the remaining task. It had been four days since my arrival, and I hadn't ventured beyond the confines of my new abode.

"Sure, pick me up. I'll get ready," I agreed, deciding that a change of scenery and a chance to connect with Jasmine in person were worth the diversion.

Half an hour later, my phone buzzed again, announcing Jasmine's arrival. I quickly informed my son, Keith, that I'll be heading out and will return later.

"Okay, Mom. Have a great time," Keith's voice echoed from his room upstairs.

"Thanks. Love you, Sweetie," I replied, excited to see Minnesota on this lovely day.

Stepping outside, I was greeted by Jasmine's friendly smile as I settled into the passenger seat of her tiny blue sedan. Despite nearly a year of virtual communication since she began dating my brother Jake, this was the first time I met her in person.

"Hi, sister," Jasmine greeted cheerfully, her smile beaming as soon as I opened the car door.

"Hello, Jasmine," I responded, the excitement of finally meeting her face-to-face evident in my tone. "It's wonderful to finally meet you in person, even though I feel like I already know you so well from our conversations."

Jasmine's affection for my brother was apparent, a complex blend of lingering emotions and unspoken hopes. She wore her heart on her sleeve, her love for him sometimes bordering on overwhelming. However, my brother wasn't quite ready for the level of commitment she desired, leaving their relationship in a delicate balance of off-again and on-again. This time, it was off. Despite these nuances, Jasmine was undeniably charming—a bit eccentric, occasionally over the top, but charming, nonetheless.

We drove to Jasmine's brother's house and waited in the car while she called him on the phone to come out. Moments later, peering out of the car window, I noticed a tall man emerging from the house we were parked in front of, moving with caution and clutching his abdomen in discomfort, a clear sign of ongoing recovery. He bore no resemblance to Jasmine. Jasmine was Black, but the man was clearly Hmong.

"Is that your brother?" I inquired, nodding towards the man approaching us.

"Yes, that's my brother," Jasmine confirmed with a laugh, quickly adding, "from another mother." She obviously noticed the slightly inquisitive expression on my face.

As her brother settled into the backseat, Jasmine introduced me, "This is my friend, Stephanie. She just moved here from California."

"Hey, nice to meet you. I'm Caleb," her brother greeted. "Sorry about the dramatic entrance; just got out of the hospital a few days ago. Almost kicked the bucket, but here I am, living the dream," he joked with a blend of sarcasm, humor, and evident relief at his recovery.

"Nice to meet you too and I'm sorry to hear. Glad you're still with us," I responded, returning a similar sentiment of his humor.

We made our way to Caleb's friend's house, perched on a hill with a picturesque view of downtown Saint Paul. The cityscape sprawled before us like a glittering tapestry. Arriving at our destination, we were greeted by a small gathering in the backyard—a lively scene of people lounging on metal folding chairs, engaged in animated conversations, and savoring food and drinks against the backdrop of the setting sun.

"Why don't you two join us? I still need a ride to my brother's house after this, and it would be nice for my friends to meet you both. It'll just be a short while, I promise," Caleb reassured us. "My friends are just happy to have me out of the hospital."

Jasmine and I exchanged a quick glance, silently deliberating the unexpected detour from our plans to tour Minnesota with only a couple of hours of sunlight left. However, mindful of Caleb's request and not wanting to seem impolite, Jasmine spoke up first. "We can stay for an hour at most," she agreed. I nodded, echoing her sentiment. "I'm okay with that."

As we stepped into the lively gathering, Caleb took the initiative to introduce us to his friends. The first person to extend a welcoming hand was a petite woman with dark, shoulder-length hair that framed her friendly smile. She wore a light gray tank top and cut-off shorts, and her skin had a dry tan that suggested she spent a lot of time in the harsh sun.

"Hi, I'm Dee. What's your name?" She greeted me with genuine interest and curiosity.

"Hi, Dee. I'm Stephanie, but call me Steph," I responded, reciprocating her friendliness.

Dee gestured toward a cluster of chairs, inviting us to make ourselves comfortable. "This is my brother's place, so feel free to make yourself at home and help yourself to anything," she said, pointing to the display of food on the table. "You have to try the food. My brother's girlfriend, Marissa, did all the cooking, and she's a really great cook. We're all just here to hang out and have fun," she added, creating an atmosphere of inclusivity and ease.

Jasmine and I settled into our seats with the panoramic view of downtown Saint Paul stretching out before us. With a sense of awe, I got up from my seat and made my way to the edge of the hill, where the view was most breathtaking. The glimmer of the cityscape captivated me, urging me to capture the scene on my phone.[8]

A sudden gesture interrupted my focus—a shot of clear liquor appeared in front of each of us, courtesy of Marissa. I hesitated, my preference for not drinking conflicting with the social etiquette of accepting hospitality graciously. Glancing at Jasmine, I could see she was mirroring the same hesitation.

I slowly leaned toward her without making it conspicuous and whispered, "Let's just take it and pretend to drink." We both accepted the small shot glasses, holding them in our hands as everyone toasted to Caleb's recovery.

As celebratory words were shared among the gathering, Jasmine caught a glimpse of my quick flick of the wrist, and the liquid was stealthily tossed behind me into the grass. Suppressing a laugh, she followed my actions, ensuring that our pretense went unnoticed by the others.

Dee joined us at our seats. She turned her attention toward me with a curious smile on her face. "So, Steph, tell me about yourself?" she inquired.

"Well, I just moved here a few days ago from California," I replied, offering a glimpse into the recent chapter of my life.

Dee's eyes lit up with enthusiasm. "Oh, that's great. Well, you're here with the best crowd in all of Saint Paul," she remarked proudly. Then, with a playful look in her eyes, she asked, "Are you single, by the

---

[8] Photo timestamped at 7:34 p.m. on August 4, 2019.

way?"

Her question came as a surprise, yet I couldn't help but smile at her directness. "Yes, I'm single," I said, then quickly shook my head. "But not looking." My focus was on self-discovery rather than romantic entanglements.

Without missing a beat, Dee leaned in. "Well, we have quite a few guys here who are single too," she teased, gesturing towards the gathering of people around us.

I couldn't help but feel a twinge of awkwardness at the sudden matchmaking attempt, but there was also a sense of amusement in the situation. *Was this normal for Minnesota gatherings?* I quietly thought as Dee proceeded to point out various individuals, highlighting their single status with playful commentary.

Then, her finger landed on a man seated at the center of the group. "That's Logan. He's single too," she announced, drawing my attention to him.

I glanced over at Logan, noticing a cigarette nudged between his fingers as he lifted it to his lips. Our eyes briefly met, a silent acknowledgment passing between us as he took a drag, exhaled smoke, and then redirected his attention to his friend who was speaking to him.

Unexpectedly, my heart fluttered. *Those eyes—captivating and deep—seemed to hold a thousand stories waiting to be told.* He was undeniably attractive—gorgeous, even. And those lips, the way they formed, carried a sense of familiarity about him that I couldn't quite understand, especially for someone I had just barely laid eyes on. It's very rare, if not non-existent, that upon first glance I find myself drawn to someone. *No, Steph! Focus!* I snapped myself out of my daze. A man of his good looks and status often comes with complications and distractions that I cannot afford to have in my life at this moment.

Stay away, he has trouble written all over him, I warned myself.

As I sat in my chair, contemplating his mysterious brown eyes and his full, slightly curved lips, the familiarity and image of someone else came to mind. A man I could have sworn I had met in a childhood dream. There was something nostalgic about Logan that reminded me of this man, who carried a sense of contentment and security emanating from his presence. Their resemblances were strikingly similar. In this dream, the man wore long khaki shorts that covered his knees, leather sandals, and a beige polo shirt. I remember him sitting on a large rock as if in deep reflection, and at another time, walking around familiar buildings with a certain charismatic charm. Feeling slightly perplexed, I disregarded the memory and brought myself back to the present.

As the evening wore on, I found myself retreating into my own thoughts, content to converse mainly with Jasmine and Dee. Our hour drew to a close, and we prepared to leave. I made the rounds to bid farewell to each person, expressing gratitude for the enjoyable evening. Lost in the exchange of pleasantries, I didn't realize that Logan, who had not exchanged a single word with me all evening, was seated to my left.

"You're very lovely. What was your name again?" Logan asked politely, suddenly breaking his silence as he extended his hand toward mine. His deep, resonant voice caught me off guard, and the unexpectedness of it momentarily took me aback.

"I'm Steph," I replied as I gently shook his hand.

"It's a pleasure to meet you. May I see your phone?" Logan asked, reaching for the device in my hand before I could even answer.

"Oh, sure," I stumbled over my words, surprised at how direct he was. I quickly unlocked my phone and handed it over to him, curious about his request.

I watched as he used my phone to make a call. Suddenly, his phone started ringing, but instead of answering, he tapped "Decline." He handed me back my phone and said, "There you go. Now we have each other's numbers. Why don't you give me a call tomorrow, and I'll show you around town?"

I retrieved my phone, a mix of surprise and amusement washing over me at his sheer confidence and lack of hesitation. He didn't talk to me all night, but when he wanted my number, he just took it.

Definitely trouble, I mused, a reminder to tread cautiously despite the intrigue his boldness sparked. Nonetheless, there was a hint of enjoyment in his audacity.

To ensure I didn't forget whose number I had just acquired, I swiftly sent Logan a text: "Thank you, Logan. It was a pleasure to meet you.[9]"

Logan received the message, glanced at it and gave me a charming wink. I smiled. *This guy could get me in so much trouble.*

---

[9] Text message timestamped at 8:04 p.m. on Sunday, August 4, 2019.

CHAPTER 4

NO SLEEP

*D*AYS HAD GONE BY, and Logan's number remained a mere entry in my phone, untouched and uncontacted. He was indeed attractive, but I couldn't shake the feeling that reaching out to him would lead down a path I wasn't ready to tread. Despite being captivated by his bold move of taking my number without asking, I had a sense that he was the kind of man who attracted attention effortlessly. It wouldn't be surprising if there were other women vying for his time and affection. I wasn't keen on becoming just another name on his long list of admirers.

Moreover, I knew myself well enough to recognize my tendencies. While being empathetic had its advantages, it also meant I often found myself unintentionally diving deep into people's emotions and motivations, frequently uncovering red flags early on. Call it intuition or a sixth sense, but from the moment someone begins to speak, and I allow myself to truly take in their presence, every word, every gesture, even their silences, are meticulously analyzed, often without trying. It's as if I possess an invisible filter that translates their every offering into the underlying truth. I can discern what they might be hiding or if they're being dishonest, and I've learned to trust my instincts—they have rarely led me astray.

Relationships, especially casual ones, weren't my forte. I feared the potential for hurt, either on my part or his, or worse, becoming just a passing fancy in someone's life—none of which held much appeal for me. So, when it came to Logan, I made a conscious decision to steer clear, opting to avoid any entanglements I didn't intend to pursue.

It was Wednesday night and it marked exactly a week since my arrival in Minnesota.[10] Most of my belongings had found their place in my new room, with the exception of a few boxes containing photographs, paintings and books. I had postponed unpacking those until I settled into a more permanent home. With a new client on the horizon, the prospect of diving into work brought a sense of fulfillment and confirmation that things were gradually falling into place.

However, amidst the growing sense of contentment, a nagging migraine had decided to make an unwelcome appearance. Despite taking painkillers earlier, the throbbing persisted, making even the slightest light unbearable. Seeking relief, I retreated to my bed, covering my eyes in an attempt to block out any stimuli. Just as I was trying to find some comfort in the darkness, my phone rang, disrupting the quiet sanctuary I had sought. Reluctantly, I glanced at the Caller ID—Logan's name flashed on the screen, catching me off guard. I had not expected him to call at all.

"Hello," I answered tentatively, unsure of what Logan's unexpected call might entail.

"Are you bored yet?" Logan's cheerful voice rang through the phone. His enthusiasm was apparent even through the receiver. His question caught me off guard. There was no "Hello" or "How are you?"—he went

---

[10] August 7, 2019

straight into asking if I was bored, leaving me momentarily perplexed.

"I'm okay," I replied cautiously, not entirely sure how to interpret his inquiry.

Undeterred by my reserved response, Logan's eagerness spilled into his next statement.

"What are you doing? Let's go out," he suggested assertively, a tone that was hard to miss.

I hesitated, torn between my lingering migraine and the allure of stepping out into the world with this intriguing man who had somehow managed to capture my attention. Despite my earlier resolve to steer clear of potential distractions and "trouble," a nudging voice reminded me, *Steph, you're new in town, and you still need to make friends.*

With a tentative nod to my internal monologue, I agreed. "Sure, we can go out. Where to?" I asked, trying to keep my tone casual despite the slight flutter of nerves.

"You pick," Logan replied nonchalantly, leaving the choice in my hands.

"Sorry, I don't know this town well. How about meeting up for coffee somewhere?" I suggested, even though it was after five in the late afternoon, but my mind was drawing a blank on other options.

Logan had something else in mind. "Let's go to Mystic Lake. I'll meet you there," he proposed with easy confidence.

Mystic Lake, is that a lake? I wondered, momentarily puzzled by the unfamiliar name. Then again, just about everything in town was unfamiliar. However, I reasoned that a lake would be a serene setting, perfect for a casual meet-up. Pushing aside the remnants of my headache, I decided to make the best of the spontaneous outing.

I quickly entered "Mystic Lake" into the GPS app on my phone, only to discover that it was, in fact, Mystic Lake Casino—not quite the serene park and lake I had envisioned. Nevertheless, I reassured myself that a casino was a public place and set out on the drive to Mystic Lake.

As I arrived at the imposing structure of Mystic Lake Casino, a mild frustration gnawed at me. The expansive parking lot appeared to be filled to capacity. Unsure of where to park, I opted for valet service, allowing myself a moment to gather my thoughts before stepping into the bustling lobby. With a deep breath, I dialed Logan's number, eager to navigate this unexpected adventure.

"I just arrived. Where are you?" I inquired, scanning the lobby for any sign of Logan's familiar figure amidst the throng of people.

"I'm here too. Wait for me in the lobby. I'm parking my car and will join you," he replied with anticipation in his voice.

Immersed in the opulence of the lobby, my gaze lingered on the breathtaking crystal chandelier suspended above, casting prismatic patterns across the room. Nestled into a plush cushioned seat at a small cocktail table just across from the bar, I took a moment to check my calendar for the upcoming week. As I scrolled through appointments, the lively chatter of patrons and the sound of slot machines filled the air, a stark contrast to the quiet solitude of my recent days.

In the midst of this vibrant scene, Logan's presence caught my attention. Dressed in a casual burgundy t-shirt and jeans that accentuated his athletic build, he exuded an effortless charm. His freshly styled hair complemented his overall appeal. Our eyes met, and a warm smile spread across his face as he made his way over to where I sat. Returning his smile, I rose from my seat to meet him.

I watched as he strutted towards me; he even walked the same as the man in my dream. Not to mention, he was wearing leather sandals too. *Interesting*, I noted.

"Hello, Beautiful," he greeted me charmingly. The naturalness of his gesture offered no sense of hesitation or reservation as he extended his arms to embrace me.

Settling in beside me, Logan initiated conversation, his easy demeanor putting me at ease as he inquired about my day.

"It was good," I replied. Reciprocating his interest in our exchange, I asked, "How was yours?"

"I had to work today, hit the gym, shower, gave you a call, and now I'm here," Logan answered confidently.

I couldn't help but notice his physique, the result of dedicated time and effort spent honing his body and I knew his mention of the gym wasn't an attempt to impress but rather a glimpse into his routine and lifestyle.

As our conversation flowed, Logan offered to get drinks, a gesture I appreciated even though I didn't indulge in alcohol. "I don't drink," I politely declined, but Logan was insistent, convinced that everyone should enjoy a drink now and then.

"In that case, suggest something sweet," I said, clueless about what drinks were called these days anyway. "But whatever you order for me, you'll have to order one for yourself too because I don't want to drink alone," I compromised, hoping to find something palatable in the array of options available.

Logan decided on two piña coladas, and soon our drinks arrived. Despite my initial reluctance, I took a few sips. The tropical flavors tingled on my palate, but the hint of alcohol slightly ruined the drink for me, as I had never developed a liking for it. When it comes to alcohol, I get flashbacks of myself as a child, running away from my parents in tears to escape taking medicine whenever I was sick. It was that repulsive to me, and as an adult, the child in me still tugs on me to run every time.

Our conversation continued effortlessly, and I didn't even notice when my migraine went away. It didn't take long for Logan to express that he was beginning to feel the effects of his drink. "This drink is strong and getting to me already," he remarked, closing his eyes briefly and placing a hand on his forehead.

I couldn't help but raise an eyebrow, finding his sensitivity to alcohol comical and internally amused by the irony, especially since we've taken about the same number of sips, and I haven't felt anything.

"I don't usually drink," he confessed, a wry smile forming on his lips.

As we chuckled over the unexpected turn of events, I couldn't help but wonder why we had even bothered with drinks when neither of us had intended to indulge. We humorously remarked that a free cup of Pepsi from the concession counter would have been more enjoyable.

Earlier, when driving to Mystic Lake, a tinge of apprehension had crept into my thoughts. My previous encounter with Logan left me with the impression that he was reserved, almost silent, as he only seemed to find his voice when I was leaving. However, it was apparent that this night was different; our interaction was most interesting, like two old friends catching up after a long time apart.

Logan surprised me with how well he carried on a conversation, and his quirky sense of humor was refreshingly infectious. Many of the things he said, I couldn't believe were coming out of his mouth, which made me laugh hysterically. He was brutally honest and did not sugarcoat a single thing, which I appreciated. I did not feel my usual tendency to decipher his intentions as everything he expressed felt raw and authentic, which dissipated any reservations I had initially. Each time he laughed, it was as though he had a knack for drawing out laughter from within me.

"I'm usually very reserved and don't talk this much," said Logan with a huge grin on his face. "I don't know why I'm talking so much tonight with you, but you're really fun to talk with," he added.

Logan mostly took the lead in steering our conversations. His animated storytelling and witty remarks kept me captivated, allowing me the leisure of simply listening and enjoying his company. It was a pleasant change of pace, a chance to relax and be in the moment without the pressure of keeping the conversation afloat.

When we arrived at Mystic Lake, it was just before 7:00 pm. From the moment we sat together, our conversation had been non-stop. Now, as it draws closer to 11:00 pm, we're still here exchanging words and laughter.

Suddenly, Logan's voice broke the rhythm of our exchange, "I don't mean this in a creepy way," he began, his tone sincere and considerate, "but I already have a room here. I was planning to stay the night anyway whether you showed up or not. It has a double bed, so if you're tired, you're more than welcome to take the other bed. I promise I won't do anything to make you uncomfortable."

His offer was unexpected, but kind, and I appreciated the thoughtfulness behind it. "Thank you, Logan," I replied with a polite smile, "but I won't be staying. I prefer to head home for the night."

Undeterred, our conversation continued, transitioning from one topic to the next. Logan's curiosity piqued as he asked, "So why didn't you call me?" I bit my bottom lip slightly as I told him a half-truth, "I'm still settling in, and I didn't want to inconvenience you."

"It's not an inconvenience. I was waiting for your call, and when I didn't hear from you, I thought I'd check in to see if you were bored yet from whatever you were doing," he said, and we both laughed at how he initiated the call.

Then he asked, "What made you agree to come out tonight?"

I took a moment to consider his question before responding, "Since we didn't say much to each other the other day, I thought, why not take this time to discover more about what else is so intriguing about you."

The interest was mutual as Logan inquired further, "What about me was intriguing?" His question caught me off guard, causing a faint blush to rise to my cheeks. I was not expecting him to catch that and question me.

"Well," I confessed with a blushing smile, "first of all, your eyes. They're deep and seem to reflect a beautiful soul. I feel like there are so many stories behind them, and I'm intrigued to know them."

As I heard myself speaking those words, I couldn't help but wonder why I was flirting with him when I hadn't intended to. Logan's face lit up with a genuine smile, his eyes sparkling with newfound delight.

"Really? My eyes?" he said, glancing at me. "No one has ever said that to me before," he exclaimed, his expression turning boyishly endearing and I couldn't help but be drawn in by him.

Time seemed to lose its relevance as we immersed ourselves in our dialogues, oblivious to the passage of hours. The lobby still buzzed with activity around us, yet our focus remained steadfast on each other. When I finally glanced at the time, the realization dawned that it was already 5:00 in the morning.

Startled by the time, "I should head out," I remarked, the late hour registering as I prepared to leave.

But Logan insisted with concern in his voice as he stood up, "I don't want you to be too tired to drive. You can have the keys to the room, and I'll just stay out here in the lobby," he suggested, his consideration evident.

Despite his thoughtful offer, I declined. "It's okay, I'm not that tired yet. I'll make it home just fine," I assured him, pushing in the chair I had occupied for hours.

Logan then offered to walk me to my car, displaying his chivalry without hesitation. "Where did you park?" he inquired.

"I valeted," I replied, appreciating his gesture.

Without a moment's delay, Logan handed me some cash, an offering meant to ease my travel back home. However, accepting money from others wasn't something I did easily unless I had earned it.

"Thank you, but that's unnecessary," I politely declined, although his thoughtfulness was noted.

We made our way to the valet stand together, Logan patiently waiting as my car was retrieved. Once it was brought around, Logan tipped the valet driver generously, a small act of kindness that spoke volumes about his character. As he approached my passenger window, leaning in slightly, he wished me well with a warm smile.

"Have a good day. I really enjoyed our conversation. Let me know when you get home safely," he said, his genuine concern echoing in his parting words.

As I drove away from Mystic Lake, I smiled at the highlights of our conversations replaying in my mind, leaving me with a sense of appreciation for the unexpected connection and turn of events that had unfolded amidst the buzz of the casino lobby.

"I guess Logan wasn't so much 'trouble' after all," I said aloud in the car as I turned on some music to accompany my drive home. I liked how genuinely and straightforwardly honest he was, which made me feel at ease about spending such long hours with him.

CHAPTER 5

STILLWATER

THE MOMENT I CROSSED THE THRESHOLD into my bedroom, exhaustion swept over me. Hastily, I gathered my unruly hair into a messy bun and splashed my face with warm water and soap to wash off the day. I brushed my teeth, slipped into my usual pajamas, and collapsed onto my bed, craving the embrace of sleep.

The silence of slumber felt short-lived when my phone started ringing. Rubbing my bleary eyes, I flickered towards the time on my phone, registering the time—just past 10:00 am. Pleasantly surprised it was Logan calling.

"Hello," I greeted, my voice thick with drowsiness.

"Did you get some sleep?" Logan asked in a gentle concern tone.

"I was until you decided to wake me up," I teased lightly, a playful smile tugging at my lips.

"Sorry. I didn't mean to wake you up. I just wanted to make sure you got home safely since I didn't hear from you," he explained.

Hearing that he had been waiting for my call or text to ensure I got home safely, I felt bad. "I'm sorry. I appreciate your thoughtfulness. I didn't realize how drained I would be when I got home and knocked out as soon as I touched my bed. I should have let you know. But I'm up now and I'm fine," I reassured him, feeling a warm sense of gratitude for his consideration.

Without further hesitation, Logan inquired, "So, any plans for today?"

"Nothing yet," I admitted, the day was still a blank canvas, and I was too tired to think.

"Well, I want to see you again. How about you come out to meet me at Phalen Lake around 2:00 pm?" Logan proposed with a gentle eagerness.

Phalen Lake—that, I know, is an actual lake. I said, "Sure, I've heard about the infamous Phalen Lake where all Hmong people in town congregate but haven't had the chance to explore it yet. I'll see you there at 2:00 pm," I accepted with a flicker of excitement at the prospect of another rendezvous with Logan and happily surprised that he wanted to see me again so soon. It had only been five hours.

After hanging up, a question dawned on me—*had Logan even slept since our late-night conversations?* The hours had slipped away unnoticed and now, his eagerness to meet again revealed his interest, and I couldn't help but smile.

Despite the remnants of tiredness clinging to my eyes and limbs, Logan's call infused a seed of warm energy within me. I crawled from bed, feeling a sense of anticipation as I began preparing for the day ahead. My heart was brimming with anticipation at the thought of seeing Logan again.

It was 1:30 pm when I began my drive over to Phalen Lake. The sun bathed the surroundings in a warm golden hue, casting playful shadows across the landscape as I navigated the unfamiliar roads.

Approaching the lake, I give Logan a quick call, "Hi, Logan. I'm here by the lake. Where should I meet you?" I asked.

"I'm already here. Drive around the lake along the east side until you reach the furthest northern part. There is a turn there, make a left and follow it until you come to a small fishing dock. I'll be there waiting. Look for a white cargo van," Logan instructed.

Following his directions, I soon found myself cruising along the serene expanse of the lake, the gentle ripples on the water mirroring the tranquility of the moment. And then, just as Logan had described, I spotted him standing next to a white cargo van near a small fishing dock.

The sight of him sent an expected flutter of excitement through my nerves. I noticed the roof of his van was equipped with a ladder rack, suggesting that his vehicle was most likely used for work. As I approached, I could see him tidying up a few tools at the back of his van before striding towards the front where a couple more power tools lay on the ground alongside his vehicle.

Looking at Logan, I took a deep breath as my heart seemed to echo in my ears—a rhythmic drumbeat of anticipation and nerves. I had never seen such a beautiful man make a simple white T-shirt, jeans, and leather sandals look so good.

"My gosh, he is gorgeous," I whispered as I finally exhaled. He wasn't trying to impress, yet he exuded a magnetic appeal that was hard to ignore.

My eyes traced the contours of his sculpted, golden-tan arms as he picked up his tools one by one from the ground and diligently placed them into the side of his van. I noted how his jeans accentuated his long legs, and I was extremely attracted to his rugged masculinity.

He stood at exactly 5'8". I hadn't noticed his height when we first met because he had been sitting the entire time. However, when he greeted me with a hug last night, his towering presence over me was hard to miss. I couldn't help but ask for his height, entertained as I recalled my joke from a few weeks ago about snagging myself a five-foot-eight Minnesota man, enhancing his allure.

Despite my initial reservations not to entangle myself, I couldn't help but be drawn to him and his effortless charm that was beginning to appear more sincere than trouble. This meeting was shaping up to be more than just a casual encounter.

I exited the car and walked toward him, feeling a profound sense of familiarity with each step, as if we had known each other for much longer than just a few days. Unlike past relationships, where I constantly felt the need to uphold a perfect image, fearing my flaws would be exposed or rejected, with him, there was no such unease. His presence was a safe haven where I could let my guard down and simply be myself. I felt no pressure to be anything other than who I truly was, and that realization filled me with an unexpected sense of peace and comfort.

Approaching him, his smile was warm, and his words, "I'm glad you made it," felt like a welcoming embrace.

We settled by the dock, where the gentle breeze carried the scent of the lake—a fresh, earthy aroma mixed with the subtle fragrance of pine and wildflowers—and the warmth of the August sun enveloped us. The ambiance was serene, with the rippling water providing a soothing soundtrack to our conversations.

"Did you even sleep at all since I left Mystic?" I asked him curiously.

"I did, but only after finally hearing your voice this morning and knew you were home safely. Before that, I was so worried I couldn't sleep a wink," he said.

I turned to look at him with a serious expression, hoping he is joking. For a brief second, he didn't say anything, then chuckled, "Seriously. I was worried, and I did not sleep until after I called you, but it was mostly because I just couldn't sleep."

I chuckled with him and shook my head. "You're such a jokester."

As we delved into various topics again, picking up right where we left off at Mystic, I was mesmerized by Logan's easygoing nature and genuine laughter. After an hour of pleasant conversation, Logan suggested, "Let's grab something to eat. I'm sorry I enjoyed our conversation last night a little too much and forgot to feed you. I'll make up for it."

"Oh, I enjoyed it too," I said. "I actually don't remember being hungry at all," I continued with a laugh.

Logan suggested we head over to Destiny Café 2 for some pho since it was close by, another place I had heard of prior to my move. I followed him in my car. When we arrived at the restaurant, we settled into a booth. Logan continued speaking with an infectious smile and laughter. Unable to resist, I slyly took a picture of him smiling with my phone, pretending to look at something on my screen.[11] I felt a bit silly, like I was being a "creeper" on only the second date! But I was completely charmed and too embarrassed to ask for a photo directly. I wanted to capture his boyish smile. It was as if this man had cast a spell on me, and I didn't want to leave his sight. I genuinely wanted to get to know him better.

Reflecting on when I saw him tidying his tools by the lake, I asked, "What do you do?"

"I work in construction. I've been doing that for 20 something years now," he replied.

"Ah," I said, "explains your cargo van."

When he said that, I couldn't help but notice Logan's calloused hands, a testament to years of hard work in construction. His dedication and perseverance were evident in every detail. He had big, masculine hands that looked like they hadn't taken a break for a day in his life. I secretly wanted to reach over and touch his hand but kept myself reserved, smiling as I continued to listen to Logan talk.

We ordered our pho and enjoyed our dinner together. Logan sure loves his protein; he ordered double servings of it. When the bill arrived,

---

[11] Photo timestamped at 6:23 p.m. on August 8, 2019.

I took it from our waitress and insisted on paying for our meals. I've never believed a man should pay just because he's a man or because we're on a date. However, Logan quickly reached for the bill from my hand and firmly said, "No, I've got this. I said I would make up for last night, and it's my responsibility." I gasped as I watched him take the bill from my hand. He looked at me and started laughing at my expression.

When we reached the parking lot, the evening was still young, and sunlight still graced the sky. It promised more time together, and neither of us was willing to end the night just yet. Logan suggested, "If you don't mind, we can leave my vehicle here and take yours. That way, we can continue our conversations while I show you around."

"I don't mind at all. That's a great idea actually," I agreed.

While I was driving, Logan glanced down at my hand swiftly shifting gears. His surprise was evident in his voice as he said, "You drive stick? That's pretty cool. And you handle it so smoothly, too. I don't know any women who drive stick."

I chuckled at his remark. "Seriously? Lots of women drive stick," I said as I pulled out onto the street.

Logan took the opportunity to guide me as we drove. His directions led us to Stillwater. We parked in a lot by the St. Croix River, the calm waters mirroring the vibrant hues of the sky as the sun prepared for its nightly descent. With about 45 minutes until sunset, we strolled along the water's edge until we found a peaceful spot by some stone steps. Logan sat down first, gesturing for me to join him.

What began as a lively exchange gradually transitioned into a more somber and intimate conversation. Logan shared poignant memories from his life, opening up about his regrets and the dreams he still clung to despite the passage of time in his 40s. It was a vulnerable moment, offering a glimpse into the weight of his past and the complexities he carried within.

As Logan spoke, his gaze fixed on the water with an intensity that held many deep and unspoken thoughts. I sensed the profound sadness in his eyes as he talked about his disappointments and the lack of dependable support in his life.

"There isn't a single person I could truly count on if my life depended on it," Logan confided. "I always believed I was destined for greatness, but now I feel like time is slipping away, and I lack the belief system I long for to make my dreams a reality."

His words resonated deeply with me, stirring a sense of empathy. "The world is full of endless possibilities," I replied, my voice soft yet resolute. "Nothing is set in stone until we draw our last breath. You still possess the potential for greatness. The key is to determine what you truly want and then pursue it with unwavering determination. The most capable people out there aren't inherently different from us; what sets them apart is their unyielding belief in their dreams, giving them more reasons to make them happen than excuses not to."

Logan's gaze remained fixed on the water, his expression contemplative. In a low and gentle tone, he spoke, "You're right... You're absolutely right."

We sat in silence on the cool stone steps, the soft glow of the post-sunset sky casting an ethereal light around us. In that tranquil moment, as I continued to gaze at Logan, an inexplicable connection came over me, and a lingering sense of familiarity that defied logic; a feeling that I had not been able to shake off since meeting him. His vulnerability and transparency had stirred something deep within me, a feeling that whispered, *if you're not careful, you can fall in love with this man forever.*

A sudden urge to capture the essence of this moment seized me, prompting my courage to pull out my phone—an unusual act for me, as I wasn't one for selfies or impromptu snapshots. Yet, there was something about this shared moment that felt like it would hold significant meaning someday.

"I have a feeling this is the beginning of something extraordinary," I said to Logan, lifting my phone. "Would you mind taking a selfie with me?"

The remaining soft glow of the evening sky painted a warm hue around us, creating a picturesque backdrop for our impromptu photo. With gentle smiles, we immortalized our first picture together.[12]

As we settled back into conversation, Logan's words caught me off guard. "Where have you been all my life? You're the key. I wish I had met you 20 years ago. You're so driven and you know exactly what you want. I believe my life would have been so different had I met you sooner."

His sentiment struck a melancholic chord within me, tugging at emotions I hadn't expected. "I don't always have it together or figured out," I confessed, my voice soft but sincere. "In fact, I'm here in Minnesota because I'm trying to figure things out. Professionally, I'm not worried, but my personal life is lacking a sense of direction and motivation."

Logan's gaze softened, a flicker of understanding in his eyes, as I continued, "Time is a funny thing. Perhaps if we had met at any other time, we wouldn't appreciate this conversation as much as we do now. Maybe we needed all those years to deepen our experiences, so that we could be ready for this chapter of our lives where we crave more stability than temporary thrills."

A playful glint appeared in his eyes, as to lighten the mood of the moment after sensing a hint of sadness in my tone. He changed the subject with a grin. "How about we head to the best place in the world?"

I raised an eyebrow, intrigued. "Best place? Where's that?"

"Hinckley!" he exclaimed. His enthusiasm infectious as he expressed his excitement.

---

[12] Photo timestamped at 8:04 p.m. on August 8, 2019.

Though unfamiliar with Hinckley, I agreed with a smile. "Sounds like an adventure. Lead the way."

Logan got up and held my hand to help me up from the stone steps. "I'll drive," he eagerly volunteered.

CHAPTER 6

BEST PLACE

I HANDED LOGAN THE KEYS and settled into the passenger seat. The engine came to life as he turned on the ignition. "It's been a long while since I've driven a stick. This should be fun," Logan said as he shifted into reverse and then into first gear to pull forward, making his way out of the parking lot

"It's a dying art," I responded. "My very first car had a manual transmission, and I've stuck with it ever since. I've driven an automatic a few times, but the lack of control doesn't appeal to me."

Unsurprisingly, our dialogue continued to flow from one topic fluidly to the next. It was a long-awaited experience to harmoniously connect with someone on such a deep level, especially considering my usual introverted nature. I marveled at how we hadn't run out of things to say.

As we continued our drive, Logan's words reverberated in my mind: "You're the key." It struck me as both unusual and intriguing. Fueled by curiosity, I turned to him and asked, "What did you mean by 'I am the key'?" With a grin and a hint of mystery in his eyes, Logan explained,

"It's a feeling I get sometimes. I have these intuitions about people and their significance in my life, whether it's just a fleeting moment or something more profound. I am never wrong about these instincts. With you, it feels like you're the key."

Still puzzled, I pressed for more clarity, but Logan simply smiled and replied, "I know it's you, but I don't want to jinx myself by saying too much. I promise I'll explain one day." I nodded, not exactly disappointed that he didn't elaborate, but reassured myself that *if it's genuinely significant, he'll share it when the time is right.*

It was approximately 9:30 p.m. when we arrived in Hinckley, I couldn't help but note how short our drive felt, despite the time indicating that it was an hour long. While Logan searched for a parking space, I glanced over to the blinkering establishment. *Another casino,* I thought with a wry smile. *This guy sure spends a lot of time in casinos.*

Entering the lobby, the sound of slot machines and excited chatter immediately greeted us. Logan suggested that we stay the night, considering the late hour and the length of time we planned to spend there. Initially, I hadn't realized how late it would be by the time we arrived, but his practical suggestion made sense as it would probably be after midnight by the time we start heading back. I agreed to his proposal with little hesitation, knowing that if tonight was anything like the other night at Mystic Lake, we'd be up all night talking.

After swiftly checking into our room at the casino's hotel concierge desk, we ventured back into the lively casino lobby. My understanding of gambling was limited, so I observed Logan as he deftly navigated the games, explaining their intricacies and strategies while I sat beside him. I hung on to his every word, captivated, not due to the game itself, but because I loved watching him talk; the way his lips curled when he enunciated his words and the occasional smile or laughter that graced his face.

Around 2:00 a.m., we finally retired to our room. Despite the availability of two queen beds, we chose to lie next to each other, our faces inches apart in the dimly lit room. I could feel his gentle warm breath dancing on the corner of my lips and cheeks as we laid quietly facing one another.

Though I did not inquire, Logan confessed, "It's not that I like gambling," his voice soft and tired, as he settled into the comfort of the bedding. "I don't have much interest in it, but I find myself spending time in casinos simply because they are always open, even at the wee hours of the night, and bustling with people. The lively atmosphere and constant chatter are a distraction from my daily routines and troubles, and for a moment, I forget about being depressed or alone," he shared with slight somberness in his voice.

"What about your family and other relationships?" I probed gently, curious about the depths of his past experiences and the immediate people in his circle, "I doubt you're entirely alone." Logan's gaze drifted towards the ceiling as he reflected, "I've never been with anyone where I didn't feel alone. I was the black sheep of my family, and they had their own life. In my other relationships, we didn't talk effortlessly like you and me. With you, I feel like we can talk forever about anything."

"We can," I softly assured him, feeling a warm connection between us that transcended mere conversation.

Genuinely interested in getting to know him, I asked Logan, "Were you married before? Any kids?" Logan paused, seeming to search for the right words. "Yes, I was married once," he began. "I was 18, young and naive, hardly ready for the responsibilities of marriage, let alone fatherhood. My ex-wife, a few years my senior, had been married before and had a son who was less than a year old when we got married. We didn't date long. I stepped into the role of a father almost immediately."

I listened intently as Logan recounted his youthful foray into family life. "We were married for almost two years when my daughter was born."

Eager to know more, I asked, "Tell me about your daughter."

A proud smile spread across his face. "She's my only child, and she's bright, incredibly sharp—didn't get that from me," he chuckled. "But she definitely inherited my attitude and fire." His eyes lit up at the mention of her, and I could see how much he adores her.

"Well then, that only means she has a big heart," I added. I couldn't help but smile as he talked about his daughter. His affection for her tugged at my heart, and I was happy to learn that his daughter and my firstborn were only a few months apart in age.

"What does she enjoy?" I probed further.

Logan's face softened. "Oh, typical girly things—shopping, dresses, purses. That sort of stuff."

"And are you two close?" I ventured.

The light in his eyes dimmed as he hesitated, his tone turning somber. "Unfortunately, no. My ex and I split when my daughter was only a few years old. She moved to another state and remarried soon after, making it hard for me to see my daughter. With her new husband in the picture, I didn't want to cause any trouble."

As he continued to share details about that part of his life, my heart sank. I thought of my own children and how I insisted that their father remain a part of their lives after our divorce.

In our divorce agreement, without any hesitation, I waived all rights to financial support and told the judge, "I only have one requirement from my ex-husband, and that is for him to make time for our children. Despite our relationship, our children need to know that he will still be in their lives, that he loves and cares for them."

He may not have been a good husband to me, but he was a decent father, and I was adamant about preserving their relationship. Children should never be pawns in the aftermath of a divorce, used to score points against each other. They deserve unwavering love that isn't tainted by our adult conflicts.

As we lingered in the quiet of the room, I observed Logan, his eyes betraying the weariness of the night's events. Slowly, they closed, and he drifted into sleep, his breathing becoming steady and peaceful. It was a stark contrast to his animated self when awake, and I couldn't help but find this gentler side of him endearing, like a hidden facet of his personality that only surfaced in moments of vulnerability.

I smiled softly, appreciating the moment, then reached behind me to switch off the bedside lamp, casting the room into darkness with only a faint glow filtering in through the sheer curtains from outside. Lying next to Logan, I closed my eyes, feeling the weight of exhaustion finally catching up with me. Sleep embraced us, offering a temporary respite from the complexities of life and whatever hopes lay ahead.

The night passed without disturbance. It wasn't until the gentle rays of morning light broke through the curtains that I stirred from slumber. As consciousness returned, I became aware of the sensation of being cradled in Logan's arm, my face nestled against his chest—a position I hadn't anticipated but found surprisingly comforting. Unlike past experiences sharing a bed, where I often felt overheated and restricted, and usually ended up retreating to reclaim my own space on another side of the bed; our bodies seemed to harmonize in temperature, resulting in a restful and serene sleep, a feeling I had never encountered with anyone else, not even when sleeping alone. It was as though our beings were in perfect alignment, creating a haven of tranquility and peace.

Reluctant to disturb his peaceful sleep, I stayed still, savoring the warmth of his embrace and the steady rhythm of his breathing. His breath brushed softly against the top of my head, tickling through my hair and evoking a sense of contentment within me. I closed my eyes and gently absorbed the serenity of the morning, feeling attuned to the safe and comforting energy emanating from Logan.

I could feel the gravity of his life's journey, the complexity of his emotions, and his yearning for genuine affection. It seemed as though he sought unconditional love despite the shortcomings he saw within himself, and it was clear that peaceful nights had been rare for him lately. In the intimate quiet of that moment, I simply wanted to shelter and embrace this man completely—a sentiment I couldn't entirely grasp, yet was ready to welcome.

As minutes passed, the coziness and warmth pulled me into a gentle slumber, where dreams danced on the edge of consciousness. Later, I sensed a change in his movements, indicating he was waking up. Opening my eyes, I met his gaze as he softly greeted me with "Good morning."

Returning his greeting, I couldn't help but notice the unspoken tension in the air, charged with anticipation and possibility. Without hesitation, as if guided by an instinctive sense of comfort, Logan leaned forward, and his lips met mine in a tender, first kiss. Initially, I hesitated, concerned about my morning breath, but it was quickly replaced by a sense of calm acceptance as I relaxed into the moment and his embrace, savoring the sweetness of his kiss and the unspoken affection.

We continued to lie in bed as Logan asked me how I slept. "I was quite comfortable," I said before cautiously inquiring if I snored.

"If you did, I didn't hear it. I was so tired, I blinked, and it was morning," he said as he wrapped his arms snugly around me, pulling me tighter into his embrace. Then he let out a rumbling groan as if he was shaking off the tiredness and continued, "I cannot recall the last time I slept so well, and you're a sweet sight to see first thing in the morning."

I chuckled at the sound he made, feeling the full breadth of his body vibrating against me. He was certainly strong.

After half an hour of casual banter in bed, we finally roused ourselves to prepare for heading back into town.[13] Just before merging

---

[13] Friday, August 9, 2019, at approximately 11:30 a.m.

onto the highway, Logan veered into a gas station. Parking alongside a pump, he inquired if I needed anything, to which I lightly shook my head. Shutting off the engine, he stepped out and disappeared into the station to pre-pay for the fuel.

A few moments later, I spotted him emerging from the station carrying a large brown paper bag with handles at his side. It bulged with something sizable, likely a large box. He approached the driver's side, deftly opened the back passenger door, and announced, "I got you some cinnamon rolls," carefully placing the bag inside and closing the door.

After completing the fuel refill, he settled back into the driver's seat. Turning on the ignition, his face suddenly lit up with a grin. He turned to me, proclaiming, "These cinnamon rolls are the best in the state. People come from all over just to stop at this station for them. I grabbed you two dozen to take home."

I smiled, amused by how easily he was excited over cinnamon rolls, but surprised at the mention of two dozen. There's no way I can finish all of these. Keith was never much for sweets. His idea of indulging his sweet tooth consisted of strawberries and bananas. My dad and stepmom aren't any different. So, I suggested, "I can take half a dozen, but you should take the rest for your family."

"I live alone," he said.

In all our conversations over the last few days, we hadn't delved much into Logan's family background. They were mentioned sporadically but very vaguely. His past sorrows had seeped into many of our discussion multiple times, revealing a void where familial support should have been. Driven by a desire to understand him better, I ventured to ask, "Tell me about your family?"

"There's not much to say," he replied tersely, igniting a hint of intrigue within me.

"Are you the youngest or oldest?" I pressed on, hoping to gain a little more insight.

"I'm the youngest son," he answered, his tone closing off any further discussion on the topic. Sensing his reluctance, I respected his boundaries, reassuring myself with the thought, "He'll share when he's ready."

We drove for what felt like 20 minutes, and for the first time in the car together, the hum of the engine filling the space between us was the only sound before Logan finally broke the silence. "My father had two marriages. My mom was his second wife, and he passed away a decade ago. He and I were not close," he disclosed, his voice carrying the weight of memories.

I turned to Logan, offering my silent attention, respecting his pace as he shared intricate details about his family dynamics.

"I'm the youngest son, but I drew the shortest straw," Logan spoke with a depth that showed years of deep thought and insight.

"I wasn't an orphan, but often I felt like one," he confided. "I'll admit, I was quite mischievous as a kid, but it was mainly because I felt neglected. No one seemed to pay much attention to what I did, so I practically did whatever I wanted."

Pausing for a moment to collect his thoughts, Logan's gaze on the road ahead softened as he delved deeper into his past. "I was my dad's least favorite son. He was very stern and always hard on me. I don't know why, but I think he hated me. Even as a kid, I saw a difference in how he treated me versus my older brothers. There was a time when I was in the kitchen looking for food. There was a plate of covered chicken wings on the table, and he yelled at me not to eat it. He said he was saving it for his favorite son. He didn't even ask if I was hungry. Sadly, that difference only grew as I got older." My heart broke hearing him share that. I couldn't fathom how a parent could do that to their own child, but I listened in silence as he continued.

"He once accused me of stealing $500 from him and demanded that I pay him, or he'll kick me out of the house. I told him I hadn't seen it and didn't take it, but he wouldn't relent. I ended up paying him anyway because that was the only way to keep a roof over my head. He eventually found his money a week later, realizing he had misplaced it."

I was astonished and asked, "Did he pay you back? Did he apologize?"

"Nope," Logan responded abruptly.

I felt disheartened and had no words to comfort him except only to offer my ears.

"My father had children with his first wife, and while they were part of our lives, the closeness was never quite there. We had our separate paths. However, my stepmom from his first marriage was compassionate and caring towards me. I think she was the only person who understood the sacrifices of love and pain."

Though I was hurt to hear about the relationship between Logan and his dad, hearing him speak kindly of his stepmom was a fleeting moment of happiness, knowing that he at least had someone who cared about him. It marked the first time he opened up about such sentiments, yet the past tense in his voice suggested a loss, casting a veil of sadness over my heart.

"What about your mom?" I asked, noticing he hadn't mentioned anything about her at all.

"She had her favorite too, and sadly, it wasn't me either," he replied. His words seemed to carry the weight of unspoken pain and longing.

As Logan shared more about his family, each story unveiled layers of his past, revealing the intricate web of experiences that shaped him into the person I was beginning to understand.

In one of Logan's most heartfelt moments, he shared a poignant memory about his brother Scott. "I had hit rock bottom and was living hours away from the Twin Cities. My brother Scott was the only person who cared enough to drive all the way out to visit me," Logan confided, his voice tinged with somber. "I didn't have anything at the time, but he came out and spent some time with me. Before he left, he bought me a television. It was a simple gesture, but his thoughtfulness meant the world to me. Growing up, he was the only brother who ever gave me a few bucks when I needed it, and if I had to say there's one person in this world who loves me, it would be him." As Logan shared this vulnerable moment, I listened attentively, offering reassurance and a safe space for him to open up.

As a mother of four, I couldn't possibly love any one of my children more or less than the others. Therefore, it was difficult for me to comprehend how his parents or some members of his family didn't love him, and I wanted him to be wrong in his assessment of their love. However, I reminded myself that these were his feelings. Regardless of how his family treated him—whether lovingly or not—his feelings were valid. If he felt hurt by their treatment or words, who am I or anyone to say that he shouldn't be hurt or is wrong for feeling that way? But I hope that with time, I can change that familial perspective for him.

CHAPTER 7

HEAD OVER HEELS

A FEW DAYS LATER, I received an unexpected call from Caleb. I hadn't seen or spoken to him since we first met a week ago and was surprised by his call.

I answered, "Hi, Caleb."

"Hey, Steph. How's Minnesota treating you?" he inquired.

I shared with him that I was still in the process of exploring and getting to know Minnesota, but overall, I was enjoying my time here.

Caleb then mentioned that his doctor had advised him to go on more walks during his recovery but was reluctant to go alone. "So, I talked to Jasmine and wondered if you'd join me for walks. Would you be available?" he asked with hopefulness in his tone.

After a thoughtful pause, I responded, "Sure, I can join you. When and where?"

He suggested Keller Park within the next half hour, describing the picturesque boardwalk along the lake's edge as quite romantic. Intrigued by the boardwalk, I agreed, eager to experience what awaited us at the park. He also mentioned he wouldn't be driving for a while, so I offered to pick him up. Exploring a new place sounded like a great way to spend the afternoon.

As we strolled along the boardwalk, the peaceful surroundings captured my attention. The lush greenery, tangled vines on the trees, and wildlife going about their day made it feel like a hidden oasis. It reminded me of parks back in San Diego, especially Balboa Park with its natural charm. Wanting to remember this beautiful place, I took a picture of the boardwalk with the lake and greenery in the backdrop.[14]

What struck me the most was how close this tranquil lake was to our neighborhood. Minnesota truly lives up to its reputation as the Land of Ten Thousand Lakes. It seems like there's a hidden lake waiting to be discovered around every corner.

Exploring Keller Park and its serene beauty was a refreshing experience. It's moments like these that make me appreciate the simple pleasures of nature, right in our own backyard.

"So, how is your recovery coming along?" I inquired, trying to strike up a conversation.

"I'm getting better. This experience has definitely opened my eyes to the importance of taking care of my health," Caleb replied, his tone reflecting a mix of seriousness and gratitude.

"I'm really glad to hear that," I responded. Curious about his life before the hospital visit, I asked what he did for a living. He revealed he was a hairstylist, jokingly mentioning that his sensitive hands were exclusively made for beauty. His humor lightened the conversation, eliciting a laugh from me.

Caleb, standing tall at 5'11", was quite a rarity for a Hmong man. He was handsome, with a witty sense of humor, fair skin, and stylishly combed thick hair.

"Since you're on leave from work now, what do you do all day?" I

---

[14] Photo timestamped at 4:43 p.m. on August 11, 2019.

asked, imagining how I would struggle with boredom in his shoes.

"I stay in bed and watch Korean dramas all day," he admitted with a chuckle. "And that's why my doctor told me to get out and walk."

The mention of Korean dramas caught me by surprise, and I laughed in response. "What genre of K-drama do you indulge in?" I asked.

"I like the romantic ones that make you cry," Caleb confessed, prompting another round of laughter from me. He was initially serious but joined in the laughter too. I found it quite hilarious to learn about his unexpected passion for K-dramas, especially coming from a heterosexual Hmong man.

"You look like you could be a leading actor in one of those K-dramas," I said, hinting at his good looks. Caleb laughed and quipped, "Thank you. I think I've watched enough to memorize every monologue from 'Crash Landing on You' in English. I don't even need to watch it with the subtitles anymore." His comment sparked more laughter between us.

Just as our amusement began to subside, my phone rang, breaking the lighthearted moment. It was Logan. I answered quickly, and he caught the trailing echoes of our laughter. "It's good to hear you're having a great time," Logan remarked. "What are you doing?" His voice carried a mix of curiosity and perhaps a tinge of something else.

I paused for a moment, not just to hear his question, but to absorb the irresistible low timbre of his voice that always seems to slow down the world for me. "I'm out for a walk with Caleb," I replied, "but we're almost finished here."

There was a subtle shift in Logan's demeanor, a quietness that crept into his tone. I couldn't quite decipher his emotions—was he disappointed, curious, or simply lost in thought? Without hesitation, I reassured him, "We're about to leave the lake. I'll be dropping Caleb off at home shortly."

There was a moment of silence before Logan spoke, "Okay. No need to rush. I'll see you later?" His question carried a note of uncertainty, as if he needed confirmation.

"Yes, I will definitely see you as soon as I drop off Caleb," I confirmed, hoping to ease any lingering doubts or concerns he might have had.

After dropping Caleb off, I hurried to see Logan, eager to spend our evening together. As soon as he spotted me, he smiled and wasted no time in asking if I like ice cream. My eyes lit up at the mention of my weakness; indulging in ice cream was an irresistible prospect. Logan suggested we go out for ice cream then spend some time at the park. The simplicity of his plan was perfect, aligning with my love for uncomplicated pleasures.

We sat on a park bench, relishing the cool August breeze that tousled our hair as we quietly savored our ice cream. It was a peaceful moment, exactly what I needed at the end of every day. Suddenly, our calm was interrupted when Logan mentioned Caleb.

"So, Caleb, huh?" Logan's question, delivered with a subtle edge and curiosity, caught me mid-bite. His tone carried a hint of jealousy as he probed, "Are you and Caleb close?"

Taken aback by his sudden question, I reassured him, "I met him the same day I met you, but we're not close." Despite my surprise, I couldn't help but feel a twinge of amusement about Logan's reaction.

Logan embodied everything I desired in a man—tall, dark, and handsome, with a magnetic mix of qualities that drew me to him. He had a captivating blend of physical strength, ruggedness, honesty, humor, sentimentality, and generosity. If only he knew how mesmerizing he was to me whenever he's within my sight or how he takes my breath away, he wouldn't think to ask such a question.

Despite our budding connection and my increasing fondness for him, it had only been a week, and I wasn't in a hurry to label or define anything just yet. Nor did I want to deter him by coming off as clingy or desperate, because I genuinely liked him. However, I also wanted to be mindful of Logan's feelings. I didn't want him to feel uneasy or unsure about our interactions with other people. Having come from past relationships where my partner showed little concern for my well-being or whereabouts, Logan's attentiveness was a refreshing change, and I admire him for caring enough to say something.

Approaching the topic with care, I said, "I know it's early for us to put labels on things, but I've genuinely enjoyed getting to know you, and I care about you very much. I sensed a bit of concern regarding my walk with Caleb, and I just want to make sure you're comfortable with everything."

A smile played at the corners of Logan's lips as he glanced down at the grass beneath our feet. "I'm fine. Caleb's a good-looking guy, and if you were interested in him, I'd genuinely be happy for you," he replied.

His response left me feeling a bit disheartened, and I gazed at him intently. "Please don't say that unless you mean it, because that stings. I really like you, and you're constantly on my mind when we're apart."

The small smile that had graced Logan's face widened into a genuine grin. I leaned in to kiss his cheek while placing my hand on the other, but he turned slightly, and I kissed the corner of his lips instead. Not dismayed by the unexpected turn, I remarked, "Caleb is a very nice guy, but he doesn't tug at my heartstrings."

What I truly wanted to express was that Logan had been tugging at my heartstrings from the very moment I laid eyes on him. He was a blend of fantasy and dream, but also tangible reality. I couldn't comprehend how fortunate I was to encounter him and have the pleasure of his attention, because I've never been the kind of girl who "gets the guy," who takes her breath away at first sight.

We lingered on the bench, enjoying each other's presence as we savored the last bites of our ice cream and took in the peaceful view of the sun slowly descending beyond the glistening lake in front of us. When Logan finished his ice cream, he stood up excitedly to share about an event he wanted to host, something he had always dreamed of doing. His enthusiasm was contagious as he started to dance and sing, his face lighting up with the biggest smile. I couldn't help but steal a glance before turning away to conceal the beaming crimson red that filled my blushing cheeks. It was clear, and unequivocal, that I was beyond head over heels for this man.

CHAPTER 8

I Love You

*T*HREE WEEKS HAD GONE BY since I met Logan, and it seemed as though he had seamlessly woven himself into the fabric of my life. We spent every day together after our memorable evening at Mystic Lake, where we stayed up all night talking. Whether during lunch breaks, after work, or on weekends, his presence was a constant source of joy and comfort in my otherwise busy and often solitary routine. Yet, I treaded cautiously, mindful of past experiences where relationships fell apart just when things felt comfortable and promising.

It was a bright and breezy Sunday morning. [15] My dad and stepmom had been away since yesterday, visiting my stepmom's sister in Sacramento. To break the quietness of the room, I played one of my favorite playlists on my phone that always gets me into a creative mood.

---

[15] Sunday, August 24, 2019

I kept the volume low so as not to disturb Keith, whom I presumed was still asleep since I hadn't heard him come out of his room. My bedroom window faces north, so there was barely enough sunlight filtering in even on the brightest day. However, with my frequent migraines, I preferred it this way.

I began arranging my clothes on the newly acquired clothing rack I had ordered from Amazon. Thank goodness for Amazon and online shopping. I don't enjoy shopping and dislike the tediousness of traditional retail, where I would wander through endless aisles when I needed only a single item. Despite my minimalist approach to fashion, the modest four-foot-wide closet in my room was starting to groan under the weight of my wardrobe.

As I reached for a soft blue sweater from the basket to be hung up, my phone buzzed, and Logan's name lit up on the Caller ID, setting my heart aflutter.

"Hi Logan," I answered with a smile, eagerly anticipating his warm voice on the other end. However, instead of his usual greeting, I heard a distant murmur. "Logan? Can you hear me?" I queried, only to be met with silence. In the background, I caught snippets of another familiar voice—Jacob, Dee's brother and Logan's childhood friend. It seemed Logan had accidentally called me amidst a conversation with Jacob.

"Hello?" I spoke a bit more assertively, hoping to capture Logan's attention. He seemed engrossed in sharing something with Jacob; his voice was animated and enthusiastic. Intrigued, I shamelessly remained on the line, eavesdropping as Logan began speaking about me.

"It's only been a few weeks, but I feel like I've known her for a very long time. Whenever we talk, I can't help myself from wanting to keep talking to her," Logan continued.

Jacob abruptly interjected, "Bro, you always did like the sound of your own voice," laughing as Logan joined in. I couldn't help but chuckle hearing Logan's laughter. There's something about the sound of his laugh that always draws me in.

"Seriously. It's different with her. She really cares about me. I know it. I could be talking nonsense for hours, and she would always listen without making me feel like she had to rush off somewhere. And when she responds, it's like whatever she says is the best thing in the world. She makes me think about things I have not thought about before," Logan said with passion in his voice as I melted onto my bed, listening more intently and in awe that I made him feel that way.

"I've never met anyone like her. She's amazing, works in IT, and is incredibly smart. I don't know what she sees in me. I'm just a fool," Logan gushed. Hearing his words, I couldn't help but smile broadly. I was completely touched and pleasantly surprised that he would speak of me in such fond ways.

"I know she's genuine about you," Jacob remarked. "When Marissa asked her about Caleb, she said, 'he's nice, but he's not Logan.' That says a lot about how she feels."

It was strange, yet flattering, to hear someone talking about me in such a context.

I wrestled with guilt for eavesdropping, yet I couldn't resist listening to what else Logan had to say about me. All this time, I knew he was interested in me, but I didn't know how deep his affection was. I remained on the call, placing myself on mute, spellbound as Logan poured his heart out, speaking passionately about our bond and the deep connection he felt with me. Each word he uttered felt like a sweet serenade to my ears. Yet, amidst the joy, a nagging thought crept in—*He literally talked only about me for almost half an hour now. Did Logan know I was listening? Was this a deliberate display to impress me?*

Quickly dismissing the notion, I reminded myself of Logan's genuine nature. He didn't need theatrics or pretense; his authenticity was one of the things that drew me to him. Feeling conflicted, I quietly disconnected the call, content in knowing that the affection in his words was as genuine as the man himself. It reassured me to know that his feelings mirrored mine.

Hours later, Logan called, expressing his desire to see me and suggesting he would swing by to pick me up. We drove to a serene spot in a small park along the Mississippi River. It was my first time there. As Logan parked the car, I sensed some anticipation from him. As soon as he turned off the engine, he seemed eager to talk. "What's on your mind?" I asked.

Logan hesitated for a moment, his expression pensive, as he began to speak. "I know I'm not the only person you're talking to. I'm sure Caleb calls you sometimes, and he's probably not the only other guy, too," his voice tinged with uncertainty.

This was unlike the confident and assertive Logan I met, who took my number without asking. I listened intently, interested in where he was steering the conversation. "What are you trying to say?" I asked, genuinely wanting to understand.

I was hesitant but admitted that I also knew I wasn't the only one he was talking to. Sometimes when we were together, his phone would ring, catching my attention as I saw other women's names flashing on the caller ID. Despite him never answering their calls while with me, I silently acknowledged it and never asked him about them, choosing instead to maintain our unspoken understanding. Our relationship existed in a liminal space, undefined yet filled with deep emotions—a product of our relatively short time together.

"I don't know how to commit to you. I want to, but I worry you may not want to because you have other options," he confessed with a raw intensity that caught me off guard. "I feel like you have me under your spell, but you're talking to these other guys, and I'm not the jealous type, yet I am with you."

His words hung in the air, heavy with emotions he had not expressed to me directly before. I sensed that he had been down this road more times than he should have, where previous partners may not have been honest with him. I grounded myself to remain understanding, but my heart quickened upon hearing the passion in his words, a stark contrast to the guy who had just nonchalantly mentioned not too long ago that he would be content as long as I was happy, regardless of who I ended up with. Yet, this sudden shift in his demeanor left me wondering: does he want more, or does he want to reduce spending so much time together? I hoped it wasn't the latter.

Without waiting for clarification, I said, "Isn't it obvious that I spend every waking moment with you when I'm not working or sleeping? I see you more than my own son, and he lives with me." I paused, observing his reaction before continuing, "I want all of you, every part that makes you uniquely you."

Logan looked at me, his expression a mix of relief and warmth as he seemed to be gathering his thoughts, then he said, "I want to be exclusive."

Without saying anything, I look down at his hand and held it affectionately, intertwining my fingers with his, then returning to his gaze, I replied, "I do too." He raised the back of my hand to his lips and kissed it tenderly before turning to kiss me.

"I don't care about other women," he murmured, his voice filled with conviction. "They were women I knew and used to talk to before I met you, but I never had anything serious with them. Talking to them was like talking to empty echoes. They only wanted to be heard, but they never heard me. I don't want you to ever worry about them."

Logan's words forged a deeper connection and devotion within me, one that I had been hoping for but hadn't expected to hear so soon. Nonetheless, I was glad we finally had this conversation. Part of me couldn't help but wonder, was he blind to his own attractiveness compared to my plainness, or did he see something in me that I'm just not seeing?

The next day,[16] while engrossed in my work at the client's office, my phone rang, and I glanced to see Logan's name on the Caller ID. As usual, a smile naturally formed on my lips as I answered his call with a warm greeting, "Good morning."

"Good morning, Beautiful," Logan's voice came through in a soft, low tone.

"It's always nice to hear from you," I replied.

In his characteristic joking yet somewhat serious tone, Logan teased, "You don't miss me."

His comment caught me off guard, and I lightly laughed before responding, "Why would you say that?"

"Because you never call me. It's always me calling you," he replied playfully.

Feeling a twinge of guilt mixed with understanding, I admitted, "I'm sorry about that. I promise to call you more often. It's just that I'm always caught up with work when I'm in the office, so I don't call you during this time. Also, I know you're working too, and I didn't want to bother you. You know I'll see you as soon as I get off work anyway."

It was a nice surprise to hear Logan express his desire for more frequent communication from me. In my 20-year marriage, calling my ex-husband during business trips often elicited annoyance from him. Even in my post-divorce relationships, communication remained minimal and primarily functional. Thus, I had become accustomed to the notion that less communication equated to normalcy, despite harboring a silent yearning for deeper connection. Learning that Logan

---

[16] Monday, August 26, 2019

shared this desire was both refreshing and reassuring, offering a glimpse of the fulfilling connection I had longed for.

"I'm working in the area today and thought I'd swing by to have lunch with you," Logan announced.

"I would love that," I replied, my smile widening at the thought of spending even more time with him.

"I'll pick you up at noon," Logan affirmed.

We exchanged a few more words before ending the call.

It was 12:00 p.m., and my heart quickened with anticipation, a familiar thrill every time I was about to see Logan, despite seeing him every day. Stepping outside, I found him waiting for me in the parking lot. One thing about Logan that I love is that he is always punctual. His mere presence instantly brings me a sense of calm and happiness.

When he spotted me, a smile formed on his face. I couldn't get over how gorgeous he was, even in his construction attire, which consisted of a cap, worn-out jeans, a faded t-shirt, and construction boots often covered in dirt or sawdust. The sight of him never failed to take my breath away. I also couldn't get over the fact that this beautiful man wanted to be with me, plain Jane in a ponytail.

I settled into the passenger seat of Logan's car, "Where are we going to eat?"

"Let's go to Noodles!" Logan suggested with excitement. I love how he loves food. The way his eyes lit up when seeing his favorite dishes.

Sitting with our meals at Noodles, the casual atmosphere allowed for an intimate conversation to unfold. Logan turned to me with a smile on his face. "I feel incredibly fortunate to have you," he confessed, his words weaving warmth within me. "I'm surprised you're not tired of me yet," he added.

"Never!" I said playfully.

His declaration touched a heartfelt chord within me, and I leaned toward him, feeling the urge to express my own emotions with a kiss.

After lunch, we returned to my office with 15 minutes to spare before my next meeting. Despite the ticking clock, neither of us felt rushed. We lingered in the car, savoring these moments together, our conversation ongoing as if time had paused just for us.

As the minutes slipped by, I became aware of the impending need to return to work. Turning to Logan, I softened my voice, "I'll see you after work." I gave him a quick affectionate kiss before reaching for the door handle.

However, the chivalry in Logan was unwilling to let me walk. "Let me drop you off right by the door," he insisted.

"It's just a few steps. I'll walk," I replied with my leg already halfway out the door. I bid him a wonderful afternoon and closed the door behind me as I made my way towards the entrance.

Just when I thought he had left the parking lot for his construction site, I saw him circling his car back around. I paused to watch him. He stopped in front of the entrance, rolled down his window to meet my gaze, and a genuine smile lit up his features, his eyes sparkling with affection as he declared, "Kuv hlub koj tshaj nplaws.[17]" I had never heard anyone speak these words to me in Hmong before, and it felt profoundly different as it tugged at my heartstrings. I didn't anticipate his heartfelt announcement, yet it felt undeniably right. Any other time and with anyone else, I might have thought this was corny, but without hesitation, I replied with all my heart, "Kuv hlub koj thiab.[18]"

In that moment, surrounded by the bustling rhythm of daily life, I realized that love, true and genuine, knows no timeline. It blooms in unexpected moments, filling the spaces between words and actions with a warmth that transcends all doubts and ambiguities.

---

[17] In Hmong, translate to "I love you so much."

[18] In Hmong, translate to "I love you, too."

After work, since Logan was working nearby, I asked him to text me the address of his construction site. I had not seen his work before, although I had seen plenty of before-and-after pictures of projects he had completed. I wanted to stop by and see him in action and observe his work up close.

I arrived at the address and noticed Logan's car parked in front of a charming, beige-colored house in a newly developed neighborhood. I pulled up behind his vehicle, parked, and got out of my car. A group of construction workers caught my eye as they walked toward the rear of the house. Assuming they were his crew, I decided to follow them.

As I entered the backyard, I spotted Logan on one knee, overseeing the construction of a grand composite deck. He was using a power drill to secure the final handrail into place. The deck had a second-story elevation connected to the house and featured an elegantly crafted L-shaped stairway that gracefully descended to an unfinished patio below. The wooden framing around the patios indicated that concrete would be poured later.

Logan noticed my smile as I watched him work and responded with a playful wink, inviting me to join him on top of the deck. I nodded and headed toward the concrete stair landing. As I ascended, I placed my hand on the white-coated steel handrail, admiring its perfect match with the house's trim. The decking boards displayed two shades of sandalwood and white, complementing the house's siding color. With my trained eye, I carefully inspected every board and rail for perfection and alignment, noting every concealed screw and its placement.

Having overseen numerous construction projects while in California, I could recognize exquisite craftsmanship when I saw it. Logan's work reflected his years of experience in the field, leaving me thoroughly impressed and deepening my admiration for him even more. When I reached him, I immediately gave him a hug, kissed him, and complimented him on his work, saying, "I would love a deck like this someday. It's gorgeous, and every detail is so clean. You did a really great job." He laughed and said, "You're just being too kind." I assured him, "I wouldn't have said anything at all and would have just greeted you if I thought the deck was mediocre."

After asking him if he was finished for the day, I said, "Let's go to dinner. My treat."

With a wave, Logan directed his crew to wrap things up and tidy all the tools and building materials. They sprang into action immediately, efficiently picking up tools, boards, and excess trimmings scattered around the yard. Within a few minutes, everything was neatly put away, showcasing Logan's leadership skills and the reliability of his crew. I couldn't help but smile at him and remarked, "I love a man in charge."

As we settled into a nearby restaurant, the aroma of sizzling meat, onions, bell peppers, and garlic surrounded us, prompting us to know exactly what we wanted from the menu. The waitress promptly brought us a bowl of chips and salsa. Watching Logan enjoy his appetizer, I couldn't help but ponder the deep connection between food and love. The way flavors mingle and bring joy, filling our stomachs with warmth. *Perhaps this is why couples often gain weight as they find comfort in indulging together*, I mused to myself and smiled.

While waiting for our food, I asked Logan, "How did you get started in construction?" He took a sip of his water to wash down the chips and salsa and began to share, "I didn't really know what I wanted to do. I've had various jobs: bus driver, truck driver, bartender, pizza delivery, and even worked in a warehouse once. But I always disliked the rigid hours and low pay. I wanted something more hands-on and to have more control over my work." Taking another chip, dipping it in salsa, he continued, "I saw an opportunity to take a vocational course in construction, which seemed like something I could be good at and fits into what I wanted to do. The training led me to work on several construction projects. I built homes for a construction company for a few years before branching out on my own to have more control over my hours and the kind of work I wanted to focus on."

The food had finally arrived, and I was still intrigued, so I asked him to continue. He talked about his first deck project and how his cousin had given him the opportunity to build a wooden deck. It was a decent-sized deck, and he earned $1,000—a sum that was significantly small compared to what he earns now, but it was the first project he could add to his portfolio of experiences. He was grateful for the opportunity.

I asked him how he came up with his business name, Among Builders, and he chuckled as he explained, "It didn't start out as Among Builders." I smiled, intrigued by his answer. "When I started, I was a one-man crew, a Hmong man. So, I called it 'A Hmong Builder,' but as my business grew and word started to spread, everyone confused the name with 'Among Builders,' so the name just stuck." I laughed when I heard that and said, "I love the name. It's very clever and fitting now that you have a crew and are constructing among builders."

As I listened to him share his experiences, from his first deck to the countless projects he had completed around the Twin Cities, I envisioned construction as if I were there to witness it all. His career experiences truly made him a jack-of-all-trades and a master at deck building.

As we finished our meal, Logan called the waitress over to order some food to go. As she approached our table, he turned to me and said, "Why don't we get something for Keith too? What does he enjoy?" His thoughtfulness was unexpected and a pleasant surprise. After all, Logan hadn't met Keith and had only heard me talk about him, my pride and joy. It truly warmed my heart that he was thinking about my son.

Even though I had insisted on treating him to dinner, Logan sneakily excused himself to the restroom and took care of the bill. I playfully chided him for his sneaky move but couldn't help appreciating his generosity. As we waited for our to-go order, I felt it was the appropriate time to share that I would be going out of town soon.

"I'll be heading back to California in a few days," I began, watching his expression shift with curiosity.

His brows furrowed slightly. "California? For how long?"

"Just under a week," I replied.

He paused, contemplating my words for a moment before a spark of excitement lit up his eyes. "I want to go with you too!"

Surprised but pleasantly so, I leaned in, a smile tugging at my lips. "Really?"

"Absolutely!" His enthusiasm matched my own. "It's been more than a decade since I've been to California. If you don't mind me coming with you, it'd be fun."

"I don't mind at all. That would be incredible," I responded. Traveling alone had never been my favorite thing to do. I dreaded it. The thought of exploring California with Logan filled me with anticipation, whereas before, I was not looking forward to this trip at all. If I wasn't a keynote speaker, I wouldn't be going.

Feeling a sense of relief and genuine happiness, I leaned back into my seat and said, "Well, then I'm glad I mentioned it with enough time to book your flight and make other plans while we're there."

A couple of days later, my mom called me with a request: she wanted a chest freezer. She lamented the inadequacy of her current freezer, expressing her wish for a spacious chest freezer like everyone else seemed to have, especially for storing her frozen goods. She mentioned with sarcasm, "Seems like everyone else's kids love them enough to buy them multiple chest freezers. I have eight children, and none have bought me one." I couldn't help but roll my eyes at her insinuation that none of her children loved her, though deep down, I found her tone comical.

In Minnesota, it was a common sight to see families with two to three chest freezers, often because they have at least one family member who enjoys hunting or fishing. These freezers are usually stocked with a variety of meat, as I noticed at my dad's and stepmom's place. They had a dedicated freezer for each type of protein: one for pork, another for beef, and yet another for fish.

I responded to my mom, "Yes, Mom. I'll get you a chest freezer."

Logan was right beside me in his car when I answered her call, so naturally, I turned to him and asked, "Where can I find a chest freezer?" Since arriving here, I hadn't explored Minnesota much. My days were mainly filled with spending time with Logan. If I didn't initiate a call, he would reach out to me, and our days always ended up being spent together.

"I know exactly where," Logan affirmed as he started the car. We drove to a local department store and browsed through the extensive appliance section for a chest freezer. Given my mom's compact living space, we aimed for something small. We explored various options before finally selecting one that I believed would be perfect for her tiny place.

"Do they offer delivery?" I asked Logan.

"Yes, but there's usually a fee. I can just drop it off for your mom," Logan kindly suggested.

I was taken aback. I wasn't quite prepared for Logan to meet my mom just yet. I knew the barrage of questions she'd throw at him, likely starting from the moment he was born. I hesitated for a moment before quickly adding, "Don't worry about it. It'll be easier to have the store deliver it."

"Don't be silly. I got this!" Logan reassured me confidently.

As we were checking out of the store and paying for the chest freezer, the cashier asked me for my phone number to be entered into their purchase records. I said my number aloud to him. Just then, Logan subtly remarked, "No wonder."

I looked over at Logan, puzzled, and asked, "No wonder what?"

"You have so many 5s in your phone number. It's no wonder we connected so well. 5s are always a good sign for me," he explained.

I smiled at him. I didn't take him for a guy who looked for signs.

After finalizing the purchase of the chest freezer, the sales rep enlisted one of the department floor guys to assist us in loading it into the car. I was thankful that Logan was driving his work vehicle, a large cargo van. As we drove over to my mom's place, I couldn't shake off a slight nervousness. I had never introduced a man to my mom before, as I tended to keep my romantic life quite private. With my ex-husband, I didn't introduce him until we were about to get married.

Pulling up to the house, I turned to Logan and mentioned that I'd go in first to inform my mom of our arrival. Firstly, I wanted to let her know about the chest freezer. Secondly, I aimed to prepare her for meeting my "gentleman caller" and cautioned her against asking too many questions. Lastly, I planned to clear a space in her small kitchen to accommodate the freezer.

As soon as my mom opened the door, she was surprised at how quickly I responded to her request. She hugged me tightly and exclaimed, "You do love me." With a slight smile, I rolled my eyes and replied, "Yes, Mom. Of course, I love you."

Just as I was about to begin clearing the space, Logan made his entrance, effortlessly carrying the freezer—about the size of a washing machine—in his arms. He wore a dark gray t-shirt, and his bulging biceps were impossible to miss. My mom's excitement distracted me, and I hadn't had the chance to inform her that he was accompanying me, adding an unexpected twist to the situation.

She looked at Logan in surprise and asked, "Are you here to deliver the freezer?" assuming he was the delivery guy. Immediately, I deliberated whether to let her assume he was the delivery person, thus avoiding her inevitable questioning. However, I didn't want to make Logan feel uneasy, especially since he had expressed excitement about meeting my mom during our drive to her place.

"Mom, this is my good friend, Logan," I said hesitantly. The heat rushed to my cheeks, and I couldn't bear touching my face, fearful of discovering it might be sweating with anxiousness. At 40 years old, I hadn't uttered the words "my boyfriend" since I was a teenager. The other guys I dated after my divorce were only referred to as "partners," and it felt awkwardly foreign and strange to tell my mom that Logan was my boyfriend. So, "good friend" it was.

"Oh," my mom exclaimed with a wide smile, her tone full of surprise, as if she already knew he was more than just a friend.

"Me tub,[19]" she affectionately addressed him in Hmong.

Then came the inevitable barrage of questions—about his parents, his profession, the duration of our acquaintance, and his intentions toward her daughter, whether it would lead to marriage or in her words, "ua si xwb.[20]" Silently, behind my mom's back, I mouthed the words to Logan, "I'm sorry," feeling the weight of the unexpected interrogation he was facing. It was an awkward situation I hadn't prepared him for.

He stole a quick glance at me, offering a smile that didn't waver as he politely fielded every question my mom fired at him. Even as he diligently unpacked and set up the chest freezer in my mom's tiny kitchen, he remained composed and gracious.

When Logan finished with the installation, my mom's questions were still unending. Sensing the need to wrap things up, I intervened, saying, "Sorry, Mom. We've got a lot of errands to run today, so we have

---

[19] In Hmong, "me tub" (pronounced: me thu) translates to "son."

[20] In Hmong, "ua si xwb" (pronounced: ua she xú) translates to "playing only."

to get going," as I made my way toward the door and signaled Logan to go to the car first.

Logan politely excused himself, telling my mom he was happy to meet her, and stepped out. I wrapped my arms around my mom in a warm hug, saying, "I hope you like your new freezer, Mom. I'll come back and visit soon." However, her response caught me off guard. "He's husband material, you know. He's tall, strong, and handsome. You were blind before, but you were young and didn't know any better. I'm happy that you have good eyes now and can finally see clearly," she asserted confidently, her words carrying an unexpected weight. "Thanks, Mom," I replied, a mix of awkwardness and gratitude at her newfound approval of Logan.

Joining Logan in the car, I couldn't help but apologize profusely for the intense questioning my mom had subjected him to. "It's okay. I'm good with moms. They all love me," he responded with a confident grin, his humor bringing a lightness to the situation. I kissed his cheek and said, "Yes, she does. She already thinks you're 'husband material'," adding to his confidence.

CHAPTER 9

TOES IN THE SAND

THE MORNING OF OUR FLIGHT TO CALIFORNIA,[21] we met up early to take a ride-share, arriving at the airport just after 5:30. The airport was already filled with the usual buzz of early travelers starting their weekend getaways or business ventures. With our boarding time swiftly approaching, the hustle and bustle of the airport made me slightly anxious about making our flight on time.

However, Logan caught sight of an old friend from a construction project they had worked on together a few years back, who had now become a TSA agent. I watched as Logan walked over to him to exchange waves and engage in playful banter with his friend. I couldn't hear their conversation over the airport chatter, but Logan returned a minute later with a grin on his face and announced, "My buddy here can fast-track us through TSA.

---

[21] Thursday, August 29, 2019

Grateful for the shortcut, I followed Logan as his friend guided us past the regular security line, allowing us to efficiently check our carry-on bags and move through security with ease. It was a relief to have Logan's connections working in our favor.

Having spent most of his life in Minnesota and not having much leisure for travel, Logan was excited about our first trip. I made sure to book a window seat for him on our non-stop flight to San Francisco, wanting him to enjoy the view. As we settled into our assigned seats, I reached over to hold his hand, feeling a rush of excitement and gratitude.

"Thank you for joining me on this trip," I said. "I hope you're prepared for the surprises I have planned."

The thrill of the upcoming days filled me with anticipation. My conference was scheduled for the weekend, leaving us with Friday to settle in and explore, and Monday and Tuesday for leisurely activities. I had planned a one-day stopover in Las Vegas on our way back to Minnesota on Wednesday, as Logan had mentioned he had never been there before.

Our flight from Minneapolis to San Francisco lasted a little over four hours, during which we leaned on each other and dozed off for most of the journey. The gentle humming of the airplane engines and the warmth of Logan's presence made the time pass comfortably and swiftly. As the plane began its descent, I gently nudged Logan awake, urging him to peer out the window. His eyes widened as he caught sight of the expansive Pacific vista in the distance, the waters sparkling under the morning sunlight. With a sense of nostalgia, I shared with him, "This view is what I miss most about California."

Touching down in San Francisco just before noon, we eagerly disembarked from the plane and made our way to baggage claim to retrieve our luggage. The air was crisp and refreshing, carrying with it the familiar scent of salt from the ocean. The blue sky overhead and cool breeze greeted us with a warm embrace, welcoming me back to the

Golden State. It was a pleasant feeling to be back in the familiarity of California's vibrant atmosphere, and this time, sharing it with Logan made the experience even more special.

After picking up our car from the rental lot, I deliberately chose the scenic route to our hotel, ensuring Logan could catch glimpses of the ocean along the way. Despite visiting California a couple of times before, he never had the chance to witness the vastness of the ocean up close. I was determined to ensure he experienced the joy of dipping his toes in the sand and ocean before we returned home. The thought of sharing this moment with him filled me with anticipation, adding an extra layer of magic to our trip.

Minutes after we checked into our hotel room, Logan's exhaustion caught up with him, and he fell asleep almost instantly. I watched him, knowing how little rest he usually got back home. More than likely, he didn't sleep at all before arriving at the airport. His nights were often restless battles against insomnia, and days consisted of grueling hours at a construction site under the scorching sun, with barely any breaks. Despite being in charge, he would give his crew breaks but not take them himself. Some days, I'd read my books while keeping him company as he slept. The slightest noise would jolt him awake, his demeanor almost resembling that of someone with post-traumatic stress disorder. It was clear that life hadn't been gentle on him, yet his heart remained incredibly kind and resilient. I couldn't help but feel protective of him because he deserved so much more than the constant hardships he faced.

I silently made a vow to myself as I lay beside him, gently running my fingers through his hair—a comfort that seemed to soothe him in his sleep. I didn't just want to witness his dreams coming true; I wanted to stand beside him through every struggle and triumph, ensuring he never had to face a day of hardship alone.

This desire stemmed from more than just affection; it reflected his unwavering support for me. A week ago, I called him when my car broke down. When I learned that he was in the midst of a demanding construction project, I assured him I could manage with a ride-share. Yet, he dropped everything without a moment's hesitation to come to my aid, ensuring everything would be fine. When he arrived, he greeted me with a term that took me by surprise, "I could never leave my Queen waiting."

The title felt foreign and somewhat misplaced to me. I smiled at him, dismissing the endearment. "Oh, don't call me that. It makes me feel weird," I protested. No matter what he had going on, he always made me a priority, and that meant more to me than any tangible gift.

Lying beside Logan, I couldn't help but admire how peacefully he slept. His features seemed even more beautiful in this serene state—his perfect nose, his perfect lips—tempting me to lean in for a gentle kiss. Yet, I refrained, not wanting to disturb his slumber or worse, jolt him awake.

Our relationship had deepened over the past month, but a subtle thought lingered in my mind. It was a minor concern, but curiosity nagged at me. Despite our closeness, our physical intimacy hadn't progressed beyond kissing and cuddling, leaving me to ponder his level of attraction toward me. Even in moments that felt like they could escalate, he would pull back. *Shouldn't we have moved forward by now?* I wondered, my thoughts edging toward overthinking.

Yet, just as swiftly as the doubts arose, I quashed them, scolding myself for succumbing to old insecurities. Reminding myself that Logan had openly expressed his love for me just a few days ago, a declaration that held profound weight in our relationship and wasn't based on our physical intimacy. *Stop overthinking, Steph!* I chided myself internally. *You're allowing past doubts to cloud the present. Appreciate what you have—a remarkable man who loves you without the demand for physical intimacy.*

By the time Logan stirred awake, evening had begun to descend upon us. As we perused the directory of dining options, a nearby sushi restaurant caught our attention, and we decided to indulge in the fresh seafood that San Francisco had to offer. I mentioned to Logan how San Francisco boasts some of the freshest seafood around, a delightful perk of its proximity to the ocean. Logan's excitement was noticeable as he eagerly anticipated indulging in the coastal freshness of the city's daily catch.

After dinner, I took Logan on a tour of some of my favorite San Francisco landmarks. We visited the iconic Golden Gate Bridge, soaked in the vibrant atmosphere of Fisherman's Wharf, strolled through outdoor markets, and enjoyed moments of tranquility along the docks. The city's nocturnal charm unfolded before us, aglow with twinkling lights and caressed by the ocean breeze, creating a memorable evening for our first time together in San Francisco.

We walked to the edge of a dock and paused, taking in the night's view over the dark waters. The shimmering lights of homes scattered along the hillsides added to the enchanting scene. The absence of the moon only heightened the beauty of the cityscape, casting a veil of mystery and romance over us. Logan turned towards me and placed a tender kiss on my forehead where it meets my hairline, adding to the magic of the moment. However, the night was starting to chill, so we decided to return to our hotel.

Back in our hotel room, I laid out the outfits I would be wearing for the next two days at the conference, while also informing Logan about the guest pass I had secured for him. He playfully suggested he'd be my personal assistant for the next few days, which made me laugh. "Please don't do that," I responded, appreciating his humor.

I handed him the conference agenda and excused myself to take a shower. The hot water cascading over my back felt soothing, a familiar sensation I often indulged in back home. However, with Logan waiting just outside, I hastened my shower, eager to return to his company.

I quickly dried my hair and put on my pajamas before easing into bed beside him. I noticed him staring up at the ceiling with a contemplative expression. "What's on your mind?" I inquired, curious about the thoughts swirling in his head. His lips formed a brief pout, hinting at a suppressed thought before he simply replied, "Nothing," and continued to gaze at the ceiling. I adjusted my position and settled on my back to join him in looking upwards. "What's on your mind?" he echoed my question.

"I was thinking about our plans after the conference," I shared, breaking the silence. "We'll be heading up north to Sonoma for zip-lining on Monday." Logan's eyes lit up with excitement. "Oh, I've always wanted to do that. That'll be so much fun!" he exclaimed; his enthusiasm contagious. "I know. I remember you mentioned that" I replied with a grin. "And then on Tuesday, we'll be off to Sacramento to meet up with my cousins for horseback riding. One of them has a friend who owns a horse ranch. Since you enjoy riding horses, I can't wait to see you in action."

Logan's joy was evident, and I couldn't help but feel a surge of happiness witnessing his excitement. His demeanor transformed, glowing like a child on Christmas morning.

As we turned to face each other in bed, his fingers delicately played with my hair, gently pulling on my bangs and then letting them go, causing my natural curls to bounce playfully across my face. I laughed softly at the ticklish sensation and his silly amusement with my hair. In the midst of this tender moment, he spoke, with a tinge of concern and vulnerability, "You're so smart. I worry that I won't be able to keep up with you because I'm so dumb. You'll eventually get bored of me."

My heart clenched at his words, sensing the weight of his worries. "Don't say that. Don't ever say that," I responded genuinely, wanting to reassure him.

Logan continued, voicing his subtle doubts about his worthiness compared to others I might have been with in the past. It hurt to hear him question his value, and I felt an overwhelming need to convey just how much he meant to me.

"Hun, I may have dated men with degrees and wealth, but if I were to strip away everything and leave only what truly matters, you would still outshine them all," I asserted, wanting him to understand his irreplaceable qualities. "You have the best heart of anyone I've ever met. You love deeply, care passionately, and always put me first. Your intangible qualities are rare and special. I know that for a fact. Anyone can obtain a degree and material things and can lose it all overnight or choose to do nothing with it, but not everyone possesses your heart qualities, which are a core essence of who you are. It's what I love most about you," I said with sincere earnestness.

Wanting to lift his spirits further, I expressed, "You know how I see you? I see you as more than just a self-made and accomplished man; you're brilliant. You've built your own construction company from the ground up and possess an engineering mind that effortlessly visualizes everything in 3D. Your mental math skills far surpass mine; you have the answer while I'm still working out the equation with a calculator. And your beautiful, generous heart is the crown on top. Your heart, Logan, is your greatest asset, and that's what makes you truly special to me. Let's not forget, you're breathtakingly gorgeous," I continued, emphasizing both his inner and outer qualities.

I moved in closer to reassuringly wrap my arms around him. His presence always felt like a sense of familiarity and calmness. Though I had only begun to truly understand him, there was a sense of belonging, as if he was the missing piece of home I had long been searching for.

As Logan gently lifted my face to meet his gaze, he leaned toward me and placed a gentle kiss on my lips, deepening our connection beyond what we had before. It was a moment of accelerated intimacy and vulnerability, where our hearts spoke volumes without the need for words. In that ultimate embrace, I knew that Logan's place in my heart would always be safe, and I never wanted him to doubt his significance in my life.

The next day dawned with a sense of anticipation as we prepared to leave for my conference. I glanced at Logan and was taken aback by the sight of him in an all-black, sleek suit without a tie, paired with fancy shoes that caught my eye—a departure from his usual casual attire of jeans and a t-shirt. His appearance was striking, and I couldn't help but feel a flutter in my heart over how dashing he looked.

It was certainly a different side of him. The way his suit accentuated his broad shoulders and masculine features, adding a touch of sophistication to his presence, left me momentarily speechless and unable to take my eyes off him. He approached me with a confident smile and a wink, clearly aware of the impact his appearance had on me. Tenderly, he gave me a hug and a kiss, asking if I was ready to start the day with breakfast before heading over to the conference room on the main floor.

Downstairs, the ambiance of the breakfast nook was cozy, with a view of the San Francisco Bay visible in the distance. Soft morning light broke through between the sky-blue curtains, casting a gentle glow over our table. Lost in my daze, I absently twirled my fork in my hash browns, mixing them with my eggs, my mind drifting back to the intimate moments shared with Logan the previous night. A contented smile lingered on my lips.

Across from me, Logan's eyes flickered with amusement as he observed my thoughtful expression. With a teasing grin, he quipped, "Is your mind in the gutter this morning?" His playful tone sparked a blush that crept across my cheeks, caught off guard by his lighthearted remark. I slightly bit my bottom lip, trying to find the right words to respond to his teasing before finally admitting, "Well, I was reminiscing about last night, and I couldn't help but wonder what took you so long," as I laughed lightly, almost embarrassed at what I was saying.

Logan's expression softened. "I can explain," he began, leaning in slightly as if sharing a secret. "I'm actually a bit of a germaphobe," he confessed. "It's not that I don't want your germs or anything like that. I just have this cautiousness about getting too intimate with people too easily or too early before getting to know what kind of person they are," pausing for a second, then quickly added, "and I don't want 'their' germs." He said, emphasizing "their" with air quotes, his expression was evidently serious. "You might see me talking to a beautiful woman at a bar," he continued, "but you'll never see me take anyone home, and anyone who has known me for most of my life can attest to that. I prefer to get to know someone deeply, to fall in love with their mind and heart before exploring any physical intimacy. And you never know how many partners they've been with. Thoughts like that scare me."

His words resonated with me on a profound level. The way he valued meaningful connections over superficial encounters revealed much about the quality of his character, and I found that deeply admirable. I've always held intimacy in high regard, seeing it as a sacred bond shared between individuals with intense emotions for each other. As I pondered his perspective, I couldn't help but marvel, *could he be any more perfect?* His approach to intimacy was a breath of fresh air in a world often driven by instant gratification.

As we continued our breakfast, our conversation shifted to lighter topics, but Logan's words lingered in my mind. It was another thread in the intricate fabric of our relationship, one that continuously increased my appreciation for him.

CHAPTER 10

WANDERLUST

MY TWO-DAY CONFERENCE HAD WRAPPED UP, and our adventure continued with anticipation for the next leg of our trip. We spent the morning in Sonoma County zip-lining amidst the towering redwoods, a first experience for both of us. After zipping through and above treetops, Logan and I agreed that it wasn't as thrilling as we had hoped. Neither of us had a fear of heights, and we joked that the next time we ziplined, it should be somewhere over the Grand Canyon. Despite it being less exhilarating, it was enjoyable just to be in each other's company, and this experience allowed me to see a spontaneous and lighthearted side of Logan. He's among the hardest-working people I've encountered, with little time for leisure, so witnessing this carefree side of him made me genuinely happy.

We made a stop at Glass Beach, where the rugged cliffs and untamed terrain welcomed us with their wild beauty. I didn't hesitate to make my way down the steep paths to the water's edge, an act that was natural for me and didn't give it a second thought, but Logan was concerned for my safety. He offered a steadying hand, and I reassured him with a smile, "I appreciate it, but I'm more sure-footed with both hands free." He watched me with admiration as I descended. "You truly are amazing," he said, his voice filled with awe. "I'm surprised at how agile you are. Fearless on a zip-line and now scaling cliffs like it's a stroll in the park. I feel like I don't need to worry about you; you handle pretty much anything that comes your way."

Amused by his remark, I shared, "I was quite the tomboy and a gymnast during my youth. When I wasn't at home tending to my chores, I was on the farm climbing trees, leaping from heights, or competing in sports alongside the boys at school. I sometimes forget that age has crept up on me," I paused for a moment before adding, "I should be more careful though; I'm not as young as I used to be—I could seriously break a hip," and laughed.

The water's edge was lavish, revealing a hidden world teeming with life—fish darting among the rocks and reefs, starfish clinging to crevices, and tiny black crabs scurrying about. Logan lifted a crab he found in the water nestled beside a rock. I took a quick photo of it in his hand before he released it back into its habitat.[22]

We didn't stay long at Glass Beach. There wasn't much to explore anymore, and it was sad to see that the once glistening shore, adorned with shimmering glass pebbles, had been depleted by hordes of tourists collecting souvenirs over the years. What remained was a bittersweet reminder of the beach's former splendor, a poignant reflection of the passage of time and human impact on natural treasures. I had been hoping it'd be as picturesque as the photos we had seen circulating on the internet.

---

[22] Photo timestamped at 4:35 p.m. on September 2, 2019.

On our way back to the car, Logan carefully helped me up the cliffside and terrain. His strong arms made it look effortless. For the first time, it felt nice to be cared for—a role I hadn't fully embraced for myself before. When other men saw that I was capable, they tended to leave me to my own devices, and for the most part, it never bothered me. Being capable and independent had become second nature to me, not by choice but out of necessity, as I never had anyone I could rely on or any man who was insistent enough to lend a helping hand despite my capability. I had grown accustomed to handling everything on my own.

However, with Logan, there was a different dynamic: an old soul with a sense of nobility that compelled him to ensure my well-being, despite my self-sufficiency. I appreciated him for allowing me to let my guard down and embrace my femininity. It was a simple reminder that even a strong woman likes to have her hand held sometimes and that having a man who cares for her enough to support her and share the load is a true gift. Logan's presence showed me that I didn't always have to be invincible; it was okay to rely on someone else and let them care for me.

Logan took the wheel, insisting on driving as we navigated the winding curves of Highway 1 to Half Moon Bay. Sitting beside him, I felt a sense of ease and contentment. I rolled down the window, inviting the crisp ocean breeze to tousle through our hair. It carried a scent of salt and freedom, mingling with the tranquil rhythms of the sea. As I gazed out, taking in the expansive views of the ocean, a wave of gratitude washed over me at being back along the coast, and this time, with Logan. He made all the simpler things more beautiful and worth savoring, as I didn't have this anxiousness in my heart to be anywhere else than in the present.

He noticed my gaze lost in the ocean horizon and reached over, gently taking my hand and placing it on his heart. I turned to look at him, and a smile graced my face. He made every moment feel like everything was just as it was supposed to be. Our eyes met briefly, and in that simple gesture, I felt the depth of our bond—unspoken yet profoundly understood.

We arrived at Half Moon Bay just as the sun was beginning to dip toward the horizon, painting the sky in hues of orange and pink. I was still determined to have Logan walk barefoot on the wet sands, so we made our way to the beach. I eagerly kicked off my shoes, letting them fall to the sand with a satisfying thud, and gestured for Logan to do the same.

"You must experience the feeling of the salty water and wet sands between your toes. It's a quintessential part of being in California," I explained, raising my voice over the crashing waves and coastal winds. "Plus, it's like a natural spa treatment. After a few walks along the beach, your feet will be baby soft," I added with a playful grin.

Following my lead, Logan shed his shoes just as easily. We placed them on a nearby fallen log before venturing barefoot onto the damp sands. The cool sand provided a soft contrast to the day's lingering warmth. We stepped closer to the water's edge, ready to welcome the evening tide under the fading light of the setting sun. The cool ocean waves lapped at our feet, creating a soothing rhythm as we walked along the shoreline.

Logan drew me in, wrapping his arm around my shoulders as I tucked myself into his embrace. I found myself standing on tiptoe, stretching to match his height, though not nearly tall enough. He adjusted his height to nestle closer to me as we captured a series of selfies against the breathtaking backdrop of the ocean.

Just as the sun began its final descent below the horizon, I picked up a stick from the beach and etched into the wet sand, "Logan was here 9/2/2019," preserving our memory against the timeless ebb and flow of the waves.

"There! Proof that you graced this beach with your presence today,"

I exclaimed, snapping a photo of the inscription beside Logan, immortalizing his first beach experience.

As the evening deepened, we seated ourselves side by side on the soft sands, utterly captivated by the remnants of the sun's light still illuminating the sky. A gentle breeze whispered secrets by our ears, its soft melodies harmonizing perfectly with the tranquil imagery before us. Nestling closer to Logan, I rested my head against the strong curve of his shoulder. He then wrapped his arm around me, pulling me into the warmth and security of his embrace. In that moment, I felt a profound sense of peace and happiness I hadn't experienced in a long time.

We continued to sit in quiet observation as thoughts ran through my mind. The same year I got divorced, my twin daughters embarked on their college journey and moved to Colorado, leaving only me and my son in San Diego.[23] A year later,[24] I decided to take on a project in Long Beach, so we relocated to a penthouse condo in the bustling scene of downtown Long Beach with a view of the marina. It was something I'd always wanted to do before I was married.

This move marked a pivotal moment for me—an opportunity to reclaim my independence and redefine my identity. For the first time in over twenty years, I was not someone's wife. This new place was a chance to create a living space that reflected my personal tastes and dreams, from the carefully selected furniture to the color palette adorning the walls. Every detail was of my choosing, a liberating experience that breathed new life into my sense of self—whereas before, I was confined to whatever my ex-husband wanted.

While Keith and I enjoyed our life in Long Beach, filling our evenings and weekends with enriching activities like exploring

---

[23] Summer, 2016 – Divorced a month after twins' graduation from high school.

[24] Summer, 2017 – Moved to Long Beach.

museums, diving into discovery centers, and marveling at aquarium wonders, there was an undeniable void. The absence of family and the lingering loneliness of being just the two of us cast a somber shadow over our otherwise fulfilling adventures. There was also the fear that if anything happened to me, Keith, who was only 11 years old at the time, would be left alone, and our closest relative was more than two hours away.

Our stayed in Long Beach was only for a year and a half before I made the decision to relocate again,[25] seeking a gentler life in Fresno to be closer to Charlotte, and my sister Kay. Having spent my childhood years in Fresno, I hoped to rediscover a sense of home there. However, after less than a year, I realized the home I thought I would find did not exist, and it only left me feeling more lost.

Reflecting on the events in my life and the constant relocation, being here in front of this same ocean again, a wave of somber reflection washed over me as I recalled my last visit to the beach. It was a few days following that particularly unforgettable panic attack.[26]

Desperate for clarity and purpose, I set off on a solitary two-and-a-half-hour drive from Fresno to Carmel-by-the-Sea. I didn't inform anyone of my departure. It was a last-minute, impulsive decision spurred by the need to ensure that moving to Minnesota wouldn't be yet another senseless relocation, one I might come to regret and undo.

I parked near the beach. As soon as I opened my car door, the invigorating scent of salty ocean air greeted me, immediately soothing my troubled mind. I stood by my car with the door ajar, taking it all in, hoping that I would once again gain the clarity I so desperately sought.

It was a quiet Tuesday afternoon, and as expected, the usual throngs

---

[25] December 2018 – moved from Long Beach to Fresno.

[26] Tuesday, July 23, 2019. Panic attack was on Saturday, July 20th.

of beachgoers were nowhere in sight. I kept walking towards the water's edge until I found a spot, just feet from where the gentle waves kissed the shore, and settled down. Crossing my legs in a meditative posture, I closed my eyes and surrendered to the coastal symphony surrounding me. I embraced the Pacific breeze, intertwining with every sound, energy, and vibration from the crashing waves, deepening my connection to this serene natural sanctuary.

The vastness of the ocean always had a way of humbling me, reminding me of my place in the grand scheme of things. Each grain of sand mirrored our existence in the universe — many, yet insignificantly small when compared to the immensity of the world around us.

As I remained in quiet contemplation that day, I felt a gentle whisper, "Forgive yourself and surrender." Tears streamed down my face inconsolably, releasing years of pent-up emotions that had been suppressed during my marriage, where I had felt uncherished and neglected. It wasn't about admitting fault; it was about forgiving myself for allowing my light to dim so that my partner could shine. Forgiving myself for thinking that his abuse was acceptable because my love was self-sacrificing, while I endured years of pain, allowing him to hurt me in unimaginable ways that I would never inflict on another soul, resulting in wounds where permanent and visible scars now reside. It was about forgiving myself for forgetting my own worth and preciousness, akin to a star in the vast night sky.

With each tear that fell, I surrendered myself from believing I should always be strong, as I am only human. I surrendered to the acceptance that while pain had colored my past, it does not have to shadow my future; it does not define who I am.

I sat on the beach that day and let out all my tears, pain, and the enormous weight of being a wife, a mother, and a Hmong daughter dissipated among the winds. I let it be carried out into the ocean where it would be disposed of, as I no longer needed the burden of possessing this pain.

Though that moment was only over a month ago, it felt like a lifetime as I sat on this beach with Logan. It was a moment tinged with sorrow yet profoundness as I rediscovered my light and resilience that day. It was a significant turning point, a staunch reminder never to allow anyone to enter my life who does not recognize and appreciate my true worth.

After the sun had set, painting the sky with its fiery spectacle beyond the horizon, only a faint line blurred the boundary between the ocean and the sky. Turning to me, Logan's presence was a reassuring warmth in the evening chill as he planted a gentle kiss on my forehead—always the same spot on my hairline—and whispered into my ear, "Let's head back." Gracefully, he rose and extended his hand to help me up from the cool, grainy sand. Together, we brushed off the clinging remnants of the beach from our clothes. Hand in hand, our steps in sync, we walked back to the car, leaving behind the rhythmic lull of the ocean waves under the twilight sky.

That night, as we lay in bed with only the soft glow filtering through the sheer window curtains, I rested my head on his chest, listening to the steady rhythm of his heartbeat. "I love this sound," I whispered. He caressed my hair, his touch tender and comforting.

"Were you okay earlier, when we were on the beach?" he asked in a gentle tone. He had noticed my quiet contemplation but didn't want to disturb me, knowing I had a lot on my mind. Just as I've noticed his somber moments, he's attuned to mine as well, and his concern was palpable in the low, almost whispered tone of his voice. "Do you want to talk about it?" he asked.

I reached my arm around him, pulling him closer. "Not really," I admitted. "I'm just really glad you're here."

He pressed a gentle kiss on my head, understanding in his silence. "I'm glad to be here too," he said, his voice a soothing comfort to my restless thoughts.

I wasn't prepared to reveal that level of vulnerability. I didn't want him to see me as an emotional wreck, someone he needed to "fix." Besides, I knew that if I opened up now, I wouldn't be able to hold back the tears, especially since I was still on the cusp of recovering from past traumas. He didn't press, and I appreciated that. His strong and comforting embrace was enough.

The next day was brimming with excitement as I anticipated meeting up with my first cousins in Sacramento and introducing them to Logan for the first time. It had been several months since our last gathering, and Logan was the first man I had brought into my family circle since my divorce. Though a bit of nervousness tinged my anticipation, I was confident that my cousins would embrace him as warmly as he would them. Our plan was to convene in charming Old Town Sacramento for lunch before embarking on our horseback riding adventure at the ranch.

Stepping into the rustic tavern restaurant, I felt like I had walked onto the set of an old Western film. The ambiance exuded a nostalgic charm, reminiscent of the movies I used to watch as a child, where cowboys and outlaws would clash in dramatic showdowns. As I scanned the room, my gaze landed on the familiar faces of my cousins, already seated around a round table, chatting and laughing.

"Stephanie!" their collective voices rang out as they spotted us, rising from their seats with smiles that mirrored my own excitement.

"Hi, girls," I greeted them, embracing each one in turn as they approached.

"This is Logan," I announced proudly, looping my arm around his.

"Logan, meet my first cousins: Lara, Julie, Kristy, and Angela. All sisters, and this is only half of them!" I introduced, pointing to each cousin as I mentioned their names.

"Hello, ladies," Logan said with a friendly grin, which they reciprocated with warm hugs and greetings. We settled into our seats around the table, and soon chatter and laughter filled the air.

Sitting to the right of me, Lara leaned in with a mischievous glint in her eyes and whispered, "You've made quite an upgrade, girl." Her playful comment elicited a smile from me as I met her gaze and replied, "I agree." The teasing banter added a light-hearted touch to the reunion, and Logan's easy rapport with my cousins put any lingering nerves at ease.

We sat at the tavern's wooden table, waiting for our food as the aroma of freshly cooked meals wafted around us, teasing our senses and hungry stomachs. Logan and I had decided to skip breakfast this morning before making the drive, so this meal was much anticipated.

Logan was a natural conversationalist. He effortlessly sparked lively discussions with my cousins, and their laughter was constantly rolling in waves, creating an atmosphere brimming with joy and excitement. As the exchanges continued, with him being quite the jokester matching my cousins, more hysterical laughter erupted, making us the liveliest group in the room. It was heartwarming to witness the genuine connection forming between Logan and my family; his charismatic charm seemed to complement their spirited personalities perfectly.

When our plates were cleared, Logan leaned back in his chair with a satisfied grin, casting a glance around the table. Then he leaned into my ear and said, "Your cousins are wonderful. They're my kind of people," he quietly remarked, his eyes reflecting genuine satisfaction.

"I'm glad you think so. They are more like my sisters," I replied with a warm smile, feeling happier about this moment.

With our appetites satisfied and hearts lightened, we said goodbye to the charming tavern and set off on the drive to the horse ranch, following closely behind my cousin's car. I was excited for horseback riding as I had never done it before. As we neared the ranch, my anticipation heightened.

Upon arrival, we were greeted by Angela's friend John, a seasoned horseman who had prepared the horses for our afternoon ride. I observed as John led the horses out toward the tent where we were standing, their powerful yet graceful forms highlighting their majestic nature.

Logan was quite excited to see the horses. "I haven't ridden in years," he confessed. "I can imagine us living on a farm, surrounded by animals and nature, and our five dogs," he added, his gaze drifting into the distance as if envisioning our future together. I couldn't help but smile at his subtle inclusion of "us," not escaping my notice.

I watched as Logan effortlessly mounted the horse. His confidence was evident in the way he handled the reins. John offered a few pointers, but Logan seemed at ease and ready to ride. He nudged the horse with a confident command, and he was off on his ride, his motion blending in sync with the horse beneath him.

I stood under the shaded tent, excited and impressed, as I watched him maneuver the horse with grace and skill. The sight of him riding, his strong silhouette against the backdrop of the ranch, was a reflection of his adventurous spirit and natural charisma.

"Smile!" I called out, capturing the moment with my camera.[27] Logan quickly obliged, flashing a confident grin and flexing his arm in a playful display of strength, embodying the perfect blend of rugged charm and confidence.

As I approached the horse, I was excited, but Logan could obviously tell I was nervous. He walked over and stood by me, ready to offer

---

[27] Photo timestamped at 2:03 p.m. on Tuesday, September 3, 2019.

guidance and support. He helped me climb onto the horse's back, and I felt a surge of accomplishment once I was able to mount the horse. However, my confidence wavered as I struggled to get the horse to move.

Sensing my struggle, Logan stepped in, placing one hand on the horse and the other on my leg, calming my nerves. "Hold onto the lead rope and use the back of your heels to nudge the horse," he advised, his voice steady and encouraging. "You can also use the whip to give him a little nudge if he's not responding."

His instructions made sense, but executing them was a bit more challenging than expected. I was afraid of hurting the horse, making a mistake, or worse, being thrown off its back. Logan patiently guided me through each step, offering gentle corrections and words of encouragement.

After a few attempts, I finally succeeded in coaxing the horse forward. I trotted the horse about 10 feet before turning him around and led him back towards the tent to dismount. While horseback riding might not have been my forte, the experience left me with a newfound respect for those who mastered the art.

As evening descended, we made our way to Fisherman's Wharf for our final evening in San Francisco. We chose a seafood restaurant right on the wharf. It was lively, filled with the bustling sounds of chatter and laughter, clinking glasses, and utensils. At the entrance was an oversized clear tank filled with live lobsters and crabs.

"You have to try the Surf and Turf," I insisted to Logan as we perused the menu together. "The crabs here were most likely just caught this morning right off the bay, and the steaks are top-notch," I added, looking forward to sharing one of my favorite culinary experiences with him.

Despite it being a Tuesday night, Fisherman's Wharf was full of the usual activities. It was a hotspot among locals and tourists alike. The vibrant ambiance, coupled with the delicious aroma of seafood emanating from nearby restaurants, created a festive and inviting atmosphere.

During dinner, I couldn't help but reflect on the day's adventure. Turning to Logan, I remarked, "I was quite impressed by your performance on the horse today," with a smile I inquired, "Where did you learn to ride like that?"

"I haven't had much experience, just a couple of rides before today. But I've always believed in giving my best in everything I do," Logan replied modestly. "I guess I just have a knack for picking up new skills," he added. I was beginning to see the multi-faceted side of Logan. He was certainly a Renaissance man.

Wednesday arrived all too quickly, marking our departure from California. However, with Las Vegas on the horizon before heading home, I couldn't help but feel a surge of excitement alongside Logan. We rose early, returning our vehicle to the airport car rental center. Taking the AirTran from the car rental lot to our terminal, we finally settled into the waiting area outside our gate.

As I rested my head on Logan's shoulder, I felt an overwhelming sense of gratitude. Usually, by this point in a trip, I'm weary and eager to return home. But this time was different. Logan's reassuring presence made all the difference, transforming what would typically be a moment of exhaustion into one of contentment and alleviating many of the travel anxieties that typically occur when I travel alone. He had this calming aura that seemed to ease all the tension in me. Being an empath, traveling among large crowds was usually draining, but I hadn't noticed feeling that way this time.

"I had a wonderful time," Logan remarked, tenderly brushing his lips against my forehead. His soft breath caressed the top of my head, tickling the fine hair along my hairline. I closed my eyes to savor the moment.

Our flight from San Francisco to Las Vegas was brief, touching down around 9:30 am, affording us approximately nine hours to delve into the Strip before our return flight to Minneapolis. Despite the time constraints, I was determined to show Logan as much as I can of Las Vegas, with plans for a future visit to experience more in depth of what the city has to offer.

Las Vegas was bustling with its usual energy. We took a ride-share from the airport to the Strip, starting our exploration at Tropicana Avenue. With no set itinerary, we embraced the spontaneity of the moment, leisurely strolling along the vibrant thoroughfare. Pausing only momentarily in the opulent lobbies of major casinos. Our focus was less on indulging in games or slots and more on immersing ourselves in the ambiance and visuals surrounding us. Back home, casinos were a familiar place for Logan, so I thought he might appreciate seeing the casinos along the Strip.

As we strolled through popular landmarks and features, Logan stopped to capture photos of the Paris Hotel, vibrant street performers, and intricate sculptures. All the while, I was only captivated by his expressions and fascination with our surroundings, capturing photos of him rather than the external wonders.

It warmed my heart to see Logan free from the burdens that often weigh him down back home. In these moments, his troubles seem to melt away, leaving behind a sense of lightness and peace that I normally only see when he's asleep.

We made our way to Bacchanal Buffet for a late lunch, fortunate to avoid the prime hour rush and was able to secure a table promptly. As we settled in, I turned to Logan and asked, "How are you enjoying Las Vegas thus far?"

"It's alright," he responded with a smile. "I would have liked to explore more, but I also feel like I've seen quite a bit already. Each casino is grand, but everything seems to be spread out, so it only appears to be big. It does make me miss the less expansive casinos in Minnesota."

Hearing Logan speak of his experience, I couldn't help but notice a tinge of melancholy underlying his enjoyment of Las Vegas. It showed a side of him that often sought refuge in the distracting noise of casinos back home, using them as a sanctuary to escape his loneliness. It was a weight he carried—a silent burden that followed him even in the midst of vibrant distractions. It made me wonder about the quiet hours when the facade of lights and glamour faded, leaving behind the echoes of his own thoughts.

It became my unspoken mission to be a beacon of warmth and understanding, to fill his voids of loneliness with laughter and heartfelt conversations, weaving more memories that spoke to our genuine human connection.

After lunch, we made our way toward the Venetian, eager to make the most of the few hours we had left. Inside the grand Venetian lobby, we stumbled upon a mesmerizing waterfall atrium, adorned with oversized artificial flowers that cast an artful Alice in Wonderland vibe. Nestled in front of the cascading water, was a set of large red letters arranged to spell LOVE, adding a touch of sentiment to our trip.

Inspired by this artistic display and the essence of our first travel together, I urged Logan to pose beside the letters for a memorable snapshot. He sauntered over, positioning himself between the V and the E, and leaned against the sturdy E, crossing one leg in front of the other and tucking his hands into his pockets. He wore dark denim jeans and a burgundy V-neck t-shirt, which made his posture not only attractive but also exuded a sense of nonchalant confidence, reminiscent of an Asian James Dean—a captivating blend of charm and ease. As he glanced toward me, a playful smile graced his lips and tugged at my heart.[28]

In my years of frequent work-related trips, traveling alone was the norm. The routine was predictable: airport to hotel, client site, back to the hotel, and finally, the airport for the flight back home. This itinerary, while efficient, left little room for exploration or indulgence in the cities I visited. Quite often, I would rather just stay in, as I didn't like to explore alone.

While I adore traveling and possess a wanderlust spirit, constantly yearning to explore the far reaches of the world, I find little pleasure in the prospect of solo travel. There's a certain melancholy that accompanies experiencing a stunning destination without a companion to share it with. The loneliness weighs heavily, turning simple activities like dining into monotonous rituals devoid of lively conversation and shared laughter that make meals memorable. Passing by breathtaking sights becomes bittersweet, as the beauty of a place amplifies the absence of companionship. It serves as a poignant reminder of the joy that stems from sharing experiences with another soul, crafting cherished memories against the backdrop of captivating scenes.

Years ago, when I was married to my ex-husband, I had hoped to capture some of these joys of traveling together but our trips often ended in bitter arguments, leaving a sour taste in my mouth when it came to shared experiences. Even when we were apart due to work commitments, attempting to have casual conversation over the phone only led to disappointment, as our conversations lacked the warmth and

---

[28] Photo timestamped at 3:28 p.m. on Wednesday, September 4, 2019.

connection I craved from him.

This trip with Logan marked a significant turning point in healing the wounds of my past travels. His laid-back demeanor and optimistic perspective on life brought a sense of wholeness and peace that had long eluded me. In his presence, the weight of past traumas seemed to lift, replaced by a newfound sense of pleasure, relief, and security.

As we explored different cities and experiences, I had a profound realization: the true essence of this trip didn't lie in exotic destinations or grand adventures; it was rooted in the simple joy of being with someone who felt like home. Logan's presence became my sanctuary, a safe harbor amid the unpredictability of travel and life. His knack for finding joy in small moments and his unwavering support brought a sense of completeness I had long yearned for.

CHAPTER 11

A PRICELESS GESTURE

THE MORNING WAS SHROUDED in a relentless downpour. The September rain hammered against the pavement, creating a watery curtain that obscured the world outside.

Logan and I had planned to meet at a bakery on University Avenue for breakfast. It was a quaint idea the night before but now felt almost comical given the intensity of the rain.

As I pulled into the bakery's parking lot, Logan's white van was already there, a reassuring sight amidst the relentless rain. I smiled; he was waiting for me, his silhouette framed by the misty windows of his car.

Spotting my arrival, Logan watched as I parked my car. He hurriedly stepped out, leaving the shelter of his car to greet me. Dressed casually in jeans, a dark jacket, and Converse shoes, he held a small black umbrella, using it as a shield against the downpour. With quick strides, he ran through the rain, droplets clinging to his drenched hair and clothes, lending a charming disarray to his appearance. A warm smile graced his lips as he reached my door and deftly positioned the umbrella, sheltering me from the pouring rain.

Though I protested against him getting wet, I couldn't deny my appreciation for his chivalry. Quickly exiting my car, we clung to each other under the umbrella as we hurried to his car, our laughter mingling with the pitter-patter of raindrops. Logan helped me into the passenger seat, ensuring my comfort before circling around to the driver's side. Before I could insist that he take the umbrella to shelter himself from the rain, he had already hurriedly closed the door.

As he joined me inside the car, a faint scent of rain mixed with his cologne, creating a unique and pleasant blend of earthy sandalwood, musk, and fresh mineral aromas. Despite being drenched from the rain, Logan's spirit was undampened. He smiled, glanced at me quickly, and then reached over to turn up the heat and defroster, helping to remove some of the humidity from inside the vehicle.

"You didn't have to do that," I lovingly chided him, concerned about his well-being. "I could have simply joined you without having you step out into the rain. Now we're both soaked. And you should have taken the umbrella with you. You're even wetter than I am." I continued to lecture him, not wanting him to catch a cold in this weather.

"It's alright as long as my Queen stays dry," Logan responded, his term of endearment eliciting a playful eye roll from me. Though he had been calling me that for over a month now, I had not grown accustomed to it, no matter how often he called me his Queen.

"Don't call me that," I protested, feeling a bit awkward every time. However, before I could dwell on it further, Logan leaned in and planted a passionate kiss on my lips, momentarily erasing any lingering discomfort or concern. My shoulders relaxed as I gently placed my hand on his cheek and gave in to his kiss.

"I hope you're hungry. I've already picked up our breakfast," Logan announced, his tone brimming with anticipation.

"Oh, we're not dining in?" I inquired, surprised by his sudden change of plans.

"Not today. With this rain, I thought a change of scenery would be nice," Logan explained as he reversed his car to leave the parking lot. "We can leave your car here for now and retrieve it later."

"Where are we heading?" I pressed.

"It's a surprise," he replied with a mischievous grin, adding an element of excitement to the morning.

We drove through the rain-drenched streets for about 10 minutes until Logan turned into the parking lot of Indian Mounds Lookout Park, choosing a spot that offered the best panoramic view. Logan parked his car facing the cityscape. The rain, now a gentle cascade over the city, seemed to cast a quiet, magical spell, transforming the usually bustling and noisy streets into a serene vista.

Reaching behind him, he retrieved a bag containing the breakfast he had ordered. He handed me a warm breakfast sandwich and a cup of hot Vietnamese coffee, its aroma blending with the fresh scent of rain that seeped in from the small opening of his car window.

"This is the best Vietnamese coffee you'll ever taste," Logan proclaimed with a smile. "I always ask the barista to add a touch of hazelnut for that extra flavor. Give it a try. I know you'll love it."

I brought the cup to my lips, blowing lightly into the small opening of the lid to test the temperature of the steaming liquid against my lip. Satisfied with its warmth, I took a cautious sip. The coffee was rich and smooth, with a subtle sweetness that danced on my palate. The hint of hazelnut added a delightful depth to the flavor, perfectly complementing the robustness of the pressed coffee.

"It's really good," I admitted, taking another sip and savoring the intricate blend of flavors. "Thank you for this."

Logan's eyes gleamed with satisfaction, his gaze shifting from the cityscape to me. "I'm glad you like it, Baby," he replied. "It's just a small way to brighten up a rainy day."

We sat together in the car, amidst the tranquil setting of the rain-kissed park and the breathtaking view of downtown Saint Paul. The raindrops drummed a soft melody on the car roof, adding to the cozy ambiance of the moment. Spending this moment with Logan was a simple yet meaningful gesture, a reminder of the beauty that could be found even in the midst of a rainy morning.

As I bit into my breakfast sandwich, a dream from a few nights ago surged back into my mind with startling clarity. It felt as if I had stepped into another reality, one so vivid that it bordered on being tangible. Turning to Logan as if I needed to share before the details faded, I blurted out, "I dreamt about you." It was the first time Logan had appeared in my dreams since we started dating. "What happened in your dream?" Logan asked, clearly curious.

"It was surreal, like living in an alternate life where we were married and had children," I explained, the memory still fresh and intriguingly real.

"That's interesting. Maybe it's a premonition," Logan mused with a teasing smile.

Uncertain if this dream was a premonition, I delved into the details, describing the home we shared in that dream world and emphasizing how tangible and lifelike it all felt. "Perhaps it was another lifetime?" Logan suggested.

"I can't say for certain, but what I do know is that you're in my dreams, which means you're now a constant part of my life. I don't just dream about anyone," I confessed. Logan glanced at me and smiled. We continued to revel in the soothing sound of the rain, the mesmerizing cityscape view, and the comfort of each other's company.

As I took my last bite, Logan's question about my upcoming birthday caught me by surprise. I hadn't thought he would remember, as I had only mentioned it once when we were in California last month.

"Today is the 15th and your birthday is coming up on the 21st. Less than a week away. What would you like?" he asked.

"Oh... I never ask for anything on my birthday. I just want to spend it with you," I assured him, genuinely touched that he remembered.

Every year, when asked the same question by my children or friends, I always give the same answer. It's not about material gifts but the presence and love of those I cherish that make my birthday truly special. And if one must give a gift, handmade items are treasures of my heart.

"I can't let the day go by without getting you something special," Logan insisted with determination. He leaned back for a moment, gazing out at the cityscape as if seeking inspiration. Suddenly, his face lit up with excitement. "I know exactly what I'm going to get you!" he exclaimed, his eyes sparkling with anticipation.

Intrigued by his sudden enthusiasm, I couldn't help but ask, "What do you have in mind?"

"It's another surprise," he replied mischievously, flashing me my favorite grin. He turned on the car engine, and a gentle hum blended softly with the patter of rain on the windshield as we prepared to leave the park.

"You're just full of surprises today," I said, feeling quite happy about his good mood.

Our next destination turned out to be a store filled with colorful jewels, beads, and various crafting tools. I couldn't contain my curiosity as Logan guided me through the aisles, his hand warm and reassuring as he firmly gripped mine.

"What are you doing?" I asked, impressed by the array of vibrant glass and crystal beads around us.

Logan smiled, "Pick your favorite colors," he instructed, his eyes gleaming.

I hesitated for a moment, unsure of the purpose behind his request. "Let me know what this is for, so I know how to pick," I requested, smiling and eager for a clue.

"I'm making you a ring," Logan said confidently. My eyes lit up as the realization sank in. I had never told him I love handmade items, and now his thoughtful gift was tugging hard at my heart.

No one had ever made me a ring before, let alone given me one. Even in my last marriage, I had to purchase my own wedding band. Logan's sweet gesture touched a deep emotional chord within me, evoking a sense of warmth and gratitude. Unexpectedly, my eyes glistened with unshed tears. It was a simple yet profound act, a symbol of his love and thoughtfulness that meant more to me than any material gift ever could.

As I stood in front of the colorful array of beads, I asked Logan, "How many colors should I pick?"

He flashed my favorite smile again. "As many as you want," he replied.

Sifting through the beads, I was drawn to their vibrant hues and the way they sparkled under the light, each facet catching a different angle of brilliance. I glanced at Logan as he stood by patiently, appreciating his patience while I lingered, lost in contemplation. Finally, I selected beads in shades of gold, red, green, and a striking blue sapphire. The latter was not just for its beauty but also because it represented my birth month, adding a personal touch to my choice as his birthday gift to me.

With the chosen beads, we perused the rest of the store, gathering the necessary tools Logan needed to craft the ring. He picked up a tray lined with black velvet to lay out his tools and beads. Carefully, he placed everything he needed onto the tray, making sure to select the right tools and wiring for the chosen beads. Once everything was in place, we made our way to the register to check out and then headed back to Indian Mounds Lookout.

The rain continued to pour over the city, shrouding the view in a persistent, gentle drizzle. Logan's excitement was apparent as he had already envisioned the ring he was going to make for me.

We sat in his car as he began to work, creating a makeshift workshop right in front of me. I watched with anticipation and admiration as he carefully laid out the pieces. Logan started to assemble the ring. Each bead was carefully threaded onto a wire, forming a graceful pattern. As I observed his work, a sense of awe and gratitude came over me, moved by the effort and thought he had put into this special gift.

Hours passed as Logan continued to work on crafting the ring. Some of the materials were not bending and fitting as he needed, and I could sense his frustration. The moisture from the rain brought humidity into the car, adding to the challenge and making him perspire, increasing his discomfort. Yet, he persisted with determination, wiping sweat from his forehead.

Witnessing his struggle, I leaned toward him and said, "Hun, I appreciate you so much, and just watching your effort means a lot to me already. I genuinely mean it when I say I don't need anything. Your thoughtfulness alone already means the world to me." I tried to alleviate some of the pressure he was feeling.

Logan paused his work, setting down the tools momentarily as he looked up at me. His eyes held a mix of exhaustion from the tedious task and determination fueled by his affection for me. Wiping the sweat from his brow, he chuckled before confessing with a smile, "I must be very much in love with you, because I've never struggled this much or done anything like this for anyone before. This is hard work!" His tone carried a blend of jest and sincerity, highlighting the novelty of his efforts in crafting a ring for me. "I made a beautiful and elaborate dream catcher for my brother once, which was significantly larger, but I've never had the urge to make a ring for anyone. It's not easy making a ring. It's so small and delicate," he explained.

In response to his half-joking confession, I couldn't resist teasing him. "Well, we are driven to do unexplainable things when it's for our soulmate," I quipped with a playful tone, acknowledging the humor in the statement while also appreciating the warmth it brought to my heart. "Apparently," Logan chuckled in agreement.

On the day of my birthday, Logan took me to dinner at one of our favorite sushi restaurants. We had just settled into the cozy ambiance of our table, the warm glow of the lanterns casting a soft light on our faces, when Logan confessed, "I'm still working on your ring," his tone tinged with frustration and disappointment. But I wasn't the least bit disappointed. I smiled at him, feeling his affection. "It's okay. I love that you tried. That alone is a gift already," I assured him.

"The beads are quite delicate, and their sizes vary, while the wires are either too thick or too thin, resulting in parts of the ring being either too tight or too loose," he explained, his brow furrowed with disappointment. I noticed how he always comes through, a man of his words, and when he doesn't, he takes it hard on himself. It's very admirable, but I didn't want him to feel bad. Logan's dedication to perfection was evident in everything he did, from his meticulous craftsmanship in designing and constructing grandmaster decks to something as small and delicate as a ring.

Just then, he reached to his side and pulled out a black box the size of a shoebox and handed it to me. I looked at him, and his eyes were reflecting a mix of anticipation and sentiment. "I don't want your special day to arrive without a gift from me, so I have something else for you." With his hands still on the box, he said with an earnest tone, "Before you open it, I want you to know that this is my most treasured possession. I don't hold on to too many things in my life, but this, I've held on to it for a very long time, taking it with me wherever I went."

Looking at him with a mix of surprise and concern, I replied, "I can't accept something that precious and valuable from you, especially when you've cherished it for such a long time, and we've only been together for less than two months. It's not that I don't want it. I'm just afraid I would disappoint you."

Logan's determination to give me his precious gift persisted. "If there's anyone I'd want to give this to, you are the first and only," he said with honesty and genuine sincerity in his voice. His words tugged at my heart, but I hesitated briefly. I didn't want to disappoint him by accepting his gift if things didn't work out between us someday, nor did I want to disappoint him by declining his heartfelt gesture. I then asked him, "What makes you certain that you want to give me this gift?"

He smiled and said, "Take a look."

Taking the box from Logan, I felt a wave of emotions. I love him dearly, and his gift means so much to me, but the weight of my concern lingered. Slowly opening the lid to reveal what was inside, I was greeted by the sight of a stunningly crafted sculpture. The intricately carved sculpture lay nestled in soft white cloth, cradled within the box with utmost care, and it was evident that Logan truly took good care of it. Its surface, a polished and shiny mahogany color, caught the warm light of the restaurant, casting a mesmerizing glow.

Initially mistaking it for polished mahogany wood, the weight in my hand told a different story, akin to the solidity of marble. "Is it petrified wood?" I asked, filled with awe.

"It's actually sculpted from a mammoth tusk and is of rare quality," Logan explained.

Impressed by its beauty and material from which it was sculpted, I couldn't help but ask, "What's the story behind this?"

"It's been with me for over 20 years," Logan began, his eyes reflecting fond memories. "I acquired it from a collector who owned an antiquity store. Its rarity and elegance always appealed to me. I didn't have much at the time and couldn't afford it, but I worked all summer to complete my first two big projects just to acquire it," Logan explained with pride in his voice. "It stands as a symbol of inspiration for me to keep pushing forward so that I can have a home of my own someday. I want to build it with my own hands. I envisioned placing this sculpture on my oversized mantle as a reminder of my achievements and aspirations."

I was completely touched, but what he shared only added to the weight of this gift's value. "Hun, this is absolutely breathtaking. However, I am hesitant to accept it because it's priceless. It's not an object that you can just purchase again," I said, feeling bittersweet.

"I want you to have it because I know you will be living in this home with me, and it won't just be a symbol of my hard work, but ours," he revealed, his words unwavering with commitment that I had not heard before.

Oftentimes, when someone reveals a commitment of this magnitude to me, especially this early in a relationship, I usually retract and tell them I'm not ready to have such a conversation, or I tend to break things off. But in that poignant moment, with tears glistening in my eyes, I realized the depth of his affection and the sincerity of his intentions, and in my heart, I felt the same. It became even clearer to me that he didn't see me as just a passing romance or a transient figure in his life. His gift and words opened my heart to the possibility of a meaningful and lasting future together, where our love and aspirations would intertwine.

CHAPTER 12

PRIDE AND JOY

O CTOBER HAD ARRIVED, and the air carried a chilly crispness that hinted at the approaching winter. Logan and I had stopped at a quaint restaurant for dinner when he broached the subject of my son, Keith. Despite us dating for more than two months now, I hadn't quite thought of introducing Logan to Keith yet. Following my divorce, I had dated other men but never felt compelled to introduce them to my children. It was a maternal instinct to shield my kids from fleeting relationships.

Though with Logan, it was different, yet I hesitated because I was unsure how Keith would react to meeting someone I was romantically involved with.

"Do you want to meet Keith?" I asked, feeling both curious and concerned.

"Of course," he replied without hesitation.

His eagerness to meet my son took me by surprise, sparking a mix of happiness and hesitation, yet I was unsure about how to arrange such an introduction. Logan's excitement was palpable as he suggested, "There's a Halloween carnival in town every year! They have a haunted house, pumpkin patch, axe throwing, and turkey legs. It would be fun for all of us to go together."

I smiled, matching Logan's eager grin, nodded and responded, "Sure, let me check with Keith. If he's up for it, then let's make it happen."

His smile broadened, pleased with the plan, while I tucked away my reservations to ponder later.

The next morning, as I drove Keith to school, my mind abuzz with thoughts on how to approach the subject with him. Until now, he has only known me to speak of his dad. The prospect of introducing Logan to Keith, coupled with the uncertainties of a potential breakup, despite everything going so well, loomed heavily on my mind. I know I would be hurt, but the impact on Keith—and indeed on my daughters—could be just as profound. Amid these swirling concerns, I decided to delay the conversation until after school, giving myself time to find the right words.

Pulling up in front of the school, I stopped the car to let Keith out. "Have a good day, sweetie. I love you," I said, my words laden with more than the usual morning farewell.

"I love you too, Mom," Keith replied, his voice steady and sure.

He grabbed his backpack, slung it over his shoulder, and stepped out of the car as he headed towards the school entrance. Watching him walk away, I reflected on our unique bond. Keith, at 12, was an old soul wrapped in youthful exuberance. He shared my passions for arts, science, technology, and music, and our inside jokes resonated in a world that often felt just ours. Despite his maturity, he remained unabashedly affectionate, never hesitating to show love or receive it, even in front of his peers.

Pulling away from the school parking lot, my thoughts drifted to Logan. I've had a string of unfortunate experiences in relationships before, leading me to establish a six-month rule. If I can't see a future with someone by that mark, it's best to spare everyone's feelings and part ways.

Yet with Logan, there has been a distinct feeling, an intuition from the very beginning, that there is more than just a mere encounter or budding romance. He could be the one I'll love for the rest of my life. Our connection transcended the usual new-relationship exhilaration; it was as if our souls were aligned, resonating on a frequency that sang of old love reborn.

In just over two months, he had deeply entwined himself in the daily rhythm of my life. His presence was a constant source of reassurance and exhilaration, a force I never imagined experiencing so profoundly at this stage of my life. For a long time, I thought feelings like this only happened to others.

After school, Keith rode the bus home, while I met up with Logan. He was preparing for a construction project scheduled to start the next day. Together, we headed to the local lumberyard and hardware store to pick up the necessary supplies. After loading up, we made a brief stop at the construction site to drop off some of the smaller items.

As we navigated the increasingly busy streets of Saint Paul, the day gradually gave way to evening. Unexpectedly, delicate snowflakes began to drift down from the darkening sky, casting a serene veil over the city. I watched, enthralled by the quiet beauty of the season's first snowfall, and my first experience of snow in Minnesota.

Excitedly, I turned to Logan, I couldn't help but share the magical moment. "Look, it's snowing. Do you know what they say about the first snow?" I asked, playfully excited.

Logan glanced at me and asked, "What do they say?"

"They say whoever you're with when the first snow falls is the one you'll fall in love with and you'll both be together forever," I explained, my words tinged with whimsy.

Logan smiled, meeting my gaze. His voice was sincere as he replied, "Then we'll be together forever."

His words wrapped around my heart like a warm blanket, soothing the chilly air that seeped into the car.

Later that evening, as I prepared for bed, I paused by Keith's room to check on him. He was diligently finishing his homework at his desk.

"Hi sweetie," I greeted him. "How was your day?"

"It was good, Mom," Keith replied, barely looking up from his work.

"I'm glad to hear that. Still tackling your homework?" I inquired, leaning against the doorframe.

"Yeah, but I'm almost done," he responded.

Keith was always a bright kid, on top of his schoolwork and excelling in just about every subject without needing any extra help or tutoring. As a mother, I felt incredibly fortunate.

Encouraged by his good spirits, I decided to take the opportunity to venture forward. "I heard there's a Halloween carnival coming up," I mentioned casually. "I thought it might be fun for us to go together."

"Yeah, we can do that," Keith quickly agreed, finally looking up from his papers.

Encouraged by his response, I decided to broach the topic I had been contemplating. "So, I've been getting to someone. He's a great guy, and I really like him. I was thinking he could join us too," I said with a tinged of nervousness, hoping he didn't notice.

"Sure, that sounds great, Mom," Keith replied again without hesitation, surprising me with his easy acceptance.

"Are you sure about that? It's not too weird, is it?" I prodded, needing his reassurance.

Keith grinned and replied confidently, "It's not weird at all. I'm not a little kid anymore."

I often forget how mature he is for his age. It's as if he were a 30-year-old man in an 18-year-old body, yet he was only 12. This realization strikes me when I reflect on past conversations we've had. I recall a particularly tough conversation when his grandma passed away. She was one of his favorite people, and he spent almost every day with her. He was only eight at the time, and we had never discussed death before.

On the drive home after learning about his grandma's passing, I cautiously asked him how he was feeling because he had not said anything or even shed a tear. He paused, taking a moment to process my question before responding, "I'm sad, but I also understand that death is a natural part of life. I'm not afraid of death, Mom," he said, then quickly correcting himself, "I mean, I'm not afraid of death as an old person who has lived a long life like grandma. What scares me is if I were to die young and not experience my life fully."

His words left me speechless, unsure whether to cry at his profound response or be relieved that he was handling it so well and maturely.

As I bid Keith goodnight and left his room, a wave of gratitude washed over me for having such an exceptional son.

On the night of the carnival,[29] Logan arrived at our doorstep to pick up both Keith and me. He stood in front of the door, his confident stride

---

[29] Friday, October 25, 2019

and beaming smile suggesting at either his joy in seeing me or his eagerness to meet my son. He looked most handsome, sporting a cap, a zip-up jacket, and dark jeans. I wanted to leap forward to give him a kiss, but I refrained, considering Keith was just in the next room.

"Hi," I greeted Logan with a smile that mirrored his own radiance.

"Hi, Baby," Logan replied. "Ready to go?"

"Yes," I confirmed, then called out to Keith that it was time to leave.

Keith grabbed his jacket and joined us downstairs. As he approached the front door, I couldn't help but feel a tinge of nerves mixed with anticipation.

"Keith, this is Logan," I introduced them, holding my breath for Keith's reaction.

Keith greeted Logan with a friendly smile. "Hi. Nice to meet you," he said politely.

"Hey, Buddy. It's nice to meet you too," Logan responded, his playful tone lightening the mood.

"Ready for some turkey legs and a bit of axe throwing?"

"Yeah. Sounds fun." Keith replied with subtle excitement. He was never one to get too excited or too emotional about anything even if he was.

As we stepped out together into the chilly evening, Keith zipped up his jacket. I smiled, feeling relieved and excited about this first meeting. It has gone a lot better than I had hoped. I couldn't help but feel a sense of excitement for our first outing as a trio.

On the car ride to the carnival, the atmosphere was filled with a sense of anticipation. Logan, clearly nervous, made admirable efforts to engage Keith in conversation, bridging the gap between them with questions and shared experiences.

"So, Keith, what grade are you in now?" Logan asked, glancing at Keith in his rearview mirror to show his genuine interest.

"I'm in 7th grade," Keith replied, his voice confident.

"I remember my 7th grade year. How do you like your school?" Logan continued, his tone encouraging.

"School's good. I especially like my teachers. My science teacher is the best," Keith responded, warming up to the conversation.

"You like science?" Logan asked.

"Yeah, science and math are my favorite subjects," Keith said, a spark of enthusiasm in his voice.

Their conversation meandered through various topics, from favorite school subjects to recent science projects, and Keith's growing interest in robotics. Logan listened attentively, nodding, and occasionally adding his own childhood anecdotes, which brought occasional laughs and nods from Keith.

As we neared the carnival, the conversation had eased into a comfortable rhythm. The night sky had deepened to a velvet darkness, punctuated by the vibrant lights of the carnival—flashes of orange, purple, and gold illuminating the festive atmosphere. The air was filled with the sounds of laughter, music, and the distant screams from the haunted house, all blending into the night like a lively symphony.

Pulling into the parking lot, I could see the excitement reflected in Keith's eyes as he peered out the window at the bustling scene. Logan's efforts had clearly made an impression, helping to lay the groundwork for what promised to be a memorable evening. As we parked and prepared to step into the carnival's lively embrace, I felt a swell of gratitude for Logan's earnest attempts to connect with Keith.

The carnival buzzed with an lively energy that swept us up the moment we stepped through its gates. Wrapped in the brisk autumn air, we plunged into the heart of the festivities, determined to savor every experience it had to offer.

As we walked through the haunted house together, our group was notably subdued amidst the eerie staging of cobwebs, skeletons, and organs in dark rooms. When a zombie suddenly leaped out of a closet, I was startled and instinctively retreated into Logan's reassuring presence. Despite the shock, not a scream escaped any of our lips.

Observing Keith and Logan, their calm demeanor was striking, like patrons strolling through a museum rather than a haunted attraction. Yet, amidst the thrill, I did think there was enjoyment in the experience— a playful venture suggested by Logan, and I happily went along as a gesture of support for Logan's persistent efforts to forge a connection with Keith.

Upon exiting the haunted house, we stumbled upon a trampoline attraction just off to the side. Keith's eyes lit up at the sight of it. "Let's all try it," suggested Logan enthusiastically. Eager for the adventure, we made our way over.

Keith was the first to take on the challenge. He confidently put on his harness, stepped onto the trampoline, and was securely strapped to the bungee cords. Logan and I watched intently as the two poles holding the bungee cords ascended, creating more resistance.

With a burst of energy, Keith began to jump and perform flips, showcasing his agility and daring spirit—an easy feat for him, considering he has a black belt in Taekwondo. His movements were fluid and mesmerizing. Logan and I cheered him on as he continued.

I looked over at Logan, and his face was lit up with excitement. "Have you ever done this before?" I asked.

"No, I haven't, but I remember wanting to as a kid," he replied with anticipation evident on his face as he couldn't wait to try.

I smiled at his reaction and nodded, "me too."

After Keith finished, I suggested that Logan should go next because of how excited he was, but he insisted I take the lead. "I've seen you fearlessly tackle the zip-line and confidently scale down cliffsides. You mentioned being a gymnast; now I want to see those flips," he playfully insisted. Since he was insistent, I agreed. Once I was harnessed and strapped in, Logan's voice pierced through the crowd, "Go, Steph! You got this!" His enthusiastic encouragement brought a smile to my face, yet a playful thought emerges, *I bet he's testing me, wanting to see if this 40-year-old can prove herself.*

Standing at the center of the trampoline, I waited for the bungee poles to ascend before I began jumping. Starting with subtle bounces, I gradually built-up momentum until my jumps soared higher and higher. "I want to see you do a flip!" Logan yelled amidst the cheers. At that moment, effortlessly, I executed not just one flip but a series of flips, one after another. Logan's voice rose above the crowd, happily cheering in excitement, "Yeah, that's a gymnast right there!"

After I got off the trampoline, I was surprised that my muscle memory had served me well. The ability to maneuver my body into backflips and forward flips returned to me naturally.

It was now Logan's turn, and his excitement was still noticeable. Keith and I watched with anticipation as Logan was harnessed and securely strapped in. His grip on the bungee cords was firm, and a wide smile adorned his face. The sight was so endearing that I couldn't resist capturing this moment on video,[30] wanting to preserve the joy etched on his features forever.

As the poles ascended, Logan began his jumps. When he reached the apex of his jump and attempted to execute a flip, he struggled to get it right. Sensing his error, I shouted encouragement, "You're flipping a little too soon. Let your legs and your motion guide you." I observed as he grappled with making that first flip. Soon enough, he was able to find his rhythm and started flipping too.

Amidst his laughter and unexpected groans, Keith and I couldn't contain our excitement for Logan. We laughed and cheered, reveling in his newfound aerial prowess.

---

[30] Video footage captured at 8:23 p.m. on Friday, October 25, 2019.

As the evening unfolded, we found ourselves immersed in a bustling scene of food trucks. Logan, ever the thoughtful host, suggested that Keith and I settle down at a nearby picnic bench while he ventured off to get us something to eat. As Logan strode away, I turned to Keith and asked, "Are you enjoying yourself?"

"Yeah, I'm having a lot of fun," Keith replied.

Eager to know his thoughts on Logan, I continued, "What do you think of him?"

"He's cool. I like him," Keith answered with a smile.

Relieved and happy to hear Keith's response, I couldn't help but feel grateful that Logan and Keith seemed to hit it off effortlessly.

Moments later, Logan returned with an armful of delightful mishmash of treats from the food trucks. We indulged in crispy funnel cakes dusted with powdered sugar, hot dogs brimming with all the fixings, and sticky caramel apples that were as messy as they were delicious.

We sampled spicy cheese curds that weren't as fiery as we had hoped and joked that they lacked "Hmong peppers," which sent us into peals of laughter. We sipped steaming cups of hot cocoa that warmed us against the evening chill. As we ate, the sounds of the carnival swirled around us—the distant strains of carnival music, the rhythmic clunking of axes from the axe throwers, complemented by the occasional burst of laughter from nearby revelers. It was a night of unbridled joy, and simple pleasures.

CHAPTER 13

COLORADO

EVERY YEAR IN COLORADO, there's a tradition where one member of the small, closely-knit Hmong community is chosen to host a grand ball on the first Saturday of November to bring the community together in celebration of the year's end and achievements made. This year, [31] my brother Chase was honored with that role. Opting for a Masquerade Ball theme, he generously extended an invitation for us to partake in the festivities. Adding to the event, he asked me to be the co-master of ceremonies.

While Logan had already met some of my cousins during our trip to California a couple of months ago, meeting my siblings was a new step in our relationship. I had a strong feeling that he would charm them just as effortlessly as he did my cousins. However, given my family's familiarity with only my long-term relationship with my ex-husband since my early teens, this meeting also brought a mix of nerves and

---

[31] November 2019

excitement. It was a chance for Logan to show a different side of me and for my family to meet an incredible man who has won me over, mind and heart.

As I shared the news of our upcoming trip to Colorado with Logan, his excitement was through the roof. "I've never been to Colorado before," he exclaimed eagerly, his eyes beaming with anticipation. "And meeting your family would be wonderful," he added, expressing particular interest in meeting my twin daughters and getting to know my brothers. I was happy to see him so enthusiastic about the opportunity.

Colorado holds a special significance for me. It's where I relocated after high school, spending seven transformative years completing my college education and discovering my passion for Information Technology. Those years were pivotal in shaping who I am today. However, my career eventually led me to San Diego, where I assumed the role of an IT Healthcare Project Manager for a prominent hospital system. While Minnesota was starting to feel like home with Logan, returning to Colorado felt like revisiting my roots, a nostalgic trip to where my adult journey began. I eagerly anticipated showing Logan around, sharing the memories and landmarks of one of my favorite hometowns, and introducing him to the important people closest to my heart.

While I usually stay at one of my siblings' homes when visiting, Logan was apprehensive about imposing on their hospitality since we weren't married. He worried it might seem disrespectful and suggested staying in a hotel instead. Despite my assurance that my siblings weren't conventional in that regard, I didn't want Logan to feel uneasy, so we opted for a hotel.

We arrived at our hotel on a Friday afternoon and were only planning to stay until Monday morning. Checking in, I felt a mix of excitement and nostalgia, knowing I would soon reunite with my daughters. It had only been a little over a week since Keith met Logan, and their rapport had already blossomed. However, with my daughters being young adults, I worried it would be a different story. I wasn't entirely certain how they would receive Logan, but our pre-trip conversations had left me hopeful, as they expressed, "Mom, we just want you to be happy. As long as you're happy, we're happy too." And for the first time in decades, I truly was happy.

After settling into our hotel, our next destination was my brother Chase's house, where my twin daughters also reside. We were also informed that my other siblings and their families would be there as well to greet us. As we approached the front door, anticipation quickened my heartbeat. Cassie, the younger of my twins, greeted us cheerfully as she swung open the door.

"Hi!" she exclaimed.

"Hi Sweetie," I replied, giving her a tight hug.

Stepping inside, my brother's home was inviting with the warm embrace of my family, each offering a heartfelt welcome to Logan with smiles and hugs as I made the introductions. My brothers were accompanied by their wives and children, and my youngest sister, Leslie, added a cheerful presence to the gathering. Meanwhile, Keith arrived with his luggage, prepared to enjoy his time in Colorado at my brother Christopher's house, where he could connect with cousins closer to his age.

Chase's wife, Darlene, had already prepared dinner, filling the house with the comforting aroma of a home-cooked meal: thinly sliced pork belly stir-fried with bitter melon, boiled pork with greens, along with other traditional soul foods that always make me feel like I'm being welcomed home. It was a familiar scent that I don't often experience, as I don't cook unless necessary. The atmosphere in Chase's house was lively, filled with the joyful chatter of adults and the playful sounds of my younger nieces and nephews running around. It was the contented sound of home, a symphony of love and togetherness that surrounded us like a warm embrace.

Meeting my brother was a natural transition for Logan, as if he had been a part of our family gatherings for years. Conversations sparked effortlessly, punctuated by laughter echoing through the living room. My brothers showed genuine interest in getting to know Logan. Despite their lack of experience in construction, they were intrigued by Logan's stories and expertise in the field. They asked questions, shared their own experiences with DIY projects, and listened attentively as Logan talked about his work.

Being homeowners with a list of construction projects they wanted to tackle, Logan mentioned that he would be happy to drive to Colorado with all his tools and lend a hand anytime if my brothers ever needed any construction work done. His genuine offer was met with appreciation and camaraderie.

Christopher and his wife, Kaila, had recently bought a newly developed home and were part of a Homeowner Association. One of the requirements was to complete their backyard with a deck, sod, and some landscaping. "Let me know when you need to get it done. Your sister and I will make time to drive down and get your deck built for you," Logan insisted, promptly arranging a date with Christopher to take on the project of building them a deck at no cost for his labor, saving them almost two-thirds of the cost if they were to hire a professional and headaches if they were to tackle it themselves. Logan saw this as an opportunity to bond with my brothers, and I deeply appreciated his kind gesture.

After dinner, when everything had been cleaned and put away, and my other siblings and their families had left, the warm glow of the kitchen was filled with the soft chatter of my daughters, excited about the upcoming Masquerade Ball. Kayla, the eldest twin by mere minutes, sought my help with some alterations to her new dress—a task I happily embraced as I hadn't had the opportunity to do this since they moved away for college.

Meanwhile, Cassie sat at the kitchen table, her brow furrowed in concentration as she tried to remove her worn acrylic nails. A nail file lay out before her, silently bearing witness to her struggle.

Logan, who had been quietly observing the scene, leaned against the hallway into the kitchen with a concerned expression. "That's going to take a while," he remarked, his voice laced with empathy.

Cassie glanced up; her fingers paused mid-task. "Yeah, but I can't afford a professional job right now," she admitted, slightly frustrated and embarrassed.

Watching her struggle, Logan's face softened. "Tell you what," he proposed, stepping into the room, "put that down. I'll take you, Kayla, and your mom out tomorrow morning to get a manicure."

Cassie's eyes lit up with surprise as a smile formed on her face. "What? Really? You don't have to do that, Logan."

But Logan insisted, his experience as a former nail technician lending weight to his words. "I insist. It's going to take forever if you continue on your own, and it might not even turn out well without the proper tools." He had spent years in his 20s dabbling in various jobs, including a stint as a nail technician, which gave him an understanding of such tasks.

"Thank you so much, Logan! That is so thoughtful of you." Cassie's voice was thick with gratitude, her earlier frustration forgotten in the wake of his generous offer.

Early the following morning, we were back at Chase's house to pick up my daughters. Despite my reservations—having never indulged in a manicure due to the demands of a career that kept me perennially at my keyboard—I found myself enjoying the opportunity. Logan, with his characteristic charm, insisted, "You deserve to be pampered and treated like a queen because you are my queen." Though still unaccustomed to such praise, I couldn't help but look forward to having pristine, polished nails for the ball. It seemed a fitting complement to the elegance of the event.

As we settled into the plush chairs of the nail salon, Logan was very attentive, making sure we were taken care of as he weaved between the stations where my daughters and I were having our nails tended to. His eyes roamed from one technician to the next, a satisfied grin playing on his lips whenever he caught my eye, silently questioning if I was enjoying myself.

When the nail technician asked me what I needed done, I had not a clue. Logan walked over and told her, "Give her a classy ombre finish with square rounded tips. Make the colors as natural as possible. She'll like that." The nail technician looked at me to confirm, but what Logan said was foreign to me, so I said, "Whatever he said," with a smile.

In this simple act of getting a manicure, I found myself embraced with a kind of love I hadn't known before; the luxury of being cared for with such attentiveness was also foreign to me.

After my nails were perfectly shaped and polished, I carefully examined them, and Logan was right—my nails had never looked this nice. As we pushed in our chairs, Logan approached the counter to take care of the bill. He chatted amiably with the technicians, expressing his gratitude and leaving a generous tip that went beyond mere words.

The twins were quite happy with the result of their nails. Cassie leaned close to me, her voice low and earnest, "Mom, he is a keeper." Those simple yet profound words made my heart full.

After getting into the car, Logan asked to see my nails. I showed him my hand, and he gently held it to get a closer look at them, saying, "They're beautiful," then affectionately kissed my hand. My eyes glistened at his thoughtfulness. It's the littlest things that pull on my heartstrings the hardest.

As the afternoon faded into the hues of evening, it was time for the

Masquerade Ball. Logan, ever the iconoclast, chose a dark charcoal sleek suit sans tie, paired with leather dress shoes sporting intricate designs that complemented his entire outfit. His casual defiance of conventional dress codes only enhanced his charm, as he has a way of always taking my breath away with his appeal. Meanwhile, I had selected a classic long black dress that flowed effortlessly around my ankles.

After a final flurry of preparation, I emerged from the bathroom with my hair styled into soft curls, pulled back into a simple low ponytail, leaving some bangs to frame my face. Catching sight of Logan, I approached him, the back of my dress slightly undone. "Could you help me with the zipper?" I asked, turning my back towards him. With a gentle touch, he pulled the zipper up, securing the fabric with a soft click. Then, tenderly, he spun me around to face him. His eyes charmed with a mix of pride and admiration as he whispered, "You look beautiful, Baby."

I've always considered myself a plain Jane, finding comfort in simplicity. Yet, the way Logan sees me and makes me feel defies the self-image I've held for most of my life. Even my own mom, who is very beautiful with fair skin and delicate features, would tell me, "You're not very beautiful, so you must learn to always be kind, so others will like you." Those words, repeated over the years, colored my self-perception. But with Logan, he makes me believe that I am beautiful inside and out.

The Masquerade Ball unfolded in the grandeur of a hotel, its decorations a perfect echo of opulence with a touch of black and gold shimmer. Each table was a spectacle of elegance, adorned with tall vases filled with ostrich feathers, shimmering beads, and balloons that danced in the air, creating a scene reminiscent of a bygone era. A corner of the grand ballroom was transformed into a photographer's dream, featuring a festive backdrop in the night's thematic colors, inviting guests to immortalize their masked revelries.

My brothers and their wives had been at the hotel all day

orchestrating this spectacle, ensuring every detail in the grand ballroom was flawless. For convenience they had rented rooms at the hotel, preparing themselves for the night and were planning to stay over, should the festivities extend into the wee hours.

As we entered, we were escorted to a table near the lively dance floor, where a live band had already begun to serenade the gathering with vibrant, traditional melodies. Soon, my brothers, sisters-in-law, my sister, and twin daughters joined us, each in their finery, their outfits, a dazzling display of the night's elegance.

With the responsibility of co-emceeing the event, I found myself oscillating between the spotlight on the stage and the warm gathering at our table. Despite the demands of my role, Logan was holding himself quite well, striking up conversations with my family, and pulling me aside for a dance whenever my hosting duties allowed a brief reprieve.

As Logan pulled me into his arms on the dance floor, he leaned in close and spoke into my ear, "Are you enjoying the evening?"

"I am, especially because you're here," I replied, my voice nearly lost in the swell of the music.

He smiled. "I'm here for you. You're doing a great job as the emcee. I knew you were great with words, hearing you speak at your conference in California, yet it always amazes me how naturally you can engage a room full of people," he said with admiration.

Returning his smile, I briefly let my gaze wander over the room and the gathering around us. "I've had many years of practice," I said to him, turning back to meet his gaze.

"You're an amazing woman, Baby," Logan murmured, his eyes softening as he looked at me, the band was playing a gentle melody in the background of the dimly lit ballroom.

"I really enjoy getting to know your family too," he continued. His voice held a warmth that belied the hint of sadness that followed. "I wish my family was a lot more like yours. You all know how to love each other."

The music surrounded us in a bittersweet symphony that seemed to echo the complexity of emotions in Logan's words. Reflecting his sadness, I removed my arms from around his shoulders and encircled his waist, tightening my embrace and resting my head on his chest as he reciprocated by wrapping his arms around me. I always loved being in his embrace—strong and broad.

When the song ended, we returned to our table. A few of my cousins pulled me aside and asked, "Is he your new man?" I smiled shyly and answered, "Yes, he is." They took one more peek at him and said, "He is quite handsome," while another cousin exclaimed, "Damn girl, he's hot!" They playfully nudged me with smiles and chuckles. I returned a smile and nodded in agreement.

Moments later, amidst the laughter and music, a young lady approached our table, her arms laden with a large bouquet of red, pink, and white roses. Spotting her, Logan waved her over invitingly. He selected a rose and presented one to each of my sisters-in-law and my sister with a charming smile.

Then, in a sweeping gesture of romance, he took the remainder of the bouquet from the young lady's embrace and presented it to me with a tender look in his eyes. "These are for you, Baby," he declared, his voice a soft murmur over the music, transforming a simple moment into an unforgettable gesture of affection. He even gave the young lady more than what the flowers were worth.

I hadn't expected such a gesture, and the evening was turning out to be more enchanting than I had imagined.

Sunday was the last full day in Colorado, and I intentionally reserved this day to show Logan and Keith around all my favorite places. Keith was born in California and never had the chance to live in Colorado, so this was a treat for him just as much as it was for Logan.

The first stop was downtown Denver. Having spent most of my years in Colorado working in Larimer Square downtown, it became my favorite part of the city, especially during winter when the streets are covered in snow and festive lights are strung. Christmas wreaths hung on streetlamps, replicas of old-fashioned gas lamps positioned along the streets of the 16th Street Mall, where the entrance to the building I worked in faces.

With limited daylight hours and so much to explore, our stop downtown was brief, allowing us time for lunch at one of my favorite French bistros that served the best Coq au Vin. It's a classic French specialty, featuring tender chicken braised in rich red wine, complemented by savory mushrooms, pearl onions, and crisp lardons. The deep, flavorful sauce soaked into the accompanying crusty bread, creating a harmonious blend of textures and tastes. Knowing Logan's love for food and trying new cuisines, I wanted to ensure he experienced this aspect of my history and town.

Next was a 35-minute drive to Boulder, where I often immersed myself in nature's splendor. There's a place called Lost Gulch Overlook with a breathtaking vista of treetops, mountains stretching for miles, and the Rockies in the distance. It's the perfect spot to witness a sunset so radiant that its warm glow embraces you so gently and kindly that it makes you feel like you're touched by Heaven's love.

I married young, and during my college years, my husband at the time wasn't always supportive of my educational choices. He lacked patience and understanding, leading to frequent arguments and sometimes extreme actions like throwing my text books and schoolwork out of the car window onto the freeway, oblivious to the traffic around us. His response was often dismissive, suggesting that if my education mattered so much, I should retrieve the discarded materials myself.

Feeling ashamed and hurt, and with the danger of oncoming traffic, I would reluctantly abandon the idea of retrieving my belongings. In moments of defeat, both emotionally and physically, when my spirits were worn and battered, I sought solace alone at Lost Gulch Overlook. There, I would allow myself to cry and bask in the embrace of the sun's warmth, taking in its love and comfort, as the cracks my heart had endured slowly recuperated.

It had been a long time since I last visited Lost Gulch Overlook, but sitting on that mountainside with Logan, feeling the cool breeze lightly brushing our faces and taking in the vast view, it was a departure from the somber memories I once associated with this place. Instead, the love I felt was from Logan and his caring, protective embrace, installing within me a new memory to cherish.

CHAPTER 14

SWEETEST NOVEMBER

RETURNING TO MINNESOTA WAS BITTERSWEET as we bid farewell to my Colorado family, but it was nice to be home and get back to the routine of things. Logan's birthday was just less than a week away. I had spent the last month contemplating the ideal gift, understanding his profound love for fine arts and exquisite craftsmanship. I was looking for something deeply personal and as unique as him. Something that would reflect his soul. It took some considerable time, but I think I found that gift.

On the morning of his birthday,[32] we strolled through a park. Our path led us to a stage and amphitheater nestled within the park's serene surroundings. Logan quickly hops onto the center of the stage, his arms outstretched, as his voice carries his aspirations into the open air.

"I want to create a grand event," Logan announced, his enthusiasm painting a vivid picture. "Not just any event, but a spectacle of fashion

---

[32] Friday, November 8, 2019

and live music, where people dress to the nines for a red-carpet experience. Imagine the atmosphere, like the Emmys or Grammys, with every aspect designed to dazzle," he proclaimed with a big grin on his face—my favorite grin.

The way he expressed his vision was heartwarming, and I couldn't help but fall deeper in love with him and his boundless creativity. As he continued to elaborate, his entrepreneurship and passion were evident. In my years of experience, I knew those were essential to driving any project to fruition.

Watching him from where I was standing, I discovered that his joy and happiness became my own, igniting a sense of purpose and fulfillment within me that I had never known before. Having orchestrated numerous events and projects in the past, I understood the immense dedication, effort, and resources such an endeavor would require. Yet, that sacrifice seemed a small price to pay for the sheer happiness radiating from his face. That alone was enough for me to give him the world. Smiling at Logan, I silently vowed to help bring his dream to life. I then called out to him, "Let's make it happen."

He bounded off the stage with excitement, his smile lighting up the park. As we strolled together, my shoulder snugly tucked under his arm, the chilly air playfully tingled our noses and blushed our cheeks. Despite the cold, Logan's presence embraced me in warmth.

We paused beside a picnic table overlooking the tranquil lake. Logan perched on its edge, his animated gestures painting vivid pictures of his envisioned event. I love this version of Logan—vibrant and passionate. It was a revelation, a stark contrast to the introspective and somewhat melancholic man I first met in Stillwater just a few months ago. Here, by the serene waters, he radiated life, hope, and palpable excitement—a feeling I wanted to savor for as long as possible.

"What would you name your event?" I asked, genuinely intrigued by Logan's ideas.

"I was thinking of calling it Hmong in Style. It's the name of a magazine I started over a decade ago. I thought we could revive it," Logan replied optimistically, his eyes gleaming with enthusiasm.

"Hmong in Style?" I echoed, my eyes widening in surprise. "I had no idea you were the creator behind that magazine. I've seen it, but I only recall encountering one issue." My surprise was genuine and profound. Logan seemed equally astonished that I had stumbled upon his publication, especially considering that I've never lived in Minnesota. "Tell me, what was your vision for Hmong in Style?" I asked eagerly, curious to learn more about his inspirations and objectives for starting the magazine.

He began to share that his initial aspiration for Hmong in Style was to highlight pop culture and fashion in the Hmong communities around Saint Paul and, eventually, the world. It was something that hadn't been emphasized before in any publication.

With minimal support and a shoestring budget, he took on every role himself—writing, interviewing, casting models, photography, design, marketing, and seeking advertisers and funding. I was astounded by his remarkable ability and dedication. Despite his incredible efforts, he revealed that the lack of support and the burden of doing everything alone left him feeling defeated, causing him to discontinue halfway through the second issue. However, this epic event would be the personification of that publication on one magnificent stage.

Hearing how he had to give up a dream tinged my heart with sadness, but recognizing the potential within both of us only fueled my determination. With unwavering confidence, I said, "We got this!"

Reflecting on his choice of name, I expressed, "I love your ideas, but for an exquisite event, let's give it a name that can reflect its grandeur while still encompassing your initial expression of art and culture."

"How about Hmong Novice?" Logan suggested.

I paused, letting his suggestion sink in before responding, "Novice might imply inexperience, which isn't the message you want to convey for something as spectacular as you've envisioned," I explained.

As Logan's suggestion lingered in my thoughts, a similar sounding word came to mind. "What about 'Nouveau'?" I proposed. "It's French, signifying newness, innovation, and modernity, capturing the essence of what we aim to achieve."

"Yes, that's perfect!" Logan exclaimed confidently, his face lighting up with excitement and approval as he said, "Hmong Nouveau. Hmoob tshiab.[33]" His spirit was suddenly renewed as he continued to share all his ideas for the event. Seeing him in his element filled me with joy, prompting me to take out my phone and capture this radiant moment of him smiling so brightly.[34]

For the evening, I had arranged a special birthday dinner for Logan at a Brazilian steakhouse, urging him to don his finest formal attire. Knowing his fondness for meat and the diverse offerings at the restaurant, I anticipated a culinary delight that would surely please his palate. I had been carrying around his gift in my coat all day, eagerly awaiting the moment to present it to him during our dinner celebration.

As we arrived at the Brazilian Steakhouse nestled in the heart of downtown Minneapolis, we opted for the convenience of valet parking. Logan's presence was striking as he stepped out of the car, clad in a dark suit that perfectly accentuated his muscular frame. His crimson button-

---

[33] Hmoob tshiab (pronounced: Hmong chia) means "new Hmong."

[34] Photo timestamped at 11:24 a.m. on Friday, November 8, 2019.

up shirt, paired with a black trench coat and stylish scarf, added an air of sophistication to his ensemble. His leather dress shoes were pristinely polished and elegant. His innate sense of style never failed to impress, radiating an effortless charm that drew admiring glances from passersby.

In contrast, dressing up was a rare occasion for me; my typical attire consisted of jeans and sweaters, often with my hair in a messy bun or ponytail. However, for Logan's special day, I carefully selected a black cocktail dress adorned with intricate crimson floral patterns to compliment the color of his button-up shirt. The rich colors added a touch of elegance and celebration to the evening. Completing the outfit was a delicate pearl necklace that draped gracefully around my neck, adding a subtle yet refined touch.

I chose to wear my hair down, allowing my natural curls to cascade freely around my face. The gentle movement of the curls framed my features softly, adding a touch of whimsy and femininity to the overall look. Together, our attire reflected the mood of the evening—sophisticated yet celebratory, a perfect match for the special occasion.

"You should wear your hair like this more often," Logan remarked, his gaze affectionate as he admired my look. "It suits you perfectly," he added, flashing my favorite smile, the one that always tugs at my heart.

We settled into our seats, draping our coats over the backs of our chairs. Logan and I seldom indulge in alcohol, yet tonight was an occasion to celebrate the birth of an extraordinary man, so we decided to savor some champagne—a departure from our usual habits. I asked the waiter to bring us a bottle of their finest.

The ambiance around us was enchanting, with soft candlelight casting a warm glow over the well-set table. Soon, a group of servers approached us, each carrying an array of meats on oversized skewers, poised to carve delectable portions onto our awaiting plates.

Our champaign glasses shimmered with the sparkling pale gold hue of honey, a surprising but delightful choice to accompany our feast. After the waiter poured us each a glass, I raised mine and toasted to Logan's birthday. "May you always be celebrated and loved beyond measure," I said with heartfelt sincerity.

Moments later, after we finished our meal, the waiter presented a sleek slice of rich chocolate cake, adorned with the words "Happy Birthday" delicately drizzled in raspberry coulis along the plate. The candle's flame danced, casting a warm glow in the dimly lit restaurant and adding a shimmer of celebration to the atmosphere.

Leaning closer to Logan, I whispered affectionately, "Happy birthday, my love. You've been a gift since the day you were born, and I want to always cherish and celebrate you," my voice tender with deepest affection. I sealed the sentiment with a soft kiss on his lips.

After Logan took a moment to enjoy a bite of his cake, I reached into my coat pocket and retrieved his gift, a thoughtfully wrapped blue package with a shimmering silver bow. As I handed it to him, I couldn't help but notice a glint of appreciation in Logan's eyes.

"It's very rare that I celebrate my birthday and receive a gift," Logan remarked. He was genuinely surprised. His words struck a chord with me, and my heart sank, realizing that someone as giving as Logan had rarely been on the receiving end of genuine gestures. It was a poignant reminder of the depth of his generosity and the understated simplicity of his desires. But I swiftly composed myself, masking my emotions with a smile. It was a silent promise to make his birthday and every day thereafter filled with moments of warmth and appreciation.

"It's the least I could do," I replied. "I wanted to make your birthday memorable and show you how much you mean to me." The warmth in Logan's eyes reflected my sentiment. In that fleeting moment, I knew I wanted to celebrate this man for the rest of my life because of his genuine humility and generous kindness.

My pulse quickened in anticipation as Logan unwrapped his gift.

"Wow, this is exquisite," he exclaimed upon opening the box, revealing a custom watch crafted from titanium and ebony wood, its marble-blue face showcasing the intricate workings within. "I had ebony wood added to the band because of your fine carpentry skills," I explained, "and the exposed inner workings symbolize your intricate nature. You're like a timeless piece, just like this watch. Check the back." Logan turned the watch over, discovering the engraving:

To my Logan, with all my love for ∞.

"That's your symbol," he noted, recognizing the infinity symbol from my business' logo. "Yes," I said, "because it's forever."

Logan smiled and placed the watch on his wrist, extending his arm in front of him to admire his gift. "I love it. Thank you, Baby," he said with appreciation as he leaned in to give me a kiss.

After we left the restaurant, we arrived at our hotel. While passing by the concierge desk, Logan grabbed a roll of breath mints from the counter behind the lobby and paid for it. As we stepped into the elevator, I glanced at him and said, "Thanks for getting the mints. I'm sure we'll need them after that dinner," and chuckled. Logan responded with a smirk and a playful wink.

Entering our hotel room, we were captivated by the breathtaking scenery, where the city lights painted a romantic and hopeful atmosphere below. The shimmering lights cast a magical radiance, setting the scene for our continued celebration.

Following our walk in the park, I told Logan that I needed to go home and get ready for his birthday dinner, which gave me some time to check in early to our room and thoughtfully arrange candles in decorative glass jars throughout. After lighting each one, I walked over to Logan. He stood leaning with one arm above him, his elbow pressed against the window, and his other hand in his pocket, gazing out at the majestic skyline of downtown Minneapolis.

Leaning close to Logan, I breathed in his cologne—a sophisticated blend of crisp citrus notes intertwined with aromatic herbs and warm undertones of amber and sandalwood. The fragrance was both invigorating and comforting, perfectly encapsulating his essence. Its intoxicating allure made it impossible for me to pull away, drawing me irresistibly closer to him. I wrapped my arms around him, and the warmth of his body felt inviting.

Whispering once more, "Happy birthday, my love. You deserve the world," my words carried a soft and tender tone in the dimly lit room, illuminated by flickering candlelight. I knew in my soul that my feelings for Logan ran deep, and in such a short time, I had grown to love him more than words could express.

Logan turned to me, his eyes brimming with affection. "I'm so grateful for you," he murmured, his hand tenderly lifting my chin to meet his gaze. In that intimate moment, with the city's twinkling lights as our backdrop, he leaned in and pressed his lips to mine, sealing his affection and appreciation with a deep and mesmerizing kiss.

Breaking from his lips and embrace, I stepped back to sit on the edge of the bed to admire his beautiful form. The soft flickering of candles cast a warm glow on the contours of his physique, while the night cityscape provided a mesmerizing view. In silent stillness, I watched as he slowly removed his black blazer, draping it over the desk chair before turning his attention back to me.

As I watched, he knew exactly what he was doing, confident that my eyes would follow his every move while he relished his ability to captivate me. My heart quickened as I tried to steady its rhythm, unable to look away. Even after nearly four months together, I still found myself in awe, cherishing every moment and knowing he was devoted to me completely.

With intense focus, I watched as his hands slowly unfastened each button on his shirt, every movement purposeful and measured, amplifying the suspense. When his crimson shirt was fully undone, he peeled it off, revealing his perfectly sculpted chest and abs—a testament to his lifelong dedication to fitness. A large tattoo of a magnificent tiger wrapped from the right side of his torso to his abdomen, seeming to come alive with his every flex and movement.

Observing him take his time to undress was both torturous and satisfying; my eyes traced the contours of his broad shoulders and defined arms, each muscle captivating. No matter how many times I've seen him bare, he still takes my breath away as if it were the very first time.

My body began to tremble lightly as I shifted onto the bed, inching closer to the center, my eyes fixed on him as he slowly unbuckled his leather belt. He drew it away from his pants in a tantalizingly slow motion, almost as if to tease me, before letting it fall to the floor with a soft thud. Instantly, my heart fluttered. His fingers then traced his waistband, unclipping the fastener and unzipping his pants with the same care. He gently eased them down, allowing the fabric to glide over his hips and sculpted thighs, letting them fall softly to his ankles before stepping out of them.

The perfection of his bare, chiseled body caused my heart to race with exhilaration as heat surged through my cheeks. His muscular physique was a feature I had never cared to notice on anyone else before, but watching Logan in this moment made me feel intensely vulnerable. My breath grew heavier, as if my heart were in my throat. I had never experienced such fervor, where the intensity of someone's presence ignited such a strong reaction within me, stripping away all my inhibitions and leaving me completely enthralled by him.

In a moment of self-awareness, I discreetly raised the back of my hand to my lips to ensure I wasn't inadvertently drooling. I bit my bottom lip, my mind racing, and completely captivated by the magnetic pull of his gaze and the fiery tension between us.

When his final garment gracefully fell to the floor, he flashed a flirtatious smirk, fully aware of the effect he had on me, causing my heart to quicken its pace. He then moved toward me with such slowness that it felt like time stretched between us. His eyes locked onto mine, and began to undress me, each gesture heightening my longing as he tossed my clothes effortlessly onto the floor.

Unable to contain myself any longer, I pulled him in for an ardent kiss, each touch awakening my senses and sending waves of desire through me. To my pleasant surprise, he had two breath mints in his mouth, passing one into mine with a gentle seductiveness that I happily accepted, savoring the sweetness on his lips.

His hands, gentle yet firm, caressed my breast with a tenderness that left me breathless. He then kissed it, blending softness and intensity, deepening the connection between us with every touch.

As he traced kisses down my body, his lips moved with purposeful slowness, sending tingles of anticipation through every inch of my skin. The warmth of his breath, combined with his loving caress, created a sensory symphony that heightened my senses. When he reached between my legs, his lips parted with gentle insistence, leaving a trail of soft, teasing kisses along my inner thigh, each one a delicate display of his devoted affection.

His deliberate pace, every movement filled with intent, only served to increase my desire. Then, with gradual slowness, he took me in, and I felt the warmth of his mouth as his tongue explored with a mix of coolness and intensity from the mint, gradually tingling every inch of my body where his tongue had traced. I had no idea this was his intention when he winked at me in the elevator, leaving me even more breathless and intoxicated—feeling blissfully thankful for his creative endeavor.

Every flicker of his tongue, every caress, planted seeds of euphoria that seemed to expand like wild vines, intensifying with each passing moment. The world around us faded into a blur as I was enveloped by the overwhelming sensation of his touch. It was a dance of tenderness and desire, a melody of intimate connection that left me utterly and completely consumed.

With his face nestled between my legs and his hands bracing my hips, he lavished me with his attention, unrushed, his steadfast conviction evident in every touch and kiss. I felt his tongue exploring every sensitive part of my most intimate area, its warm, gentle softness teasing and tantalizing, sending shivers of pleasure through me with every stroke. He moved with masterful control, his tongue flicking and swirling in a seductive motion that made my entire body quiver. He added playful nibbles and gentle kisses, each one intensifying the sensation and making me gasp with intoxicating delight.

His fingers tenderly parted my delicate lips, his tongue sweeping in a long, invigorating stroke, savoring every bit of my arousal. The blend of warmth and coolness sent waves of sensation coursing through me. I let out a breath of sheer contentment as my fingers stroked through his hair, gently grasping it in loving encouragement for him to continue.

As his tongue worked its magic, he slid his fingers inside me with a gentle, exploring touch. Each movement was intentional and precise, his fingers curling and exploring with increasing intensity. His touch was both tender and insistent, hitting all the right spots. The interplay of his tongue and fingers created ripples of ecstasy coursing through me, each one more powerful than the last.

The combination of these movements built until I reached an intense climax that shook me to my core. Yet, he didn't relent. With unyielding devotion, he continued, holding me closer and driving me to the edge repeatedly. I clung desperately to the sheets, my body trembling and convulsing uncontrollably, yet I didn't want him to stop. Each wave of pleasure washed over me in a torrent of overwhelming desire.

As I shivered subtly from the intensity, he gracefully emerged from his position and gently rested his warm torso against mine. I could feel the heat radiating from him, soothing me with each touch as he carefully held his weight over me. Feeling the warmth of his erection firmly pressed against me sent another wave of anticipation and desire coursing through me. My body responded with a mixture of longing and readiness, eagerly anticipating what was to come.

His gaze locked with mine, a contented smile spreading across his features, silently acknowledging his exceptional performance, evident in the look of gratification and exhaustion on my face. With one hand, he caressed my flushed cheeks, carefully moving the hair away from my face as he tenderly pressed his lips against mine, igniting a fiery passion. The kiss was an intense fusion of desire and love, each movement of his lips conveying a depth of emotion that tugged at the deepest parts of my soul.

After a brief pause to let the shivers subside, he repositioned himself onto his knees, his intense gaze still locked on mine. With a tender touch, he placed his hand on my thigh and gently parted my legs wider. His fingers traced a path of desire, delicately caressing the most sensual areas between my legs, leaving me yearning for more. Slowly, he penetrated me with his fingers, sending waves of gratification through my body. His warmth moved fervently yet carefully inside me. In a husky whisper, he murmured, "You're so wet, Baby. I love it," pursing his lips in satisfaction. His words reignited the flames within me, and I let out a soft moan, a plea for him to continue.

His fingers moved with mounting intensity, teasing me just enough to keep me teetering on the edge of another climax. As his touch grew more vigorous, my hand clutched the bed sheets tightly, my nails digging into the fabric as if I would lose myself entirely if I didn't hold on. I tried to hold my breath to quiet the pleasure forcing its way from my lips, but the overwhelming sensation broke through. I couldn't help but let out a cascade of moans as a flood of wetness escaped me in ways

I'd never imagined possible. It was a reaction my limited experience had thought was only a myth.

Craving the sensation of his deeper penetration, I pleaded with him to make love to me. A smirk of contentment spread across his face, as if he had been waiting to hear those words from me all night. His eyes ablaze with desire, he did not wait a moment longer to seize my hips with both hands, lifting and pulling me irresistibly closer.

With meticulous precision, he slowly entered me, each inch of his generous mass filling me completely and igniting an inferno of elation that consumed us both. Each movement became a wave of pleasure, each connection between us propelling us to the heights of exhilaration we had anxiously awaited all day to explore and indulge. Our bodies melded together in a yearning embrace, every motion intensifying the persistent longing between us.

Without losing any momentum, he intensified his thrust, driving deeper into me with each powerful motion, feeling the full impact of his masculine strength. I surrendered completely to his desire, allowing the overwhelming surges of pleasure to wash over me and consume every fiber of my being. His increasing rhythm matched the pounding of my heart, each movement a symphony of love, promises, and devotion that echoed through the candlelit room.

My legs wrapped tightly around his, and my arms clung to him, my palms pressed firmly against his back, soaked in the outcome of his unwavering effort. I gasped and moaned, lost in the relentless intensity of our union, feeling every inch of him fill me with rapture. Each powerful thrust pierced through barriers, delving into the deepest recesses of my essence. With every stroke, he propelled me closer to the edge of bliss, his desire driving us both to the brink of ecstasy.

As our bodies moved in a frenzied rhythm, his breaths grew shorter, more urgent. Finally, in a moment of intense release, he erupted into me. The sudden warmth of his embrace was profoundly intimate, sending pulsations of intense satisfaction rippling through me. It felt like a deep, consuming heat that melted all my defenses, binding us in a moment of pure unity and overpowering fulfillment.

Exhausted from the fervor, Logan collapsed onto the bed beside me. His chest heaved as he struggled to catch his breath, each inhalation deep and labored. Sweat glistened on his skin, reflecting the soft glow of the room, his body radiating the warmth of our passionate encounter. As he lay there, the rise and fall of his chest gradually steadied, the air filling his lungs in rhythm with the slowing beat of his heart, encapsulating the serene aftermath of our shared intimacy.

Logan's controlled and meticulously honed techniques brought me to multiple peaks of pleasure, leaving us both charged and utterly spent. Nearly two hours slipped through our fingers like water cascading down a roaring waterfall, each moment a whirlwind of intensity and bliss that seemed to defy the very laws of time.

With a tender shiver running through me and perspiration on my skin, I turned to nestle on Logan's warm chest, whispering between breaths, "I feel like it was my birthday." We laughed, the sound of our happiness filling the quiet, candlelit room. "Happy birthday," he said playfully, kissing me gently on my hairline and wrapping his arms tighter around me, making me feel cherished and loved.

We lay in each other's embrace until our breathing steadied and our bodies cooled. He gently placed the sheets over us and cradled me in his arms. As always, our temperatures were perfectly in sync as he held me close, lulling me to sleep. "I love you, Baby," I whispered. "I love you more," he replied.

CHAPTER 15

STRENGTH AND SERENDIPITY

*A*S NOVEMBER DRAWS TO A CLOSE, Logan dives into finalizing his year's projects before heavy snowfall sets in. While he occasionally tackles indoor renovations like kitchen and bathroom remodels, his heart lies in exterior projects such as decking, roofing, siding, fencing, patios, and driveways.

Despite Logan running his business for over twenty years and delivering every project immaculately, he still relied solely on word of mouth (which is still the most effective, by the way) and manual processes. This often resulted in not having enough projects to keep his crew busy, and I saw an opportunity where I could contribute.

When it comes to business operations, I'm passionate about business development, process improvement, and modern-day marketing. Over the past three months since our return from California, I have dedicated myself to bolstering Logan's business image and operations. I created a professional company website showcasing his best work and client testimonials, designed a captivating logo with eye-catching colors that reflect his brand, and established a robust social media presence with engaging content to attract new clients. Taking charge of expanding his market reach, I developed a streamlined system for managing customer inquiries and intake and addressed various administrative tasks that were weighing him down.

But beyond the digital realm and paperwork, I yearned to delve into physical labor, getting my hands dirty to help him construct and build—an experience I eagerly anticipated as a fulfilling contribution to his endeavors.

Eager to lend a hand, I volunteered my weekend to help him frame a deck. Initially hesitant, Logan voiced concern about me taking on strenuous tasks, preferring to reserve that work for his crew. However, I passionately pleaded with him, expressing my love for hands-on work and the joy I'd find in collaborating with him. I mentioned that it would also give us more time to spend together, and this eventually convinced him to let me join. Of course, not without some playful eye rolling on his part.

We arrived at his worksite at the break of dawn, greeted by the damp and cold morning air. Logan quickly set up a propane heater, creating a cozy makeshift shelter to keep me warm. His thoughtfulness always touched me deeply, showing how he cared for my comfort and well-being. However, I reminded him, "I love you, but I'm here to work."

It was a quiet Saturday, just the two of us on site. Logan had given his crew the day off, a testament to his respect for their time and dedication. He rarely scheduled work on weekends unless there was an urgent project, or the team voluntarily chose to work, but because he needed to complete this deck as snow was on the forecast within the next ten days, he is using his time to get ahead.

Having built countless decks over the last two decades, sometimes single-handedly, Logan developed many crafty ways to construct a deck without the assistance of anyone else, which I found to be ingenious. I complimented him on his cleverness, and he laughed as he explained, "When I was starting my business, I did a lot of good work for cheap to build my portfolio. I couldn't afford to hire a second hand, so I was forced to make the most of my situation to get the work done." It was a skillset that has served him well over the years. Now that I'm here, I told him he would never have to work on a deck by himself again.

The winter air remained frigid, with an overcast sky looming above us. Initially concerned for my safety and well-being, Logan quickly became impressed with my agility as I moved swiftly throughout the worksite. Fetching tools, supporting my own weight, and balancing with ease, I climbed to reach heights effortlessly. By the afternoon, Logan and I had already completed most of the framing for the bi-level deck that stood eight feet high and measured 12 by 18 feet.

"You are the best laborer I've ever had. No man on my crew has worked as well and with as much common sense as you have. I don't have to explain things in detail to you; you just get it," Logan praised.

I smiled at Logan and said, "We're a good team. I enjoyed this."

Following Logan's instructions, I was impressed by his framing technique. Having managed some construction projects before, I had never seen anyone frame their decks quite like him. Typically, I had seen the posts go in first, securely cemented, and then the deck frame built on top of the sturdy posts.

However, Logan built his deck with the frame attached to the house's ledger board first and used temporary posts to hold up the framed deck, securing them with supporting 2x4s. This allowed him to get ahead with his project while waiting for the city inspector to check the depths of the postholes, which often takes two to three weeks, depending on the city. This process reduces his time spent on a project and has always worked well for him. By the time the postholes are inspected, he is already one-third of the way through the deck's workload, which his clients appreciate for its efficiency.

As we worked on the deck together, Logan was standing on an aluminum platform, giving him the height to work underneath the deck, while I stood next to him on a solid part of the yard that was elevated and by a retaining wall. Still, the deck was half a foot above my head. I was holding a handful of screws for him while he screwed in one of the last few joists when the entire frame of the deck suddenly shifted. Terrified for Logan's safety, I instinctively dropped everything in my hand and grabbed hold of the entire deck, shifting it back into place and holding its weight up in my arms above my head.

In that moment, Logan ducked to avoid being crushed underneath the deck, only to realize that my quick action had prevented the heavy structure from collapsing. Our eyes met briefly, and I saw the shock on his face. He quickly ran over to the loose post, securing it back into place and applying additional 2x4s to ensure it would not come loose again. Once it was completely secured, I let go of the deck, feeling only a minor pull in my back muscle that disappeared shortly after.

As soon as the post and deck were secure, Logan rushed over to check if I was okay, inspecting me from head to toe. Then he exclaimed, "Damn, woman. I'm wifing you!" before giving me a tight hug.

"That's enough for one day; I'll finish the rest on Monday with my crew and make sure it's done before the snow arrives at the end of the week," Logan added.

As we drove home, he reached for my hand and held it tightly, saying, "You're so strong. You saved my life today. If you hadn't been there, the deck could have crashed down on me. And you could have been seriously hurt too; I would have never forgiven myself for that." I squeezed his hand back and replied, "I'm not sure what came over me. I don't consider myself strong, but at that moment, I was just so afraid for you. Maybe it was adrenaline kicking in."

CHAPTER 16

UNTETHERED

$\mathcal{I}$T WAS THE FIRST WEEK OF DECEMBER,[35] and we were having dinner at Osaka Sushi in Maplewood. I had just confided in Logan about my feelings regarding my dad and stepmom since my move to Minnesota. While I was grateful for their generosity in welcoming me into their home during a transitional period in my life, the way my dad, stepmom, and stepbrother treated me had become disheartening, and I never saw it coming before moving here.

My parents had divorced a few years before I did, which likely contributed to their understanding when I finally made the difficult decision to file for divorce without seeking further approval or discussion from either side of the family. After my divorce papers were finalized, I called my dad to inform him. His response was a simple yet profound "Okay," devoid of the usual "be patient" dialogue that had prolonged the agony of trying to salvage a marriage that had brought more tears than

---

[35] 2019

smiles.

When my dad remarried around the time I got divorced, I understood what it meant for him to find someone with whom he could build a happy life, and I was genuinely happy for him. They visited me in Long Beach, and meeting my stepmom for the first time, I greeted her with open arms, knowing she was the woman who would love my dad and build a future with him. I had them stay with me and took them on excursions around the port of Long Beach.

Moving here, I had so much hope to build a stronger relationship with my dad as he was getting older and to get to know my stepmom and stepbrother better. However, I found myself feeling increasingly unwelcome in what I thought would be a place of refuge.

The first incident unfolded innocently enough, just two weeks after I had settled into my new life in Minnesota. I had returned home from a long day at work, eager to unwind and put my belongings in order. Little did I know that the evening held a conversation that would shake the very foundation of my sense of belonging in that household.

Silas, my stepbrother, who had graduated from high school the year before and was a few years younger than my youngest daughter, called me into the living room for what I assumed would be a casual chat. As I entered, I found him and my stepmom seated, looking relaxed and ready for conversation. Silas' initial question about my work seemed like a typical inquiry from a younger brother, as I assumed he was curious about potential career paths. I happily shared details about my role as an IT Consultant and openly answered his questions about my education and salary. However, the tone of the conversation took a sharp turn when he delved into probing about the reasons behind my move to Minnesota.

His line of questioning soon revealed an underlying intention and skepticism, culminating in a subtle accusation that I had relocated solely to freeload off his mom and my dad. I felt a mix of surprise and hurt by his insinuations, especially since I had clearly communicated to my dad and stepmom that my stay was temporary until I found my own place. Furthermore, I assured Silas that I had already spoken with my dad and informed him that I would be contributing my share of expenses while I was there. Despite my attempts to clarify and maintain composure, Silas persisted with his subtle yet impolite remarks, while my stepmom silently observed the exchange without intervening.

Later, when I mustered the courage to discuss the incident with my dad, hoping for understanding and support, his response fell short of my expectations. Instead of addressing the underlying issue of respect and trust, he seemed to have brushed off Silas' actions as merely caring too much, which only added to my sense of disillusionment and hurt.

The aftermath of that conversation lingered in the air like an unspoken tension, casting a shadow over my interactions within the household. It was a stark reminder of the challenges I faced, where even basic respect and empathy seemed to be in short supply. The incident left me feeling not just humiliated but also deeply wounded by the lack of solidarity and support from those I had hoped would provide a sense of family and belonging. Unfortunately, in the months since then, the tone had remained unchanged.

"I don't want you living there anymore," said Logan. "I can't stand the way they treat you and Keith. This is the last straw," he declared. The intensity in his voice showed how concerned and deeply upset he was, and I wasn't expecting him to have or express such strong feelings.

As Logan and I sat at the dinner table, the heaviness of his emotions was apparent. His usual hearty appetite was replaced by a solemn demeanor, his gaze fixed on his plate as if searching for answers in the pieces of rice and sashimi before him.

"You know..." His voice broke the silence, followed by a meaningful pause that seemed to carry the weight of unspoken thoughts and emotions. He took a deep breath, as if gathering his resolve, before continuing with firmness in his tone. "Just because the people in your life are family, it doesn't guarantee that they love or care about you," he asserted with raw honesty that reflected his own experience. "I've only known you for almost five months now, and yet you feel more like family to me than my own. Seeing you treated this way hurts me too." The intensity of his emotions mirrored my own inner turmoil.

I was hesitant, but I shared with Logan that I'm considering moving to Colorado. At least there, I would have my daughters, and my siblings would always welcome me. Logan's face immediately turned somber, and in a soft, melancholy tone, he said, "What about me? Are you planning to leave me?" His question caught me off guard, and I carelessly hadn't considered how he would feel. Hearing him speak those words, my heart sank, and suddenly, I couldn't imagine leaving anymore. It was a stark reminder that I would be breaking all the silent promises I made to Logan.

Before I could respond with reassurances, he made a proposal that left me without words. "You're moving in with me," he stated, his eyes locking onto mine with unwavering determination.

Logan's living situation was unconventional, to say the least. His job in construction often took him far and wide across the Twin Cities, and he had converted his van into a functional camper to accommodate his nomadic lifestyle.

It wasn't until we met that he would travel closer to town every evening to spend time with me and then find a safe location, often the parking lot of a 24-hour shopping center, to park his camper and sleep for the night. Every now and then, when I worried about him or didn't want him to be alone, I would spend the night with him in his camper, so the idea of cohabiting in his camper was not new or an outrageous request.

But it was now winter, and the city was starting to get colder.

Additional layers of blankets would not suffice as they had up until now, and his camper would basically be a metal icebox. I looked at Logan, my expression gravely concerned, feeling devastated about how he would stay warm in his camper van.

"No worries. I'll have a diesel heater installed tomorrow. It's the same type of heaters used in RVs. It's safe and will keep the vehicle toasty all night without requiring the engine to be running," Logan assured me with a sense of confidence that eased at least one of my concerns.

Still feeling disheartened, I said, "I still have Keith to worry about." I couldn't bear to have my son stay living with my dad if I wasn't there, and we wouldn't all fit in the cramped space of Logan's vehicle. It might be okay for just the two of us because we always slept snugly in each other's embrace, but certainly not for three.

"Leave that to me. I'll reconfigure everything, make space for you and Keith. I just don't want to see you suffer in that house any longer," he replied, his eyes reflecting a mixture of concern and determination. I looked at him with somber yet hopeful eyes, appreciating how unwavering his love was for me and my son, but I was still worried.

The next day, Logan's offer lingered in my mind as I grappled with the implications of his words and my own turmoil regarding the living situation for my son and me. I looked at apartments, but decent ones in the areas I preferred, where Keith wouldn't have to transfer schools, weren't available until the end of January. I didn't want to wait two months.

While at work, I reached out to my brother Jake, my only sibling in Minnesota. After explaining the situation, he remarked, "I was afraid that would happen. It's why I moved out shortly after relocating there from Colorado, but I had hoped you would have a better experience." He then offered a solution that eased some of my worries. "I have roommates, but it's just us guys. Keith can stay with me until you figure things out," Jake suggested, his support becoming a beacon of reassurance amidst the uncertainty.

Logan's support extended beyond just helping me move my belongings into storage. It was a tangible demonstration of his commitment to ensuring mine and Keith's well-being. As we unloaded boxes from his vehicle into a storage unit, I expressed my determination to find a place as soon as possible so that Keith could return to living with me under a stable roof. Logan listened attentively, his reassurance echoing steadfast support that had become a constant in our evolving relationship.

"Absolutely, Baby," Logan affirmed, his voice a warmth that countered the chill of the winter air. "But don't feel the need to rush. We can always work something out."

As we lay in bed on the first night in Logan's camper van, it was dark outside, and sleet was falling gently. The pitter-patter on the camper's rooftop provided soothing comfort as he held me snug in his arms, surrounded by soft blankets and the warmth from Logan's newly installed diesel heater. Just as I closed my eyes, feeling content in his embrace, he asked, "Would you be happier with me if I had a traditional home like everyone else?"

My answer was quick: "No. That's not important to me."

"Having you here feels good, but I also feel guilty for not providing better because I'm poor," Logan confessed.

"Honey, over the past few months, I've helped you sort your business and I've seen all your transactions. You make as much as some of these doctors in town. You're not poor; you're just not saving as much as others. Your choice of lifestyle and material possessions doesn't define your wealth. You could be a billionaire with opulent mansions, yachts, and personal jets and still be broke. You don't have any credit, but you also have no debt whatsoever because you pay for everything in cash. Honestly, I'd rather be you," I eagerly expressed to Logan, letting him know he actually has the lifestyle I wish I had the courage to embark on.

I continued to share with Logan that, in my life, I've acquired expensive, materialistic things, but none have ever brought me joy. Living in San Diego, the large home we lived in had actually made me depressed. Unlike others who may feel claustrophobic in tight spaces, large homes have the same effect on me. It was too big for comfort, and I preferred smaller spaces where everything is within reach. Moreover, I dislike being tied down, so the idea of buying a home never really appealed to me, especially as I was always on the move and shedding possessions without a second thought. What really brings joy are experiences and being able to share those experiences with someone important to me. Those are the things that money cannot buy, nor can others take away.

Reflecting on my life in California shortly before my move to Minnesota, I yearned for freedom and the thrill of liberation. I recalled a post I had shared on social media back then—a meme that captured the essence of embracing the unknown with nothing more than the essentials packed into a single bag. The image depicted a woman in complete solitude, camping in the wilderness. Before her, a morning campfire and fire-brewed coffee; cup in hand, she sat back to enjoy the scenic mountain vista, looking as though she had no worries or burdens at all and was completely at peace.

I desperately wanted to experience the bliss she felt. It was a sentiment I had longed to embody, but the path to achieving that was elusive, especially when I had been conditioned to a traditional lifestyle of living in a house my whole life. Breaking away felt as difficult as remaining.

Nestled within the compact of a tiny camper van, with no rush to be anywhere at any given time, I felt like I had captured some of that essence of liberation. There, amidst the simplicity of minimalist living, I unearthed a profound sense of fulfillment that had eluded me for years, revealing the true richness of life I had been seeking. It was an ironic turn of events that brought an unexpected sense of contentment.

Contrary to my initial concerns about the cramped space being a challenge, it was surprisingly inviting. The small space, rather than limiting us, seemed to amplify our intimacy, turning every moment into an opportunity for closeness. Whether we spent our time in conversation, delving deeper into each other's pasts, or indulging in long nights of intimacy in each other's embrace, the confined quarters heightened the pleasure of being untethered, making our connection feel even more profound and heartfelt.

My consulting work's mobility and flexibility allowed me to travel with Logan throughout the state effortlessly, enhancing my newfound sense of unbounded freedom that I had long desired.

As December advanced, the world outside fell into a profound and peaceful silence under the weight of the snow, transforming everything into a tranquil, white blanket.

This was the time when Logan would put all his tools into storage and rest for the long winter. From the comfort of our snug, one-room abode on wheels, peering through the frosted windshield, the scene was tinged with an almost ethereal magic.

We nestled together in bed, enveloped by the soft glow of the camper's interior that cast a gentle ambiance around us. Logan's favorite playlist created a soothing backdrop to the moment, enhancing our intimacy.

Resting my head on his arm and listening to the faint rhythm of his heartbeat, I felt his tender touch as he took my hand, caressing my fingers and intertwining them with his. Logan's gaze wandered to the back of my hand, where faint scars told stories of battles fought and wounds healed. With a genuine desire to know me on a deeper level, he gently inquired about their origins, his voice low and filled with tenderness. "I just want to understand how to love you better," he said.

Though initially hesitant to open up about that part of my past,

Logan's gentle persistence and unwavering love encouraged me to share. I confided that these scars were souvenirs from my previous marriage, remnants of a journey filled with both pain and growth. His response was not one of judgment or pity but of compassion and acceptance.

As our conversation unfolded, Logan's request to see what other scars I had made me feel vulnerable. I worried about his reaction to my imperfections. However, as I revealed each scar, Logan responded not with words, but with tender gestures that spoke volumes. He kissed each scar ever so tenderly, his love evident. His lips whispered promises of healing and understanding. Like a soothing balm, his touch caressed each mark with the tenderness of his thumb, a silent vow to mend all my visible and hidden wounds.

In that moment, I felt an overwhelming sense of gratitude and love. Logan's willingness to embrace all of me, scars and all, was a testament to the depth of his love and instilled in me a deep trust in another person that I never had.

We continued to talk late into the night, driven by curiosity, I turned to him and asked, "Why haven't you ever settled down into a house or a place with an actual roof and running water?"

Logan paused, reflecting, before he replied in a low, gentle tone, "I tried to, but nothing ever really felt right, and my financials weren't always stable during the time when I was still searching to find my footing. Plus, I always felt like I didn't belong anywhere in one place and realized a stagnant life wasn't really for me."

Hearing him express his reasons resonated with how I've felt for most of my life: constantly moving and never feeling like I belonged to one place either, always yearning for something that wasn't there in those places.

I then asked, "How did you begin this untethered life?"

"It has been off and on over the last twenty-something years, but the last place I shared was with my brother Scott a few years ago, and then I moved in with a girlfriend. Neither arrangement worked out," he said with a note of resignation. "I love my brother, and I appreciate that he got an apartment for us when I moved back from my brief stay in South Dakota, but I was hardly home, which defeated the purpose of living together. And with the girlfriend, well, the relationship fizzled out—you know how that goes," he continued. "Being unmarried and without kids, the thought of returning to an empty home was depressing and pointless—all I really needed was a place to sleep. Often, I would end up crashing on the couch, never making it to the bedroom. With the demands of my job, it just made sense to stay wherever I was working, avoiding the needless commute when there was no pressing reason to be elsewhere. And a camper van eliminated the hassle and unnecessary expense of renting a hotel all the time."

His words painted a picture of a life shaped more by practicality than choice, a journey towards simplicity that led him here, to a life less ordinary but rich in freedom.

Adjusting to life in Logan's camper brought unexpected challenges, ones I hadn't fully anticipated. Chief among them was the bathroom situation. While Logan navigated this with ease, for me, it meant vacating our current location and enduring discomfort until we found facilities. The luxurious, warm baths that had once washed away my daily stresses were now a lost indulgence. Instead, we relied on the showers at LA Fitness, where we held memberships, to cleanse after our workouts.

Winter in Minnesota transformed the landscape into a stark tundra, where temperatures plummeted to 25 degrees below zero, turning even short journeys from a heated building to our camper into a frigid ordeal. With my natural curls rebelling against the harsh heat of a hairdryer, I opted to let them air-dry, which inevitably led to them freezing solid once I stepped back into the camper.

Each time, Logan would chide me with concern, saying, "You need to dry your hair every time. I can't let you get sick. You're too important to me." His words, always tinged with affection, underscored the small sacrifices and adjustments we navigated together in our compact, nomadic home.

And because we didn't have to pay rent or a mortgage, our lifestyle allowed us to eat out all the time, which was perfectly fine by me because, again, I don't really cook. It's a rare enjoyment for me.

On clear winter nights, beneath the vast expanse of a star-studded sky, Logan and I found ourselves lost in deep, meandering conversations about our shared aspirations and dreams. With the constellations as our only ceiling, we let our thoughts wander freely, exploring the limitless possibilities of what we might achieve and where we might venture if money were no object. Each glittering star seemed to echo our desires, amplifying our sense of wonder and the boundless potential of our future together.

As we gazed up at the expansive night sky, I shared with Logan a vivid childhood memory from when I was perhaps only five or six years old. The house had long since quieted, everyone else asleep, but there I was, a small figure perched on the edge of my bed, peering out the window into the infinite cosmos. I spoke softly to the universe, confiding in it as if it were God or some vast, unknowable creator. Though unfamiliar with the world, it was a presence far grander than anything I could comprehend, and I poured out my heart, asking questions, seeking solace, sometimes even crying out my woes, with a sense of knowing that there was always someone out there, constantly watching over me.

There were moments when a profound sadness would wash over me, a sense of homesickness even though I was in the very heart of my home, with my parents and siblings merely a wall away. My parents, baffled and perhaps a bit helpless at the sight of my tears, would simply let me be, allowing the sobs to run their course until silence or sleep reclaimed me. In those quiet conversations with the stars, I found a bittersweet comfort, wrestling with feelings too vast and deep for a child to fully grasp.

Logan listened intently, then responded resonantly, "That was me too. I always felt alone in the quiet moments, yet had a sense that someone was always watching me. At times, I felt like I was in a movie, and my life was their amusement because everyone else always seemed to have it better than me." He went on to explain that this feeling made him always watch what he did and said, which is why he is so brutally honest and authentic to who he is.

We lay next to each other in silence, savoring the shared memories and the calmness enveloping us. No matter how dim or deserted the evening, it all faded into soothing familiarity. His presence transformed any setting into a sanctuary where I felt profoundly at peace—a deep-seated sense of belonging resonated within me. I realized that home wasn't just a physical space but a person I could connect with and belong to—a feeling I hadn't encountered elsewhere. As we treasured these quiet moments, I knew I could happily spend a lifetime like this, unattached to a specific place yet embraced in the tranquility and love Logan brought into my life. We might not have belonged anywhere individually, but we certainly belonged to each other.

CHAPTER 17

COZY HAVEN

BY THE END JANUARY OF 2020, after nearly two months of embracing the nomadic van life, Logan and I stumbled upon a charming apartment that beckoned us to settle down and create a haven we could call our own. This newfound space encapsulated the very essence of our adventurous spirits—a three-bedroom gem nestled on the top floor, graced with a delightful bay window that offered glimpses of the quiet suburban street below.

Keith claimed one of the smaller bedrooms adjacent to the living room. Meanwhile, Logan and I had the master bedroom at the far end of the hallway.

Prior to Logan, the idea of cohabitation with any man before marriage while my son lived with me was something I never considered. However, with him, it felt like the most natural progression of our relationship—a seamless merging of lives that mirrored the depth of our growing connection, surpassing my six-month rule and rendering it non-existent.

The living room, bathed in natural light, quickly became our sanctuary. It was where we'd lose ourselves in conversations about our future plans and reminisce about the fateful day we first met. Logan would playfully tease, "I knew you couldn't resist once you laid eyes on me. My good looks had you hooked." I'd chuckle and playfully retort, "You're so cocky-humble." Despite his modesty, his jokes had a hint of cockiness that I found endearing, and "cocky-humble" was a term I coined for him. He wasn't wrong, though. Logan was undeniably gorgeous, and from the moment we met, I couldn't look away.

Curious about why he didn't approach me when we first met until I was leaving, I asked. He replied, "Seeing how everyone was eager to meet you, being the new face in town, I thought I'd let them have their turn first. Besides, Matt was tripping over chairs and pushing people out of the way just to get over to you and say hi the moment Dee mentioned 'single'." I burst out laughing and said, "That's a bit of an exaggeration. He only almost tripped over one chair."

Logan then added, "I wanted to be the last person to make an impression. That way, you'd be thinking of me until we see each other again," playfully smiling as he winked at me. "Still cocky-humble, Honey," I replied with a light laugh. "And you were so sly too with the way you took my number."

Logan chuckled, "I actually have never done that before. I rarely ask a woman for her number. They usually ask for mine. But with you, I knew if I didn't, I would never see you again, and I didn't want to take a chance on getting a wrong number. It was instinctual to just take your phone and call myself."

I responded that I was glad he took my number because I didn't know anyone there, and the chances of me ever going back and meeting any of them again were rare and would most likely not happen. Logan agreed, saying he rarely hangs out like that as he usually keeps to his own company.

In the corner of our kitchen stood a spiral staircase, winding its way up to a spacious attic we had transformed into our creative sanctuary. This lofty room, softly illuminated by light streaming through a skylight, housed Logan's assortment of construction tools alongside boxes brimming with keepsakes from our lives before our paths intertwined. Each item was a tangible echo of our separate pasts, now coexisting in this shared haven.

Sitting on the floor of our attic, we delved into boxes filled with memories, each item a window into our pasts. Among them was a small shoebox Logan had filled with pictures of his childhood and younger years—himself as a kid, friends he used to hang out with, and even old flames and crushes. Seeing what I was looking at, he quickly said, "Don't mind those pictures," referring to those of his old flames.

"They're your memories," I replied as I sorted through the photographs. "You should cherish them, and holding onto pictures of people you used to fancy is no big deal." Then, with a playful smirk, I added, "However, if I keep finding you up here crying and looking at these pictures, we might have a problem." We both shared a laugh, the light-heartedness of the moment weaving into our history.

As I continued to explore his memories, I stumbled upon a small, worn photo of him sitting at a table in what seemed like a school cafeteria. The edges of the photo were bleached by time and creased from years of handling. He looked to be about five or six years old, with a beautiful, shy smile gracing his face as he gazed into the camera. He wore a blue coat with the hood over his head, and I couldn't help but fall in love with his little face as I imagined what our own child might look like someday if we were to have children. I noticed that his coat was a size or two too small, which tugged at my heartstrings, but I kept that observation to myself.

"Is this you?" I asked, turning the photo around to show him. Logan laughed and confirmed, "Yeah, that's me. I remember that exact moment too." He took the photo from my hand, a smile spreading across his face.

"I had just gotten to school, had breakfast, and then my teacher came over and took this picture." I watched as he studied the photo, his eyes filled with nostalgia.

The remaining photos in the box captured Logan at various stages throughout his teenage years. I marveled at how effortlessly fashionable he appeared in every era—rocking long punk spiked hair, military jackets, and designer trench coats with flair. "You were truly a fashion icon," I remarked with a smile. "Meanwhile, I've been a plain Jane in every era when it comes to style and wardrobe."

As I flipped through the pictures, I continued, "While many of my peers chased after name brands and the latest trends, I found comfort in ordinary jeans, sweaters, and my hair in a simple ponytail."

Logan chuckled as we reminisced over the snapshots. "Well, you're The Immortal," he playfully teased, using his endearing nickname for me. "You didn't need all the fancy accessories and trends to be cool, unlike the rest of us."

I couldn't help but roll my eyes at his exaggeration. "The Immortal," I repeated with a smile. It was his way of expressing that I transcended time, and his former nickname of "Queen" was no longer sufficient.

Gazing at a particular black and white photo of him with his teenage-spiked hair, Logan reflected, "I was ahead of my time—a trendsetter rather than a trend follower."

"I have no doubt," I replied, sharing in his nostalgic pride. Though I believed we met at the perfect time, I often wondered what it would have been like if we had crossed paths in our teens or early twenties. Would we still have ended up together, or would we have been too foolish to even notice each other? *He definitely wouldn't have noticed me. I was a nerd, and president of every club I joined.*

CHAPTER 18

NOUVEAU 2020

*I*N FEBRUARY, while the ground was still covered in snow, Logan and I hosted our first Hmong Nouveau Fashion Show & Concert. We had only three months of planning following our fortuitous encounter in the park, where Logan stood on the stage of an amphitheater and shared his vision for a grand fusion of fashion and live music, designed to captivate the community. I had wondered if such an ambitious timeline was feasible for organizing an elevated red carpet event that would attract designers, models, performers, and fashion enthusiasts from across the nation. Despite our doubts and countless sleepless nights in Logan's camper, we somehow managed to bring it all together.

During our research, we attended several local fashion shows, noting that the most successful drew around three hundred attendees. Setting this as our benchmark, we hoped for a similar turnout, which would signify a triumph for us.

We chose the majestic Union Depot in downtown Saint Paul as our venue, drawn by its elegant high ceilings and ornate architectural moldings, which provided a backdrop that was nothing short of spectacular. The historical significance of the Union Depot, still an active train and bus station, added a unique charm as its grand lobby was transformed into a sumptuous ballroom for our event. Its timeless beauty and vibrant energy made it the perfect setting for our inaugural Hmong Nouveau Fashion Show & Concert, blending the city's history with the excitement of contemporary fashion and live music.

Our vision for the show was to transcend traditional runway displays. With the help of Shye, an event decorator highly recommended by an acquaintance, we were able to create an experience that melded high fashion with live musical performances and the grandeur of the Grammys. Guests were greeted by a glamorous red carpet, where a peacock made entirely of exotic flowers set the tone for the elegance of the evening. Flowy red chiffon drapes lined the walkway, accompanied by oversized red roses and faux candles atop white pillars. To ensure everyone enjoyed a moment in the spotlight, their arrivals were captured by flashing cameras before they were ushered to their tables, each elegantly draped in sleek black tablecloths. The centerpieces featured exquisite arrangements of red roses meticulously sculpted into perfect spheres atop crystal vases, adding a touch of dramatic elegance.

The show was a spectacular fusion of fashion and live music, featuring three private collectors who showcased their exquisite and authentic Hmong attire collections. In addition to these treasured collections, the event highlighted the works of eight renowned Hmong fashion designers. Each designer's runway presentation was uniquely accompanied by a performance from a well-known musical artist, creating a vibrant and harmonious blend of style and sound.

The musical highlight of the evening was the phenomenal SuddenRush band from Canada, whose tunes had been a constant source of inspiration throughout our planning process. Their dynamic energy and compelling music were integral to the ambiance we wanted to cultivate, ensuring that every aspect of the event synchronized perfectly to create an unforgettable spectacle.

A month before the show commenced, we had sold over a thousand tickets, far surpassing our original goal of three hundred. This unexpected surge meant we had to completely rearrange the layout of tables and chairs to accommodate the increased number of attendees. We eventually capped attendance at 1,200, the maximum capacity for the grand room. As the event progressed into the evening and our venue reached full capacity, we regrettably had to turn away many hopeful attendees who had not pre-purchased tickets and were looking to buy at the door.

While it might seem like a good problem to have, it also created a bit of unpleasant chaos for us, especially with those who were disappointedly turned away. It was not the tone we wanted for our first event, but this experience did provide us with many valuable lessons learned.

Although we spent the entire day at the venue, our paths rarely crossed. Our small management team consisted solely of Logan and me, though we did acquire the aid of a few volunteers to help usher attendees to their seats. Logan oversaw the entire operation, from managing guests to coordinating talents, while I managed stage production.

As the night progressed, amidst running back and forth between managing the entrance and coordinating backstage, Logan secured a single red rose bouquet adorned with ferns and baby's breath from a little girl selling them to support her dance group's endeavors. Meanwhile, I was occupied handling the night's agenda backstage, ensuring every performer, designer, and model knew their cue to go on. In the midst of this activity, Logan appeared with a gentle smile, presenting me with the rose.

"For you, my love," he said. "I don't want you to think I had forgotten you amidst all this chaos," he added sweetly before rushing off to tend to the event attendees once again.

By the end of that intense night, both Logan and I were utterly drained, having barely spared a moment for rest. Shye and her husband graciously stayed behind to help us clean up. Logan and I didn't make it home until 3:00 am. We didn't even get the chance to fully savor the culmination of our hard work in the form of our own show, but that's the price of passion.

In the days that followed, we found ourselves recuperating at home, our weary legs propped up on cushions for relief. Logan's feet bore the physical evidence of his tireless efforts—blood-tinged blisters and soreness from the relentless pace he maintained. Walking became an arduous task for him. Though I didn't have blisters, having discarded my shoes halfway through the night—the perks of wearing a long dress that covered my feet—my legs throbbed as if I had just completed a marathon.

Witnessing Logan's condition, I felt utterly helpless and saddened. "I'm so sorry, honey," I murmured, my heart aching for his discomfort. Despite his visible pain, he mustered a smile and said, "I can't believe we pulled it off." Even in such a state, his unwavering smile and resilience filled me with a profound sense of happiness and pride.

To help ease the pain in Logan's feet, I offered him a gentle foot massage, taking care to avoid any sores or blisters. As I carefully smoothed out and massaged the sole of his foot, I noticed how his toes curled, as if they had been permanently forced into that position from years of being crushed together in tight shoes. A heavy sadness settled over me as I continued to massage his feet and gently stretch each toe, realizing that he hadn't had comfortable shoes as a child.

"Honey, don't mind me asking, but did you not have proper shoes when you were younger?" I asked, my voice laced with concern and sorrow.

Logan's response came in a somber tone. "As the youngest son, I was often overlooked. I wore the same shoes for years, even when they became too tight. My feet were so cramped, but I couldn't ask for new ones; my requests were usually met with scolding."

Hearing this shattered my heart. I turned away to hide my tears as I continued to massage his feet, now with even greater tenderness and care, for these were the feet of the man I loved so dearly. I didn't want him to see me cry, knowing he would be concerned for me.

Loving him meant I never wanted him to yearn for anything beyond his grasp or for his desires to linger in the realm of impossibility. And so, I pledged to love him with a fervor that transcended the ordinary, a love that whispered, "Whatever you wish for, together we will weave it into reality."

CHAPTER 19

PANDEMIC

COUPLE OF WEEKS AFTER OUR SUCCESSFUL EVENT, when we had fully recuperated, we made plans to host an appreciation dinner for everyone who contributed—the designers, models, performers, and volunteers who helped turn our vision into reality. Invitations were sent out, but our plans were abruptly halted by the rapid spread of a highly contagious coronavirus, sweeping through countries and igniting global panic. Though it didn't seem critical yet, we prioritized everyone's health and well-being. We decided to follow guidelines from the Centers for Disease Control and Prevention (CDC) since we knew little about this virus.

Eventually, what we thought would be only a few weeks turned into months. We were advised to hunker down at home, venturing out only when absolutely necessary for essentials. Public outings to places like grocery stores required masks, and indoor dining was no longer an option. A palpable tension filled the air.

Social distancing measures were stringently enforced; we couldn't stand closer than six feet to anyone else, transforming everyday interactions into exercises in spatial awareness. The surreal nature of the situation was both terrifying and absurd—an unprecedented reality that felt ripped from the pages of dystopian fiction.

The economic impact became undeniable. Businesses shuttered, leaving streets eerily silent except for the occasional rush of ambulances or the wail of police sirens. Employees adapted to the isolation of home offices, while hospitals turned into war zones, overwhelmed with patients fighting for breath. It was like living through a horrific virus outbreak movie, where every day presented a new challenge and the world held its breath, waiting for resolution or relief.

"We were very fortunate to have had our event in February," Logan said with a sigh of gratitude. "If we had planned it for March, we would have had to cancel." The realization hit me hard, underscoring just how lucky we were. At the same time, the evolving state of the world was terrifying.

In the privacy of our room or under the stream of a shower, I often found myself overwhelmed by the world's unfolding crises, shedding tears over the collective anguish. The difficulty wasn't in the adjustment to isolation—having worked from home as a consultant for many years and being an introvert, I was well-acquainted with solitude. In fact, I preferred it.

Instead, it was the overwhelming sense of sorrow, despair, and loss that seemed to radiate from every corner of the globe, seeping into my very being. Alongside the ongoing pandemic, there was upheaval in rural neighborhoods and city streets, leaving deep scars. This was a testament to the pain and unrest echoing across our society following the unjust death of George Floyd while in police custody, which happened right in our neighboring city of Minneapolis.

From my experience in past relationships, I knew my emotional intensity was often misunderstood. Previous partners would withdraw, either leaving the conversation or the room entirely, confessing their inability to comprehend or handle my sorrow. These tears weren't the result of personal grievances but of a deep, empathetic nature.

I did my best to conceal this from Logan, fearing that he might withdraw if he saw this vulnerable side of me. He had been nothing but wonderful and patient, and the last thing I wanted was to push him away because I couldn't "get my emotions together."

One late night, unable to sleep and overwhelmed by tears at my desk, Logan awoke. Sensing I hadn't come to bed, he entered my office and asked in a low, gentle voice, "Is everything okay? Why aren't you in bed? What's on your mind?"

I remained silent, fearing my voice would crack and betray my tears. My silence only deepened his concern. He approached, gently turned my chair to face him, and squatted to my eye level, asking in a worried tone, "Did I do something wrong? Have I become too much for you?" I was speechless, struck by his inclination to question his own actions rather than assume the fault was mine.

Releasing a soft cry, I managed to whisper, "It's not you. I'm just overwhelmed by everything that's happening in the world and trying to process it all."

Logan immediately pulled me into his arms, offering reassurance with a firm embrace. "It's okay, Baby. Come here. Let me hold you. Cry as much as you need," he soothed, lifting me into his lap and cradling me as I sobbed into his shoulder, burying my face in the crook of his neck. He patted my back affectionately, murmuring, "It's okay. I've got you." While most would tell me to stop crying, he embraced my tears. In the security of his presence, the weight of my emotions began to dissipate, and the tension in my shoulders, neck, and back melted away. It was the sense of relief I had been yearning for but had been unable to reach.

We sat in silence in the dark quiet of my office until my breathing stabilized. "Are you feeling better now?" he asked in an almost whisper.

"Yes," I replied, nodding and taking a deep, recuperative breath.

"Let's go to bed. Let me hold you to sleep," Logan suggested, taking my hand and leading me to the bedroom. There, he gently enveloped me in his loving embrace, lulling me into a peaceful sleep.

What was once thought to be a containable outbreak spiraled into a global pandemic that lasted over two years. Whenever I felt overwhelmed and tears threatened to spill, Logan was there, offering the comforting sanctuary of his arms, where all tensions dissolved. It didn't matter how often it happened; he never hesitated, rushed, or probed into why my emotions ran so deep. Instead, he often created diversions to lift my spirits, providing me with the solace and support I needed.

One evening, as I bustled around the kitchen, Logan returned from work. His job in construction, being predominantly outdoors, faced minimal restrictions and his daily routine remained largely unaffected.

As soon as he entered the kitchen, Logan began to sing, improvising lyrics to a familiar tune. The sight of him so carefree lit up my face with a broad smile. He approached, took my hand, and twirled me around before pulling me close for an impromptu dance, his voice still carrying the melody. I was never much of a dancer, possessing two left feet, but Logan moved with the ease of a seasoned performer, his feet swift and sure—a sight I adored. His dancing, often employed to cheer me up, never failed.

When the confinement of home grew too stifling, we took to exploring Saint Paul in our car. Logan showed me the neighborhoods of his youth—the paths he walked, the backyard thickets where he played and let his imagination run wild, and the schools he attended. As he shared these memories, I realized that I wanted to know not just the man he was now, but also the boy he had been.

We parked in front of a grade school he once attended. Sitting in the car, he pointed to a spot near the entrance. "That's where I often ended up every recess," he said, a hint of nostalgia in his voice. "Teachers and playground chaperones would always place me there after my latest mischief."

Intrigued, I asked, "What kind of trouble did you get into?"

Logan chuckled, his laughter filling the car. "Oh, so many stupid things I can't even remember them all now," he replied, shaking his head with a smile.

I laughed along, easily picturing him as a mischievous child, imagining why he might have frequently found himself in trouble. As we sat there, Logan reminisced about old friends from school he hadn't seen in years and past puppy crushes that broke his heart.

"It's a shame, you know," I said, pausing to let the words sink in. "They didn't realize the treasure they had."

Logan looked at me, silent at first, then burst out with an excited, "I know!" as if he had just come to a revelation.

We both laughed, the sound of amusement filling up the car.

Some days, when my workload was light, I would take my laptop and accompany him to his work site. It seems like he only takes a break when I'm there, sitting with me for a moment. Otherwise, he works straight through without stopping. I make sure he rests from the scorching sun and takes time to replenish. Once my meetings are done, I join him in his projects.

I loved how seamlessly we worked together. It was almost as if we shared a telepathic connection, anticipating each other's moves without needing to speak. We moved in perfect synchronization, our actions harmonizing effortlessly. The days passed quickly, filled with a profound sense of unity and purpose.

At the end of each day, even when I was covered in sweat and dirt, I'd turn to look at him, only to meet his eyes. He would stop whatever he was doing to look at me and smile with gentle admiration, as if I were the most beautiful person he had ever laid eyes on. His long gaze would make me feel a bit self-conscious at first, and I'd tell him, "Don't look at me like that, because I don't know how to respond." He would just keep looking at me and say, "I just love you so much." Over time, I learned to appreciate the depth of his affection and the unique way he saw me.

Towards the second half of the pandemic, in early spring of 2021, I was abruptly awoken one morning by a sharp pain in my pelvis when Logan turned to hold me and his hand landed softly on the area. The touch triggered an intense pain I had never felt before, causing me to let out a soft, painful cry that woke him instantly.

In the stark darkness, I couldn't see his face, but I felt his body tense with worry. "I'm sorry, are you okay?" he asked immediately. "I don't know why, but something in my lower pelvis is hurting," I replied, making him even more concerned. He asked, "Should I take you to the hospital?" I told him no, not yet. Glancing at the clock, I saw it was four in the morning, and it was still dark outside.

"Let's wait to see if the pain goes away," I said to Logan. I adjusted myself, trying to find comfort. Logan wrapped his arm around me, carefully avoiding my abdomen, his gentle warmth soothing me back to sleep.

At the crack of dawn, I woke up to find my pelvis still tender. Placing my hand gently on the area, I felt around to pinpoint the exact location of the pain. A creeping fear began to take hold—it might be my appendix, as the sensitivity was centered in my lower right pelvis.

"Logan, I think you should take me to the hospital. I'm almost certain it's my appendix," I said.

Without a moment's hesitation, Logan sprang out of bed and swiftly came around to my side. As I tried to get up, the pain intensified, causing me to clutch my lower abdomen in agony. In the dim light of dawn, he knelt down to my eye level, his face framed with worry. "Baby, let me help carry you," he said in a firm but gentle voice. Carefully lifting me, he helped me downstairs to sit on our enclosed porch while he ran to the back of the house to pull the car around.

After pulling up to the front, Logan hurried to my side and lifted me in his arms, cradling me against his chest as he carried me to the car.

"I can try to walk on my own," I said, but he was hesitant and didn't want me to be in pain.

He gently eased me into the passenger seat, his hands steady and reassuring, ensuring I was as comfortable as possible. As we drove to the hospital, he reached over to hold my hand. "Hang in there, Baby, we're almost there," he murmured.

Every little bump in the road sent waves of pain through my pelvis, and each time, Logan's grip tightened protectively. His unwavering presence and tender care made me feel safe, even amidst the intense discomfort.

Pulling up to park outside the emergency room, I told him that I would try to walk, but he insisted that I stay put. He sprinted inside, disappearing briefly behind the automatic sliding glass doors to grab a wheelchair. Moments later, he reappeared, urgency evident in his every movement, as he carefully helped me into the wheelchair.

At the ER check-in desk, Logan anxiously told the triage nurse, "I'm her husband, and my wife is in a lot of pain." Given the pandemic, he didn't want any restrictions that might prevent him from being by my side due to our unmarried status. The staff quickly noted my symptoms and asked us to wait while they prepared a room. Thankfully, the wait was brief, and within just 15 minutes, we were swiftly checked into a private room.

Once inside, a physician promptly arrived. I shared my concerns, explaining that the pain was in my lower right abdomen, and I suspected it might be my appendix.

"Let's have a look and see what we can find," said the physician with a reassuring smile and nod. He immediately began ordering tests and scans to determine the cause of my pain. I underwent a physical examination, followed by blood tests and an ultrasound. Logan stayed by my side, sitting in his chair, offering silent support and comfort.

When the physician stepped out of the room, Logan walked over to me. "I hope everything's okay. I don't want anything to happen to you," he said in a low voice, his concern palpable.

"I'm going to be okay, Honey. If it's as I thought, they'll just remove it endoscopically, and it'll be no big deal," I assured him. Without saying anything, he went back to sit in his chair. I observed him, noting the look of concern on his face, but I appreciated how attentive and worried he was. It was a reflection of how much he cared about me.

Not much later, the physician returned with the test results. "You were right. It appears that your appendix is inflamed," the physician explained, confirming my assumption. "We'll need to perform surgery to remove it as soon as possible to prevent any complications."

Logan immediately stood up and walked back over to me. He held my hand, squeezing it reassuringly. Though I knew he was worried, he tried to mask it with a smile. "I'll be right here," he said thoughtfully. The medical team quickly prepped me for surgery, explaining the procedure and what to expect.

When I woke up from surgery, the first person I saw was Logan, his beautiful smiling face was a welcome sight. Despite feeling a bit drowsy from the anesthesia, seeing him filled me with a profound sense of thankfulness and relief.

"Hey there, Beautiful," he said softly, brushing a stray hair from my forehead. "You did great." I tried to smile back, feeling exhausted, and replied, "You did too," remembering how concerned he had been. My eyelids drooped with weariness, yet the warmth in my heart was unmistakable.

As the drowsiness faded and Logan drifted into sleep in his slightly reclined seat, I gazed at him with a profound sense of gratitude for his steadfast love and support. Yet, amidst this warmth, a somber memory resurfaced, transporting me back to a darker moment: the last time I woke up in a hospital, utterly alone.

I was married at the time and woke up with excruciatingly sharp pain. I pleaded with my then-husband to rush me to the ER, stressing that this pain was anything but ordinary. Dismissing my urgency, he accused me of having a low pain threshold and insisted I tough it out. When the pain reached an unbearable level and I resolved to drive myself to the hospital, he became upset and reluctantly agreed to take me, berating me the entire way about wasting time. He merely dropped me off and left.

Upon arrival, I was rushed into emergency surgery to address an inflamed gallbladder that required immediate removal before it could rupture. I called my then-husband to inform him about the surgery, but he saw no reason to be there since I was already being taken care of. We ended the brief call with a sense of disappointment.

It was one of the loneliest, most uncertain, and saddest moments— waking up in pain, feeling drowsy from the anesthesia, and finding myself in a dark, empty room. My throat felt parched and raw from being intubated, but I was too weak and in too much pain to ask for assistance or stay awake. I drifted back to sleep while tears rolled down my cheeks, too exhausted to wipe them away.

The stark contrast between my current situation with Logan, who never leaves my side, and my past experiences was overwhelming. It filled me with immense gratitude and relief. With Logan, I didn't have to plead or ask him to stay; his loving presence was a healing touch for the wounds of my past. It made me realize how profoundly blessed I am to have him.

The procedure was conducted endoscopically, and unlike my previous surgery, the pain wasn't as severe. An hour after waking up, I was able to get up and move around. When the physician came to check on me, I mentioned that I wanted to go home.

The physician smiled and nodded. "You're recovering remarkably well," he said. "Since the procedure was minimally invasive and your vital signs are stable, I see no reason why you can't go home today. Just remember to follow the discharge instructions carefully and take it easy for the next few days."

Logan, who had been attentively listening, chimed in, "I'll ensure she follows all the instructions and take good care of her."

The physician continued, "You'll need to keep the incision sites clean and dry, and avoid any strenuous activities for at least a week. Make sure to take the prescribed pain medication if you need it, and watch for any signs of infection, such as redness or swelling. If you experience severe pain, fever, or any unusual symptoms, don't hesitate to return."

I nodded, feeling a wave of relief. "Thank you, doctor."

As I began to gather my things, Logan insisted that I just sit in the wheelchair while he gathered all my belongings.

Once we got home, Logan made sure I was comfortably settled in bed and brought me a glass of water. "You're going to be just fine," he said, brushing my hair back and kissing my forehead. "I'll be right here if you need anything."

I smiled at him, feeling deeply grateful for his thoughtfulness, consideration, and love. "Thank you for being here, Honey. I don't know what I would have done without you. I don't even know which hospital to go to."

"I took you to the best one I know," Logan responded.

Reflecting on the day's events, I couldn't help but appreciate how far I had come. There was a time when I never imagined I would reach this point—at this age, with a second chance at finding a love so true and endearing. The fear and uncertainty that once haunted me had been replaced by a profound sense of hope and resilience.

Knowing how his presence always eases my mind and helps me sleep, he climbed into bed to spoon me, holding me close. As I closed my eyes to rest, Logan gently spoke into my ear, "I was so afraid that I'd lose you today. I don't know what I would do without you." I turned my head slightly towards him and pursed my lips, gesturing for a kiss. He raised himself slightly to meet my lips and kissed me. In that quiet moment in his embrace, I realized that true healing is not just physical—it's emotional and spiritual. It's about having someone who stands by you, through the darkest nights and the brightest days. His presence was a soothing touch for my soul, tenderly mending wounds I had long believed would never heal. As I drifted off to sleep, I knew that no matter what challenges lay ahead, I would never face them alone.

CHAPTER 20

A HEARTFELT FAREWELL

A YEAR HAD PASSED SINCE LOGAN AND I HAD BEEN TOGETHER. Amid the chaos of a global pandemic, we joyfully decided to expand our little family by adopting a Presa Canario puppy we named Cypher.

To ensure his comfort and safety, we hired a pet courier company that personally carried him through the airport and held him on the plane all the way from Florida. The other option was to put him in a crate where he would be shipped through the under-cargo storage along with passengers' luggage. The thought of it seemed harsh and traumatic and I couldn't go through with that.

It was a Saturday morning when we drove to the airport to meet Cypher at passenger pick-up. The courier handed me this little brindle eight-week-old, 17-pound puppy through our car window and placed him on my lap. As I held him for the first time, he looked up at me, and we fell in love with him instantly.

Logan had longed to adopt this breed for over fifteen years, but his nomadic lifestyle—marked by transient relationships and frequent relocations—had made it difficult to fulfill this dream. When he shared this desire with me, my response was simple, "Stop waiting. Let's just make it happen."

Every time he spoke about dogs, I could see a deep yearning in his eyes. His knowledge of different breeds, understanding their traits and characteristics, was unmatched; I was impressed as I had never met anyone with such profound insight into the canine world. His love for animals didn't stop there—he dreamed of raising chickens, goats, and horses.

Logan's ultimate aspiration was to have a hobby farm. He envisioned a green, eco-friendly home where we could live sustainably off the land, cultivating our own food and concocting natural remedies from the bounty of the earth.

However, before we could embark on this rural dream, there was a practical matter to address—our current living space. A Presa Canario is a large, powerful breed, and our three-bedroom apartment was far from suitable, especially without an enclosed yard. We needed a bigger place, a place where Cypher could roam freely.

A few months after welcoming Cypher into our home, we moved to a house with a spacious backyard—a perfect playground for him to run to his heart's content. Logan adored Cypher, often greeting him with a fond "My boy," to which Cypher responded with equal affection.

Our little Presa Canario grew to be a gentle giant; fully grown, he weighed 165 pounds and sported a light brindle coat with dark stripes that made him resemble a tiger. His feline-like movements often startled onlookers during our walks. The pandemic was still ongoing, which made our visits to the park very frequent. Sometimes, from a distance, people—particularly the elderly Hmong grandmas at the park—would mistake him for an actual tiger, which always brought a chuckle from

Logan and me.

One morning, as we returned from the store and unloaded groceries from the car, Cypher, now 15 months old, dashed excitedly back and forth along the fence in the backyard. He was always thrilled to see us, unable to contain his joy.

As we opened the front door to the house, the sound of breaking glass suddenly pierced the air. Logan exchanged a worried glance with me. "Did you hear that?" he asked. Without waiting for my reply, as if he already knew the fear of what had just happened, he dashed through the living room and kitchen into the backyard.

There, he discovered that one of the windows to the mudroom at the back of the house had been shattered. Scanning the area for the cause, his eyes widened at the sight of large puddles of blood.

"Cypher, come here, boy," Logan called. Normally, Cypher would sprint over immediately, but this time he didn't. Logan followed the blood trails and found Cypher limping around the side of the house, his expression one of guilt, as if he feared he'd be reprimanded for the broken window. As Logan approached, he saw that Cypher's two front paws and carpus were bleeding profusely; the broken glass had cut deeply, exposing the tissues and bone beneath.

"Steph!" Logan yelled frantically as I was in the kitchen putting groceries away. His tone sent a jolt of panic through me, and I dropped everything to rush outside. Seeing Logan's face, etched with fear, was shocking—he was usually so composed. "We have to get him to the hospital," he said urgently.

Immediately, I sprang into action. Understanding the gravity of the situation, Logan and I prepared to rush Cypher to emergency care. Weighing 165 pounds, he was no small burden, and although it was challenging to carry him without causing further pain, every second was precious as more blood spilled.

We hastily fashioned makeshift tourniquets around each of his wrists and, mustering all our strength, lifted Cypher into the back of Logan's cargo van, which, fortunately, had been cleared of all its tools just the day before. With no time to lose, we sped toward the nearest pet hospital.

The closest veterinary clinic was less than two miles away, but being a weekend and the ongoing pandemic, they were only accepting patients with prior appointments.

"Please, our dog's carpus is severely cut. He's in the car and he's losing a lot of blood," I desperately pleaded with the clinic attendant who answered the door. Initially hesitant, she agreed to assess Cypher after seeing the urgency in my expression. Logan, overwhelmed by distress, stayed with Cypher in the van as the attendant followed me towards them.

Upon opening the van door, we were met with a grim scene: the tourniquet had done little to stem the bleeding, and Cypher lay in a growing puddle of his own blood. His breathing was labored, and he looked up at us with weak, pleading eyes. "Please help him," I implored again, my voice cracking with emotion.

The attendant immediately called inside to the lead veterinarian on duty to explain the urgency. Within moments, a team of veterinarians rushed out with a stretcher. They carefully lifted Cypher onto it and hurried him into the hospital. Though they told us we couldn't follow into the clinic, they promised to do everything possible to help him. We exchanged contact information, and they assured us they would keep us updated on his condition.

We weren't permitted inside the hospital, and lingering by the door felt increasingly futile. Turning to Logan, I suggested, "Honey, we live less than two miles away. Let's go home, and if there's anything, I'm sure they'll call to let us know." I tried to offer comfort, but Logan's face remained expressionless, a clear sign of his inner turmoil.

Holding back my own tears, I strove to maintain a strong demeanor for his sake; he was clearly struggling, and in this moment, he needed my strength more than ever.

Hours dragged by until finally, my phone rang. It was the hospital. "Hi, we're calling for the owner of Cypher," said a voice on the other end.

"Yes, that's me," I responded as I put her on speaker, my voice trembling, bracing for the news. Logan, stirred from his despondence, looked up, his eyes filled with a mix of hope and fear.

"We were able to stop the bleeding. Cypher is stable now. As you're already aware, he suffered multiple deep cuts and will require significant surgery," the woman explained.

Without hesitation, I replied, "Whatever it is you need to do, please do it."

"The current charges amount to $1,500 for everything we've done up to this point," she continued, which was only to stabilize him and stop the bleeding. "You have two options for moving forward: we can amputate for $9,214 and continue to monitor him, or we can attempt to repair all the muscles and ligaments to save both his paws for $32,181."

My heart sank at the figures. The costs were daunting, far beyond what we could manage without serious financial strain. I told the woman that we would cover the treatment done so far but expressed concern about the affordability of further procedures. She put me on a brief hold, saying she would need to consult with the lead veterinarian.

The phone became silent, and my heart raced. Logan's face was buried in his hands. The man who had always been my rock, who shielded me from life's harsher realities, was now enveloped in despair. I felt powerless, watching him crumble, unsure how to provide the support he needed in the face of our grim options.

A little more than a minute later, another voice came on the line. "Hi, I'm the lead veterinarian. I understand the fees are substantial, and I empathize with your situation. I have three dogs at home too, and I can only imagine what you must be going through," he said, his voice laden with sympathy. Yet, his words did little to ease the weight of our decision. "I will do everything I can to restore Cypher to health, but this would require that you relinquish all care and ownership of him to the clinic."

Logan's face drained of color as he processed the veterinarian's words. The thought of parting with Cypher was unthinkable. I was torn; I loved Cypher deeply and wanted nothing more than to give him the best life possible, even if it meant letting him go. I asked the veterinarian for a moment to discuss it with Logan.

Turning to Logan, I wrapped my arms around him. "I am so sorry, Baby, but our options are limited. The best gift we can give Cypher now is a chance at the best quality of life. He loves us unconditionally, and I know he would sacrifice everything for us. Right now, we need to save him, even if it means he can't come home with us." Tears threatened to overcome me, but I held them back, my heart breaking for both Logan and Cypher.

"Do what you think is best," Logan said in a hushed, somber tone.

Returning to the phone, I informed the veterinarian that we would proceed with relinquishing Cypher. We agreed to pay for the treatment he had already received and prepared for the transition. "I am sorry for all you're going through," said the veterinarian. "I assure you, Cypher will be well cared for. Please come in to sign the paperwork and settle the fees."

When we arrived at the animal hospital, an attendant met us at the door with the necessary forms. As I reviewed the documents, Logan lingered quietly behind me. "Can we see Cypher?" I asked, hoping for a final goodbye.

"I'm sorry, but that won't be possible," the attendant replied. "If you choose to relinquish Cypher into our care, you're not permitted to see him. It's our policy." Logan, unable to bear it, turned abruptly and walked away. I watched him go, understanding his need for space. After finishing the paperwork and settling the fees, I hurried to the car where Logan sat, hands gripping the steering wheel, his head bowed in silent despair.

I slipped into the passenger seat and gently placed my hand on his shoulder. "I am so sorry, Baby. Truly, I am." Logan remained silent. "I can drive," I offered, giving him a moment to respond. We sat in quiet solidarity, allowing him space to process, yet ensuring he felt my presence. After a few silent minutes, Logan started the engine, and we drove home in hushed sorrow. I had never seen him so wounded, and I wished more than anything that I could take away his pain.

A year later, feeling the absence of a four-legged companion, we embarked on an eight-hour drive to Pocahontas, Illinois, to bring home another Presa Canario from a kennel we discovered through social media. The little guy was only eight weeks old and had a darker brindle color. I thought Logan would be okay, but upon seeing this new puppy, it was apparent that his heart was still heavy with grief. Up until that moment, he had even considered naming the new pup Cypher. However, as soon as he looked at the little guy, he said, "You're not Cypher," with a slight sadness and disappointment in his voice. It was evident that this puppy was not Cypher. I tenderly reminded him, "Baby, he cannot be Cypher. He's beautifully and uniquely himself. Let's name him Sabre."

Sabre was an exceptionally smart puppy. With just a few repetitions, he would master any trick we taught him. His agility was remarkable; he would effortlessly leap in and out of Logan's car with boundless energy. Each successful jump or newly learned trick brought a beaming smile to Logan's face, a sight that warmed my heart. Sabre quickly developed a personality all his own—full of zest, curiosity, and eagerness to please. It didn't take long for Logan to return to his old self. Though he often spoke of Cypher, it was clear that he had found a new place in his heart for Sabre.

CHAPTER 21

HOME

*W*E WERE DRIVING AROUND SAINT PAUL towards the end of autumn in 2022, ticking off errands and chatting casually when the topic of marriage surfaced. Our conversation had veered towards some friends who had recently exchanged vows and another who had just finalized a divorce. Reflecting on these contrasting situations, Logan, always philosophical about matters of the heart, remarked, "Marriage seems overrated these days. I've always believed it's not a piece of paper that keeps two people together, but rather their mutual desire to stay together."

Both previously married, we had witnessed the full spectrum of marital outcomes and felt no urgency to re-tie the knot. We had been together for a little over three years, and the topic of marriage rarely came up. Yet, we were content—happier than we had ever been. We worked very well together, seldom squabbled over the minutiae of daily life, and on the rare occasions when disagreements arose, Logan always knew exactly how to defuse the tension.

"Let's table this conversation," he would say. "We're not going to find a solution now. Just let me hold you, and we'll talk about it when we're both feeling happier." He would often pull me into his arms or onto his lap, and no matter how tense I felt, I would always melt into his embrace. The weight of the discussion would dissipate between us.

So, as the topic of marriage casually resurfaced during our conversation, I couldn't resist probing further, "You got married young and were still in your early 20s when you got divorced, yet you never remarried. Why haven't you?"

Logan replied with his typical nonchalance, "It's not that I'm opposed to marriage. I always thought I'd marry again someday. I just haven't found the right person." He paused, a reflective look crossing his face, then continued, "The relationships I've had were complicated. Whether it was financial issues, toxicity, or a combination of both, it didn't seem like a responsible decision to pursue marriage."

His admission that he hadn't found the right person stung unexpectedly. We had never broached the subject of marriage directly, and I suddenly felt exposed and vulnerable, wondering if he felt I wasn't the "right person" despite our years together and the long-term plans we had made.

"Why are you so quiet now?" he prodded, noticing my sudden withdrawal.

I hesitated, cautious not to appear too eager about marriage. "You've never mentioned wanting to marry me. While we've talked about our future plans together, marriage never seemed to be part of that equation. Does that mean you haven't found the right person?" I asked tentatively.

"That's not what I meant," he quickly clarified, stealing a glance at me before refocusing on the road. "Do you want to get married?" he asked, his question catching me off guard. "I could marry you right now," he impulsively added.

"No, Love. That's not what I want," I responded promptly.

"You don't want to marry me?" His expression turned puzzled.

"Of course, I want to marry you," I asserted, "but I don't want our decision to marry to be solely prompted by our discussion about marriage or our past commitment issues in other relationships," I explained.

"I'm sorry, Baby" he responded. "I thought since your first marriage was so long, you might not want to rush into anything just yet, especially since I'm the first serious relationship you've had after your divorce. But honestly, if there's anyone I've ever wanted to marry, it's you." Logan's words, sincere and heartfelt.

"I think I just asked you to marry me, and you said yes," he added.

"This doesn't count," I countered lightly. "We're just having a discussion." I then turned away, pretending to look out the window, and allowed myself a small, secret smile, happy by his candid expression of commitment to our future together.

A few weeks after our tentative discussion about marriage, I sat down at my computer, ready to dive into a day of work, only to find that Logan had left some of the browsers open, as he often did. Surprisingly, they were all showing different diamond engagement rings.

"Oh gosh," I murmured to myself, a flutter of excitement rising in my chest. "Could Logan be thinking of proposing?" The thought quickened my heart rate. I allowed myself to revel in the possibility, picturing a future where Logan and I were officially committed to each other. The love I felt for him was profound. He had impacted my life like no one else ever had, and the idea of spending my life with him filled me with a deep sense of contentment.

Closing the browser, I reminded myself not to get too carried away and kept my hopes in check. Still, the idea that Logan might be considering a proposal because of his recent ring searches brought a smile to my face.

However, months slipped by without a word on the subject, and I told myself not to dwell on it too much. "Maybe Logan was just curious after our conversation about marriage," I reassured myself.

One chilly February morning, as we merged onto Highway 35-E en route to Fleet Farm for some dog food, Logan shattered the drive's monotony with an unexpected serenade. It was a habit of his to do so when in high spirits, and his cheerful demeanor never failed to brighten my face with a smile as I watched him.

While the car stereo hummed softly in the background, Logan's voice took center stage, weaving his own lyrics with a soulful heartfelt melody, "Marry me, Baby, I want you as my wife. Marry me, Baby, I want you for life." His tone was deep, filled with love and infectious joy, making me chuckle and delight in his spontaneity. As he shifted from singing to speaking, he softly said, "Marry me, Baby," pausing for a breath before adding, "I'm asking you to marry me."

"Are you serious?" I asked, the smile still playing on my lips, but my heart started to race, half-expecting him to laugh and admit he was just swept up in a moment of whimsy.

"I'm serious," he affirmed earnestly as he continued to navigate the highway.

I looked at him, speechless, letting the moment sink in. Without further hesitation, I took a breath and exclaimed, "Yes! I'll marry you." Leaning over from my passenger seat, I placed my hand on his cheek furthest from me and gave him a firm kiss. He smiled and let out a light laugh.

Our drive continued, but rather than pulling into Fleet Farm, Logan took an unexpected detour into the parking lot of a jewelry store. "Come, Baby," he said, his voice a mix of excitement and tenderness as he stepped out of the car and beckoned for me to follow. He reached back towards me, his fingers wiggling invitingly—a familiar, endearing gesture meant for me to take his hand. I quickly sped up and clasped his hand eagerly, our fingers intertwining as we walked together.

Inside the jewelry store, Logan led me straight to a glass case sparkling with a breathtaking array of diamond rings. "Pick whichever ring you want, my love," he said, his voice thick with happiness.

I glanced up at him, seeing his face as happy as mine, before turning my attention to the glittering jewels below. Just then, a sales associate approached us with a welcoming smile. "Is there anything specific you'd like to see?" she inquired.

"Yes," Logan replied, his grin widening. "We're here to pick out a ring for the love of my life."

The sales associate's smile broadened at his words. "Happy wife, happy life. You've come to the right place," she responded.

"That's what I've been told," Logan said, his eyes twinkling with humor and love.

As we spoke with the associate, I felt the depth of Logan's commitment, filling me with overwhelming love and gratitude for this next chapter and level of our relationship.

"Gazing into the glass case, my eyes were immediately drawn to a bridal set that shone with exceptional brilliance. The engagement ring was a platinum band featuring a stunning 1.5-carat diamond at its center, slightly elevated above the band to catch the light. Smaller diamonds surrounded the central gem, meticulously arranged to enhance the ring's luminosity. Additional diamonds adorned the band, cascading along its length to augment its exquisite appearance. Complementing the engagement ring was a platinum wedding band, elegantly laced with diamonds, giving it a timeless, eternal look. *That's the ring*, I silently said to myself, captivated. It was the very first ring that spoke to my heart.

Noticing how I gazed at that particular piece, Logan leaned in close, his breath a gentle whisper in my ear, "That must be the one."

I smiled with affirmation. "Yes, that's the one," I confirmed.

The sales representative reached into the case from behind the glass counter, carefully extracting the brilliantly set rings and placing them on top of the glass for us to admire more closely. Logan lifted the diamond engagement ring from its velvet box and took my hand, sliding the ring onto my finger. It fit perfectly. "It's meant to be," he murmured. He then raised my hand to his lips and gently kissed the ring, as if to seal his vow.

The sales representative beamed in approval as we made our choice. "That's a very lovely set. You made a perfect selection," she complimented. "Will this complete your purchase?" she inquired. Logan nodded. She then carefully picked up the box with the wedding band still in it and guided us toward the register.

As she scanned the barcode, the total flashed on the register's screen. I caught my breath at the amount, a sum far beyond what I had anticipated. Yet Logan, without a moment's hesitation, pulled out his bank card and handled the transaction. He caught the look of astonishment on my face, but his response was affectionate and resolute.

"Anything for the love of my life," he said. He leaned forward to kiss me and added, "I just want to make you happy." His words weren't just a promise of material things but a pledge of his love and commitment to our happiness and life together.

When we got home, I placed both rings on my finger to see how it looked. I was content. Not just about the ring, but more so, the next step we would be taking together. I safely tucked away the velvet box containing the wedding band, reserving it for the day we would officially exchange our vows.

Sitting on his lap on our enclosed porch, we dreamt aloud about our ideal wedding day—imagining a whimsical garden filled with flowers and soft music, or perhaps an opulent celebration aboard a yacht sailing over glistening waters under a star-studded sky. Both were beautiful.

Logan suddenly grabbed my rear firmly with one hand and my thigh with the other, and started to playfully bounce his knees vigorously. With me perched on his lap, arms wrapped around his shoulders, I had to hold on tightly.

I burst out laughing as I said to him, "Baby, if you keep doing that, the neighbors will think we're up to something on the porch in broad daylight."

His eyes smoldered deeply, lips pursed, giving me that look that always made me melt. In a low, seductive voice, he said, "Let them. You can scream my name."

I couldn't help it and laughed even harder, unable to keep a straight face. I could never take him seriously or go along with his various roleplays, no matter how convincing he tried to be, but I always found his playful attempts very endearing as I kissed him.

Eventually, we decided on a more intimate celebration, one that would include only those who had been there for us. It became clear that the grandeur of the event was not what mattered; rather, it was the profound act of being united in a sacred ceremony, a genuine testament to our love and commitment to one another.

One evening, as twilight embraced the sky, we sat together on our porch, engaging in our usual evening conversations. The darkness surrounding us only deepened the intimacy of the moment. Logan took my hand, gently guiding me from my chair to settle on his lap, enveloping me in his arms. "It's not that it took me this long to realize you are the one," he spoke in an almost whisper, his voice tender yet firm. "In many ways, I'm convinced you've been my wife since the day we met, and I never treated you less than that. Remember those stone steps in Stillwater? When I asked, 'Where have you been all my life?' and said, 'You are the key,' I knew right then that I'd found the one person I'd been waiting for my whole life. My wife, the key to everything, had finally arrived. I've never needed a piece of paper to know you're mine. You've been mine from the start."

His words, spoken with heartfelt affection, resonated deeply within me. I listened intently and deeply touched. "You have been the home I've been searching for my whole life, a place where I belong, and my only best friend. The day I met you was the best thing that ever happened to me," he added.

I wrapped my arm around his shoulder, drawing him closer. In response to his loving confession, I pressed a kiss against his lips, then whispered my own truth, "For as long as I can remember, my heart had been searching for a sense of belonging. I looked for it in all the places I've moved to, in the walls I've lived within, and even in other people. I didn't know what I was searching for—it was just an innate feeling, a longing to belong, and I knew it was out there somewhere. Then I met you, and every part of you made me feel comforted, safe, and loved. You became my home, the missing piece I had been searching for all along. It's incredible to think that I was so afraid to move here, to the point of having a panic attack. Yet, it's been the most impactful and greatest decision I've ever made."

I caressed his hair, then gently placed my palm on his warm cheek as I kissed the other. "We were meant to meet," Logan added with conviction.

We continued to sit in the embrace of the night, feeling the world fall asleep around us, absorbing the simple yet profound truth of our deep connection. It was as if our meeting on August 4th, 2019, was no accident but rather something written in the stars long before our time. Despite our individual struggles in life, the moment we met, everything fell into place.

In the three and a half years I've known Logan, he's always placed me first. He often says, "I'd rather have the world wait and be disappointed in me than make you wait or be disappointed because I let you down. At the end of the day, if I don't see those people again, it wouldn't matter much to me, but you're the person I want to wake up to every day. I want to ensure that your days are filled with more happiness than disappointment." Hearing someone express such profound sentiments and consistently back them up with actions is a rarity, but Logan has done so many times over. I feel incredibly blessed to call this man my husband.

A few days later, I reached out to my daughters through our group chat and shared the news with them on a video call. They were overjoyed for me. My eldest daughter, Charlotte, expressed, "Mom, since Logan came into your life, I've seen your happiness and how wonderfully he treats you. I'm glad you've found love and a man who gives you everything you deserve, because that's how you should always be treated." Her words moved me to tears, resonating with the truth of our journey. My daughters have witnessed my struggles and sacrifices, but every hardship and heartache led me to this moment with Logan, making it all worthwhile.

On September 15, 2022, seven months after Logan proposed, we gathered with our closest friends and children at a secluded spot known only to us. I asked my good friend Lou to bring a bouquet rich in symbolism: delicate yellow flowers symbolizing happiness, intricately intertwined with ribbons that fluttered in the breeze, catching the light.

Before the officiant began her ceremonial speech, Keith stepped forward. Now 16, he stood as tall as Logan, his posture reflecting the confidence and warmth he had absorbed from the man who had become a pivotal figure in his life. Over the years, Logan had forged deep bonds with my children, embracing them with the same fervor and affection as if they were his own—a sentiment wholeheartedly reciprocated by each of them.

Clearing his throat and calming his nerves, Keith unfolded a piece of paper he had carefully kept in his shirt pocket. His eyes briefly met mine and Logan's, offering a silent prelude to the weight of his words.

Then, shifting his gaze down to the paper, he began to read aloud.

"When I was young, my mom always knew how to make me laugh. She faced her struggles, but she still made my world a happy place, and I knew that was love," Keith began, his voice carrying the weight of cherished memories. He paused, his eyes lifting to meet ours, allowing the significance of his words to sink in. "Over the years, I've seen how Logan made my mom laugh, even when his jokes weren't the funniest." He smiled and looked up at both of us, humorously acknowledging our lack of comedic genius, eliciting a chuckle from us. "They shared a connection, a mutual understanding that he wove into the world he created for her. She was happy, and I realized that too was love," he continued, his voice thick with emotion.

As Keith spoke, tears began to stream down my face, each word he read binding the past with the present, weaving a tapestry of love and acceptance. He continued, "All I ever wanted was for my mom to be happy, and now I know she will always be because we are here today." Pausing momentarily to steady his voice, he concluded his speech, "Logan is a cool guy, and I'm happy to call him my dad."

When Keith finished his heartfelt speech, a hush filled the room, the emotional weight of his words hanging in the air. Our officiant, her eyes glistening with unshed tears, turned to me with a tender smile. "I would cry too if my son had written something that beautiful," she murmured, her voice soft and filled with empathy. I nodded, my smile wavering as I dabbed at the tears that had spilled onto my cheeks. His words marked not only the affirmation of a new beginning for our blended family but also sealed a bond that had grown stronger with each passing day.

I turned towards Logan, and catching my gaze, he quickly pursed his lips and blew me a gentle air kiss. His gesture was brimming with affection and reassurance, anchoring me amid the wave of emotions stirred by Keith's profound words.

The officiant gently cleared her throat, drawing the attention of our intimate gathering as she began to lead us into the sacred covenant of our vows. With each carefully chosen word, she painted a portrait of love, commitment, and unity, reminding us of the profound journey we were embarking upon. Her voice carried the weight of tradition and the warmth of blessings, infusing the moment with a sense of timelessness and significance.

As we stood hand in hand, the words of the officiant became a melody of promises, each vow a note in the symphony of our devotion. She spoke of enduring love, of unwavering support, and of the sacred bond that we were forging not only between ourselves but also with our children, friends, and the divine presence that graced our gathering.

As the moment arrived to exchange rings, Logan reached over to Keith, who held two boxes, each containing our wedding bands. A smile graced Logan's face as he took the diamond-laced platinum wedding band, a treasure I had safeguarded for the past seven months. In the gentle glow of the room, the band shimmered, capturing fleeting glimmers of light as he tenderly slipped it onto my finger. Our eyes met, his gaze filled with an undying love and a promise that echoed through the sacredness of the moment.

Then came the moment for me to place the ring on Logan's finger. I turned to Keith, who held the box with a knowing grin. With a flourish, he opened it, revealing a brilliant platinum band. It was elegantly simple, adorned only with a single, solitary diamond, modest in size but set flush to ensure a smooth surface—Logan had always preferred jewelry that didn't snag on things. I had chosen this design with intention, believing wholeheartedly that men should also wear diamonds, especially a man as precious and enduring as Logan. He was forever my diamond, rare and enduring, symbolizing our unbreakable bond and everlasting love, a testament to the depth of our commitment.

As I took the ring from Keith and slipped it onto Logan's finger, I felt the weight of the commitment we were solidifying. The diamond on his band caught the light, symbolizing the brilliance and strength he has brought into my life, a constant reminder of the enduring love we share.

With a profound sense of closure and celebration, the officiant proclaimed, "I now pronounce you husband and wife. You may now kiss the bride," her words imbued with the joy and solemnity of the occasion.

In response, Logan and I turned to face each other, guided by a tender sense of purpose. As our lips met in a kiss, sealing our lifelong commitment in holy matrimony, laughter and cheers erupted from our friends and children, filling the air with joyous celebration. Hand in hand, we turned to gaze at them, our faces adorned with wide grins. Even Logan blushed a little. In that moment, we were officially united in marriage, surrounded by love and warmth.

CHAPTER 22

Nouveau 2022

WINTER HAD RETURNED TO SAINT PAUL, painting October with its crisp frosty air. With our big event just a month away, the anticipation was tangible. The chilly breeze carried a sense of urgency and excitement as we entered the final stages of planning.

Logan and I had been tirelessly preparing for what was shaping up to be our most extensive and adventurous fashion show and concert to date. Despite our adamant decision after the challenging 2020 show just two years ago that we would never again organize such a massive event, here we were, caught up in the excitement of planning once more. This time, the scale was unparalleled for us, with attendance expected to surpass 4,000— far exceeding our last show's capacity of 1,200.

Logan and I wrapped ourselves in cozy blankets as we settled into our chairs on our three-season porch. Beyond the windows, the wintry night sky stretched overhead, a canvas of stars twinkling in the cold air. Our only source of warmth was each other's presence and the soft glow of a small gas fireplace. Its flickering flames cast gentle light that danced across our faces as we pondered the looming responsibilities of our upcoming event.

"I don't know why we're doing this again," Logan confessed, his voice carrying a mix of disbelief and exhaustion.

"I don't either, Honey," I replied, shaking my head slightly. "An event of this size and magnitude—it's resource-intensive, and honestly, there's not much tangible to gain."

Logan nodded slowly, his gaze shifting to the darkness outside, before he spoke in a somber yet hopeful tone, "But for once in my life, I just want to be able to say, I did that... I made that happen."

I turned to gaze at Logan, his handsome profile etched in the soft, flickering glow of the fire. Though weariness marked his eyes, an undeniable spark illuminated his expression—a fierce determination that resonated deeply with me, reminding me that his dreams were my dreams, his hopes were my hopes. Together, we embarked on this daunting journey, spurred not only by the challenge but by a shared desire to accomplish something truly extraordinary.

During a dinner with one of our dearest friends, Susan, and her husband Nic, Susan chuckled and commented, "You and Logan are the last people I'd imagine organizing such a massive event. You're both introverts; you don't typically attend parties or indulge in drinking. And now, here you are, putting together the grandest show our community has ever witnessed."

I replied, half in jest, "I'm not sure what came over me. I moved to Minnesota to live like a hermit, to embrace peace and simplicity." Susan laughed, "You're certainly doing the opposite."

I laughed along with her, but deep down, I knew the true reason for diving into such a grand event with Logan. It was the sheer excitement in Logan's eyes whenever he talked about his vision. There was a radiant spark of passion and enthusiasm that always stirred something deep within me. His energy was captivating, filling my heart with a vibrant glow every time.

That spark ignited a promise I made years ago. We were walking through a park on a chilly day, stumbled upon an amphitheater, and in that moment, I silently vowed to help bring his dreams to fruition, no matter their scale or number. Confronted by the enormity of the task, I knew I would tackle any challenge, endure any hardship, cross through hell and back if necessary—even if it were all just to be graced with a smile from my Logan. It would all be worth it. Logan once remarked, "When someone is your soulmate, you'll discover that you'd go to any lengths for them." His words couldn't be more accurate.

My motivation was simple yet profound—a reflection of my deep, unwavering love for him. For Logan, and for that radiant smile that would inevitably light up his face as the joy in his eyes blossomed into a proud glow of achievement, I was prepared to embark on this demanding journey once more.

Over the past two years, as we dove into the intricate planning of this monumental event, sleep had become an elusive luxury. Logan spearheaded the talent acquisition for our show, propelled by a clear vision of seamless transitions and grandeur. He imagined an enthralling sequence: a grand opening combining the runway fashion show with live musical performances, transitioning into an electrifying concert, and climaxing with a dazzling DJ light show. His meticulous planning ensured that every facet of the show seamlessly flowed into the next, crafting a continuous spectacle of visuals and entertainment.

A distinctive feature of our production was the deliberate absence of an emcee. Logan firmly believed that the essence of our show resided in the seamless flow of performances, allowing the music, fashion, and lights to communicate their stories without external commentary. This strategic decision brought a level of refinement, enabling the audience to completely immerse themselves in the sensory experience without any interruptions.

Motivated by my inherent passion for meticulous organization, I dedicated myself wholeheartedly to overseeing every aspect of the event. This included coordinating with designers and models, managing performers, and refining production details, ensuring that each element was executed with unwavering precision and care.

Our nights became a battleground of restlessness; I would often wake up to the rapid thumping of my own heart, feeling the weight of responsibility tightening its grip around me. Anxiety and fear loomed large as I pondered the immense challenges of orchestrating such a complex affair. Doubts swirled through my mind with persistent intensity: Could I really bring this vision to life? The scale of the task was daunting, yet my determination to see it through spurred me on, propelling me beyond the limits of what I once believed possible.

During those moments of uncertainty, Logan's presence was my steadfast anchor. He was always there to reassure me with his unwavering confidence.

"What's on your mind, my love?" Logan inquired in a gentle, caring tone, sensing that I was awake and struggling to find peace. I heard him, but words failed me as I was still trying to process the whirlwind of thoughts in my head.

"Whatever burdens you, share them with me," he continued, wrapping me in his arms with a comforting embrace. I nestled my head against his chest, listening to the steady, reassuring rhythm of his heartbeat—a sound that always brought solace.

Without a need for words, he seemed to grasp the depth of my concerns. In the peacefulness of the night, he whispered into my ear, "Together, we are better and stronger. Whatever it takes, we will pull through."

His words weren't just comforting; they resonated as a potent reminder of our shared resilience. In Logan's presence, my anxieties dissolved, replaced by a renewed determination to confront our challenges head-on.

The Armory, our chosen venue for the grand spectacle, stood as a beacon of history and prestige in the heart of Minneapolis. Its architectural grandeur and vast interiors had witnessed a myriad of illustrious events, from performances by renowned artists to the grand stage of the Super Bowl halftime show. Accompanied by our close friends Shye and Kevin, who had become integral to our events through their décor and setup expertise, we explored the venue's halls. With each step, excitement and anticipation building within us, foreshadowing the magnificence of the forthcoming show.

During our initial tour, the immense scale and beauty of the space struck us profoundly. We instantly knew it would serve as the perfect backdrop for an event as ambitious as ours. While the cost of booking The Armory was substantial for our pockets, the priceless glow of excitement and possibility on Logan's face made it impossible for me to hesitate. Determined to bring our vision to life, I agreed, fully aware of the financial tightrope we would walk thereafter.

Later, during lunch with Shye and Kevin, Logan injected a moment of lightheartedness with a half-joking remark: "Enjoy this meal, because Steph and I will be living on ramen for the foreseeable future." His laughter filled the air, mingling with our mixed feelings of exhilaration and the stark reality of our financial commitment. However, beneath the humor lay a resolute undertone, a readiness to embrace the sacrifices necessary for our dream to flourish.

Excitement brewed not only among potential attendees but also within us as we prepared to unveil a fusion of fashion and music, aspiring to surpass our past achievements and set an entirely new standard in cultural exhibitions.

Our upcoming event mirrored our inaugural one in its promise of elegance and grandeur, featuring a red carpet to greet attendees from all corners of the nation. We extended invitations to top-tier designers, performers, and models from diverse regions. Yet, the highlight of our gathering was our headlining act—Win Vang and Houa Vue, esteemed guests from Laos. Win Vang's soulful melodies and poignant lyrics strike a chord with audiences, while Houa Vue's fusion of traditional Hmong music with hip-hop and rap brings a dynamic and captivating twist to the stage.

The announcement of Win and Houa headlining our event sparked both excitement and skepticism. Critics, including self-proclaimed 'immigration specialists,' claimed it was impossible due to U.S. sanctions against Laos, which restricted such visits. They argued that lifting these sanctions would take years. Additionally, keyboard warriors accused us of fraud, alleging that we were using this announcement solely to boost ticket sales. Nonetheless, amidst the skepticism and accusations, we were heartened by the overwhelming support we received from the majority of the community and those who personally knew us.

In moments of deep emotion, tears welled up as I turned to Logan, my voice trembling with frustration. "Why are people so quick to judge and attack us? They don't even know the effort we're putting in. We're pouring our hearts into creating something extraordinary for our community, funding much of it ourselves without expecting anything in return." Tears streamed down my cheeks, the weight of the criticisms pressing heavily on me.

"I'm sorry, Baby, that you have to endure this," Logan said, his voice a soothing comfort amidst the chaos. He drew me close, enfolding me securely in his embrace. The steady, gentle rhythm of his heartbeat against my ear grounded me, syncing with mine to quiet the storm within.

"Focus on the big picture, not the noise. We've got this," he whispered, his breath warm against my hair, reminding me of his reassuring words that "we are stronger together."

Despite the initial backlash, Logan's reminder of the extensive research and groundwork we had done fortified my confidence. I held onto a firm, instinctual belief that our meticulous planning would indeed come to fruition.

We had assembled an exceptional team, featuring some of the most connected and capable professionals in the industry. Each member was equipped and confident to navigate the complexities at hand. Miraculously, just as we had anticipated, the sanctions were lifted a mere month after our bold announcement. By summer, well ahead of our event, Win and Houa joyously informed their fans that they were indeed coming to America. This news ignited a wave of anticipation across the Hmong communities, as everyone eagerly anticipated their performance on the grand stage at Hmong Nouveau.

Amidst overseeing all the logistical aspects, we were gearing up to unveil our inaugural two fashion lines: Wings and Warriors. Little did we realize the gravity of responsibilities that would come with this endeavor. Logan and I dove into numerous late-night sessions, fully immersed in the creative journey of designing, cutting, and sewing an array of pieces for these unique collections.

Wings blossomed as a homage to ethereal beauty, showcasing ten exquisite haute couture fantasy dresses. Each dress was inspired by the vibrant plumage of exotic birds, encapsulating a blend of elegance and otherworldly charm.

On the flip side, Warriors epitomized strength and masculinity, but with a polished edge. Enriched with elements of sophistication and cultural depth, each design embodied courage and bravery, symbolizing an indomitable spirit. Every piece was carefully crafted as a testament to resilience, resonating with the essence of empowerment and self-assuredness.

Ten days prior to our event, Win and Houa arrived at Minneapolis airport after enduring a grueling twenty-three-hour flight from Laos. We closely monitored their journey, ensuring their safety and well-being at every step. It was their inaugural visit to the U.S., and they were enchanted by their first encounter with snowfall. Their excitement mirrored that of Hmong communities nationwide, all eagerly anticipating the live performance by these beloved artists.

Hmong Nouveau stood on the precipice as the most extravagant concert and fashion showcase our community had ever experienced. With each passing moment, our phones buzzed incessantly with logistical inquiries and concerns, creating an evident pressure to ensure stringent security measures and protocols were firmly established, leaving no room for errors.

Amidst the whirlwind of event planning, a different storm brewed. When Win and Houa enthusiastically shared their American journey on social media, proudly standing outside our modest home in Frogtown during their first morning, the response wasn't what we anticipated. Rather than celebrating their joy and newfound experiences, the virtual world was fixated on trivial details, like the size of our home and the perceived status of our neighborhood. It was disheartening to witness such a monumental occasion reduced to discussions about square footage and location, as if these factors determined someone's value or worthiness.

A few self-proclaimed 'social media influencers' voiced concern online about Win and Houa's supposed poor treatment in terms of accommodation. They were unaware that we had offered Win and Houa the choice of where to stay, and they preferred the comfort and familiarity of our home, where they felt safe and at ease. They expressed concerns about not knowing the language or the country well enough to be on their own in a detached hotel for an extended period.

It was difficult not to be affected by the negativity on social media, and I found myself in tears often. Logan, always my rock, would occasionally say something random yet true to redirect my thoughts and lift my spirits. "If only they knew that when we were planning our first Hmong Nouveau event, we were living out of a car. Oh, the field day the keyboard warriors would have had with that!" he chuckled heartily. His laughter was infectious, and I couldn't help but join in, feeling all the sadness and frustration melt away.

As word spread and curious fans gathered outside our home to catch glimpses of Win and Houa, a new worry surfaced. Online accusations flew, claiming that we were holding Win and Houa against their will. With my 16-year-old son at home, I feared for his safety in case an overly enthusiastic fan decided to act rashly and try to enter our house. The harsh judgments from keyboard warriors stung, but I clung to Logan's mantra: "Focus on the big picture."

There were moments when, despite my efforts to hide my distress and tears, Win and Houa would express regret for the unintended trouble they had caused. I would reassure them, explaining that I was okay and that they had nothing to worry about.

Our core values centered on cherishing life's experiences and finding joy in human connections rather than material wealth. Our humble home, though small in size, was a sanctuary brimming with love and dreams, far more valuable than any grand mansion could ever be.

Our event wasn't fueled by financial gain. While our pockets weren't deep, our passion certainly was. We took on extra projects in our respective fields to fund a significant part of the event's expenses—a sacrifice only a few could fully appreciate, and that's okay. Not everyone understands the depth of personal investment behind such endeavors. After all, if there were mountains of profits to be made, many more would be hosting events like ours. Our vision was to create something meaningful: a celebration of music, culture, and fashion that we'd love to experience in our lifetime—not just a profitable venture.

Logan's words reverberated in my mind: "For once in my life, I just want to know that I did that. I made it happen." It was about transforming dreams into reality, demonstrating that with determination and heart, even the most humble beginnings could pave the way for extraordinary achievements.

The day of the event dawned bright and early. By 6:00 a.m., I was already busy loading Logan's cargo van with runway attire. The past three days had been a whirlwind of last-minute preparations, with sleep becoming a rare commodity. My daughters, Charlotte, Cassie, and Kayla, arrived early to help diligently assemble badges for staff, volunteers, and media. Even my best friend, Lily, flew in from North Carolina to lend a hand with all the last-minute details.

"Steph, you're too kind," Lily remarked amidst the excitement and commotion of the community. "You just need to put people in their place, but instead, you stay quiet. If I were you, I'd tell everyone to shut up already," she added.

I took a deep breath and replied, "The crowd only sees the grandeur of the event. They don't see all the intricate details or the years of effort we've invested to make this happen. Right now, I can't afford the distractions or the time to explain everything. People will just have to trust that we're doing everything within our capacity to ensure their enjoyment and safety."

Every dedicated member of our staff and crew, from our outstanding designers to our talented models and performers, was expected to arrive promptly at The Armory by 7:00 a.m. This crucial moment marked the start of a challenging, yet exhilarating day filled with meticulous preparation and exhaustive rehearsals.

Security protocols were intricately laid out to ensure that only authorized personnel could access the venue during our crucial hours of preparation. As our staff and crew started to arrive, our executive assistant, Jessica, played a pivotal role. She efficiently checked in and ushered each designer, model, and performing artist into their assigned green rooms, where they would prepare for the grand spectacle ahead.

The air buzzed with anticipation as we set the stage for what promised to be an unforgettable fusion of fashion and artistic expression.

Logan and I conducted a comprehensive walkthrough of the entire venue with The Armory's management team, carefully reviewing all logistics and security measures. We made sure that signs were strategically positioned for our teams and attendees.

While I ensured that everyone was briefed on their schedules and the day's expectations, Logan worked closely with the production and engineering teams to ensure precise timing and coordination.

Among the show's grandeur were nine visionary designers, each presenting between 5 to 18 distinct creations, showcasing the depth and diversity of their artistic vision. We diligently rehearsed the runway with each design, seamlessly integrating live performances from our exceptionally talented artists, whom we handpicked, leaving no stone unturned in our quest for flawless punctuality. Our goal was clear: to achieve seamless timing and precise execution, ensuring an unforgettable experience for our audience. As Logan and I consistently emphasized, "We don't operate on Hmong time," underscoring our commitment to punctuality and professionalism in every aspect of our production.

As 5:00 p.m. drew near, The Armory buzzed with the arrival of VIP guests, each adorned in stunning attire that shimmered under the spotlights as they gracefully walked the red carpet. Cameras flashed, capturing the glamour and excitement of the evening as guests posed before taking their seats. At 7:00 p.m. sharp, the radiant interior of The Armory dimmed, creating a hushed ambiance soon replaced by the vibrant strains of a cultural melody, signaling the start of the fashion show and concert. The atmosphere crackled with energy, fueled by the anticipation and collective enthusiasm of over 4,000 attendees from across the nation.

In the weeks leading up to the event, Logan battled with nerves, wavering on whether to step onto the stage. As the crucial moment approached, his apprehension grew. He confided, "I'm not sure I can do this," voicing concerns about freezing up and feeling unsure about addressing the crowd and thanking our sponsors—these thoughts burdened him greatly.

I reminded him of the time he stood on that amphitheater stage in the park, fueled by an unstoppable passion, and how he made me a believer in his dreams. Then I added, "Honey, you're the most incredible person I know. I believe in you wholeheartedly, and I have no doubt that you'll shine. You've worked so hard, and I'm so proud of you for getting us both here. This is your moment, and you were born for this." My voice resonated with genuine conviction, aiming to boost his confidence and reaffirm his incredible potential.

Despite his inner turmoil, when his cue arrived, Logan took a deep breath and stepped onto the stage with determination, my unwavering support by his side. The audience erupted into a symphony of cheers and applause, extending a warm embrace that visibly eased his nerves. As he waved to acknowledge everyone, his presence filled the room with an undeniably charming aura.

Walking alongside him, I felt a mix of exhilaration and exhaustion. The past few weeks had been a whirlwind of activity, and I realized how little attention I had paid to my own well-being amid the chaos. My lack of proper sleep and nourishment had caught up with me, and each painstaking step felt like a challenge due to cramping legs from dehydration.

With Logan's firm arm supporting me, I summoned the strength to maintain my composure. His support went beyond the physical; it served as the emotional anchor I desperately needed in that moment. Together, we traversed the stage, our joint appearance a powerful testament to our partnership and the culmination of our tireless efforts. This was our moment, and despite the physical strain, we radiated under the spotlight, witnessing our shared vision unfold in a spectacular display as we gazed out at the sea of faces in the filled room.

"Hello, everyone!" Logan's firm and steady voice rang out through the microphone in his hand. Over 4,000 spectators filled the Armory, cheers and applause erupting from a sea of eager faces. Some stood on the first floor around the runway, which extended 60 feet and was 8 feet wide from the grand stage, while many more occupied the multi-tiers on each side and towards the back, cellphones in hand to capture this momentous occasion.

The spotlight illuminated Logan, emphasizing his presence on the stage. Standing beside him, I felt the warmth of the lights and the electric excitement of the crowd, their anticipation palpable as the cheers continued. Logan began his heartfelt speech, expressing deep gratitude to everyone present, especially acknowledging our sponsors and those who had traveled from out of state to join us for this special event.

I attempted to focus on the audience, but this was the moment I had been anticipating ever since I first saw him stand on that stage in the park three years ago, beaming with excitement about an event he wanted to create. I couldn't take my eyes off him. As I heard him address the crowd with sheer confidence and boldness, my heart swelled with emotion and a sense of accomplishment, making all those sleepless nights and tears I'd shed entirely worth it. Because my goal wasn't about Hmong Nouveau. It was about getting him here to this very moment.

As Logan's brief speech reached its conclusion, he addressed the audience before him, his words infused with excitement, "Now, I only have one more question for you. Are you ready... to party?" He paused for a moment, savoring the anticipation in the air. As the crowd cheered even louder, he lifted his arm into the air to give a fingered nod as a cue to the engineers, and said, "Then let's get the party started."

At that precise moment, a burst of glittering red and white confetti shot into the air, creating a dazzling cascade that rained down upon us and the ecstatic audience, adding an extra touch of jubilance to the atmosphere. With smiles of satisfaction and a sense of relief that our time in the spotlight was over, we gracefully made our way off the stage, leaving behind a thrilling wave of excitement and anticipation in the air.

As we retreated, the atmosphere continued to thrum with anticipation. Our next performer dashed onto the stage, accompanied by a dynamic team of backup dancers. Their high energy was invigorating, and the pulsating beat of the music signaled the exhilarating start of the concert portion of our show. The transition was seamless, and the audience's enthusiasm was undeniable, their cheers growing louder as they eagerly awaited the highly anticipated performances from Win Vang and Houa Vue, who would brilliantly close out the evening.

As soon as I retreated back to our greenroom, exhaustion hit me like a tidal wave. I collapsed onto the couch and immediately fell into a deep sleep. The world outside faded away as I sank into a much-needed rest, leaving Logan to manage the remainder of the night. I only revived later when Logan gently nudged me, a silent cue that it was time to clean up and head home.

"Oh my gosh, I fell asleep. Why didn't you wake me?" I asked, taken aback.

"Some people were asking for you, but when I peeked in to check on you, I found you sound asleep. I decided to let you rest and told everyone to give you some space. Some even joked that you must have partied too hard and passed out," he chuckled.

"I wish that were true," I replied, joining in the laughter.

CHAPTER 23

TOGETHER AND TODAY

O N THE MORNING OF MY 45TH BIRTHDAY, I deviated from my typical work-from-home routine and drove out to my client's office to meet with a few executives who had flown in from out of state. It was a rare occurrence, but with a large project on the horizon, their visit was necessary. The harsh fluorescent lights of the office often triggered migraines for me, so I didn't relish being there unless it was vital for building client relationships. By the end of the day, I was relieved and eager to head home.

Instead of parking in my usual spot at the front, I chose to park my car at the back of the house to save myself the hassle of moving it later. As I unlocked the back door and stepped inside, I found Logan already there, seemingly waiting for me. His cheerful smile greeted me, dressed in his soft navy blue zip-up sweater with a hood—my favorite because it always made him feel extra soft and cuddly whenever I hugged him. The evening air had a crispness to it, adding a touch of chill to the atmosphere.

"Hello, my love," he greeted, his smile even more radiant than usual.

"Hi, Baby," I replied, returning a smile that mirrored his, genuinely surprised by his unexpected presence and his eager anticipation of my return. This particular excitement, I knew well; it often hinted that he had something brewing, and he couldn't wait to show me. I couldn't help but be intrigued and feel loved.

Before I could utter another word, he took my hand and guided me through our kitchen, with my laptop bag slung over my shoulder. He was so eager that I had to hold onto the strap tightly to prevent it from slipping as we passed by furniture.

"What's going on?" I asked, a blend of curiosity and excitement in my voice as he held my hand firmly. Without a word, he led me through our living room and out onto our enclosed front porch.

"I was waiting here, thinking you'd come in through the front," he said, his smile widening with a hint of mischief.

On the small table on our porch sat a delightful sight: a white frosted Chantilly cake adorned delicately with fresh fruits and sugar pearls. The words "Happy Birthday Steph" were lovingly etched in red frosting, a familiar sight that never failed to warm my heart.

"Aww... Baby, this is so sweet of you," I exclaimed happily, genuinely touched but not surprised by his thoughtfulness. He never forgets my birthday and always gets me my favorite cake.

The significance of the cake was not in its flavor or decorative embellishments but in the annual tradition that Logan had upheld since my very first birthday celebrated with him shortly after we met.

On the morning of that birthday, he picked me up with unusual eagerness, refusing to disclose his plans. As we parked in front of the bakery, I had a feeling it was because of my birthday. Upon entering, he asked the baker for the cake he had ordered. She revealed a cake from behind the counter, complete with a candle.

With cake in hand, Logan led me to a small table by the window where he set up the cake. We sat together as he lit the candle. With a smile, he said, "Happy Birthday!" I playfully asked, "Are you going to sing?" He shyly replied, "I can't sing," and I smiled.

Closing my eyes, I made a wish for this wonderful man to always receive the things that make him happy. Every year since then, without fail, he has procured this special cake from the same bakery, showcasing his unwavering love and thoughtfulness, and yes, he sings.

During the challenging times of the pandemic, when the bakery shuttered its doors, Logan was determined to ensure I still had this particular cake on my birthday. He went to great lengths to track down the owner, going as far as to pay her extra just to convince her of how important this cake was. His efforts were not just about a cake; they were about preserving a cherished tradition and ensuring that my special day did not pass by without it.

Logan called Keith down from his bedroom, "Keith, your mom is home. Come sing 'Happy Birthday' for her." Then, he retrieved an unopened box of candles, their wax shimmering in a rich, golden hue under the gentle light of the room. Placing a single candle atop the cake, its flame flickered like a tiny beacon of celebration. Meanwhile, Keith's footsteps echoed down the hallway until he emerged onto the porch, a smile lighting up his face as he entered.

"Happy birthday, Mom," he greeted me with a smile as he walked over and embraced me in a heartfelt hug. I returned his smile with gratitude, my heart touched by the thoughtfulness of Logan and Keith's gesture.

Seated before my birthday cake, the single candle casting a soft golden glow, Logan and Keith sang, "Happy Birthday." My heart was filled with love and appreciation. This marked my fifth birthday celebration with Logan since the day we met, each one a precious memory cherished for his heartfelt gestures. Logan always made an effort to go out of his way to make my day memorable.

After blowing out the candle, Keith headed to the kitchen to grab some plates and a cake knife. Passing the knife to Logan, he cut slices for each of us. The cake was delicious, the flavors blending perfectly with the moist texture.

After Keith helped with cleanup, he said, "I love you, Mom" and went back upstairs to his room.

Sitting comfortably on our porch, Logan's warm smile graced me as he asked, "What would you like to do for your birthday? We can do anything you want."

I paused for a moment, gazing outside through the encased porch. The sun's radiant light still painted the sky in a gentle blend of orange and pink, casting a serene atmosphere around us. The September air carried a refreshing coolness, and a gentle breeze rustled through the leaves.

Turning back to Logan, I replied, "I just want to go for a long drive with you."

"Absolutely, my love," Logan responded cheerfully. "We can grab dinner first, if you'd like."

Logan, well aware of my love for seafood and pasta, chose an Italian restaurant nestled along Selby Street. It was a cozy gem with a charming brick exterior that promised an enchanting evening.

Stepping inside, we were greeted by the inviting warmth of the restaurant. Soft murmurs of conversation and laughter filled the air, blending harmoniously with the sounds of dishes being enjoyed. Delicate glass vases housing flickering candles added a touch of magic, casting a soft glow over the space.

Seated at our table by the window, we were treated to a captivating view of Selby Street. The scene outside was straight out of a storybook, with small businesses exuding an old-world charm. The soft, romantic glow of streetlamps bathed the street in a gentle radiance, further enhancing the enchantment of the evening.

Logan's eyes twinkled mischievously as he pointed out a tall man with unruly brown locks across the street, accompanied by a woman who radiated a mix of friendship and unspoken affection. "Ah, there goes Dave," Logan remarked, his voice carrying a hint of amusement. "Always on the hunt for that elusive spark, yet it dances just out of reach."

I raised an eyebrow, intrigued. "And who's his charming companion?"

"That's Sarah," Logan explained, a smirk playing at the corners of his lips. "Dave's partner-in-crime through a decade of highs and lows."

"He looks like he's got something on his mind," I observed, nodding toward Dave.

Logan chuckled knowingly. "He's caught in the age-old dilemma. He wants to spill his heart out to Sarah, but he's terrified it might ruin their friendship."

"Classic," I quipped, a grin spreading across my face. "Does Sarah know?"

"Not a clue," Logan replied.

I then added, "But I'd bet my last dollar that she's wrestling with the same thoughts." He smiled at me and chuckled.

Logan's talent for weaving tales from the ordinary, especially when it brings a twinkle to his eyes and a chuckle to his lips, never fails to delight and enchant me. His knack for peering beyond surface appearances, delving into the genuine essence of people, reveals truths that are truly captivating. What begins as a casual observation often evolves into profound insights and unexpected revelations. His intuitive understanding, even in the most ordinary moments, consistently surprises me, showcasing his unique perspective and depth of perception.

When Logan's intuition proves right, his excitement bubbles over with a triumphant, "I knew it!" His judgment has earned my complete trust over time. When he speaks about someone, there's a profound depth to his understanding that commands attention. He excels at deciphering the unspoken, and his accuracy is astonishing. He never misses the mark, and naturally, he shares his insights exclusively with me.

Intrigued by his insightful nature, I asked, "What were your first impressions of me?" A wide grin spread across his face as he replied, "I knew you were smitten the moment our eyes met." I burst into laughter at his playful assertion, "Is that right?" Chuckling, I playfully conceded, "You certainly have a gift!" Our laughter filled the cozy corner of the restaurant, creating a warm and memorable moment between us.

Moments later, As I swirled my fork through the pasta during dinner, a sudden realization washed over me — we had been married for a whole year. Our vows were exchanged on September 15th, 2022, and here we were on September 21st, 2023. A joyful surprise lit up my eyes as I looked at Logan and exclaimed, "We completely forgot our first wedding anniversary!" The whirlwind of searching for our forever home had occupied our minds entirely, leaving little space for anything else.

"Can you believe it's already been a year?" I asked him happily.

"It feels like it was just yesterday, yet here we are, still as giddy as newlyweds," Logan added as he laughed affectionately.

"It's incredible how time flies. It's been almost five years since we first met," I added wistfully.

"Yeah. Zoo li ib ntsais muag xwb," he replied in Hmong, which translates "It feels like it was just a blink of an eye." I sensed a touch of somberness in his voice.

With a tender smile, I reached across the table to grasp his hand, cherishing the moment and the years that had swiftly passed us by, feeling grateful to still be here in each other's presence. Our life was good.

After our enjoyable dinner, we embarked on our long drive into the countryside, guided not by a destination but by the allure of each other's company. The gentle hum of the engine provided a soothing backdrop to our conversations, while the winding road unfolded like a ribbon in the night, bordered by an endless expanse of lush, picturesque forests where the scene seemed to stretch into an eternity of quiet darkness, inviting us to lose ourselves in its tranquil charm. The waxing crescent moon hung above us like a gentle lantern, as if it were leading the way.

We drove in peaceful silence, savoring the beauty of a familiar road. As I gazed out the window, letting my eyes get lost in the night sky just above the trees, Logan reached over to me. His warm hand enveloped mine, gently intertwining our fingers and placing our joined hands over his heart. It was a gesture he often made when speaking from his soul.

"We have a really good life," he expressed, his voice overflowing with affection and unwavering certainty. "We don't argue, and we always work very well together. You're my brain, and I'm your heart. You've brought so much joy and meaning into my life; I can't imagine it without you because meeting you has been the best thing that ever happened to me. You've changed my life in ways I can't fully express." His heartfelt words resonated deeply, tugging on every one of my heartstrings.

"Throughout my life, I've always wanted to do something meaningful, something greater than myself," he continued, his gaze fixed on the road ahead. "Whether it was renovating houses or organizing grand events, my family and past relationships have dismissed my dreams, making me feel like I wasn't good enough for them to invest their time or belief in me. But you, Baby, you've never wavered. You have been the only person who believed in me, going all-in every time without questioning, and I love and appreciate you for that."

His heartfelt confession filled me with a sense of comfort as I responded, "My love, you are the best thing to happen to me too. You are my rock, my safe place, and my constant source of strength. I never doubted you regardless of how big your dreams were because you inspired me, and no matter the task or challenges, I knew we were more than capable. As you said, 'we are stronger together.' You can only fail if you do not try. Not only that, you are more than enough and deserve everything you set your heart on, and I wanted to make sure of that." I replied with love and conviction as I squeezed his hand to assure him of my sincerity.

"I want us to always be this way," said Logan. I can hear a tinge of concern in his voice.

I continued to gaze at him, the soft glow of the headlights casting a gentle radiance upon his face, revealing a quiet somberness. The road always seemed to elicit a myriad of emotions and thoughts from him, ones that he seldom shared at any other time.

A caring smile graced my lips as I spoke, "Oh Honey, I assure you... even decades from now when we're old and gray, we will find ourselves seated in our favorite chairs on our enclosed porch, basking in the sunset's warm embrace while our dogs playfully scamper about in the yard. I will turn to you with a heart full of love and say, 'we still have the best life.' We'll witness the cherished journey of our children and grandchildren, and everything will unfold just as it's meant to be. I promise you. You'll see."

As the road wound on, a smile gradually returned to Logan's face. To shift the somber tone, he began to weave jokes into our conversation, soon erupting into hearty laughter at his own wit. His knack for humor never failed to lighten the mood, and I found myself laughing alongside him.

Amidst our shared laughter, Logan confessed, "I have to laugh at myself sometimes because if I don't, I'll cry," punctuating his words with another round of chuckles. "Don't mind me. I'm just a goofball," he added playfully.

I remarked on his ability to infuse lightheartedness into any conversation, no matter how heavy it may feel. He glanced over at me briefly before refocusing on the road, saying, "You'll miss this one day."

A wave of emotion swept over me, and I replied, "Baby, if for whatever reason we are not together, I would miss more than just your silliness. I would miss everything about you." I continued to look at him, then quickly added, "But, that'll never happen, because we will always be together."

Logan gave me a quick glance then smiled. He continued to hold my hand as we drove on into the night, feeling blessed for the life we have.

CHAPTER 24

ALWAYS NORTH

SEPTEMBER USUALLY MARKS THAT TIME OF THE YEAR for Logan when he starts to slow down on projects for the winter. It's also when he prepares for his annual hunting expedition, something he plans and looks forward to all year.

Last year, amid the preparations for our big event, Logan refrained from any hunting activities. This year, he was especially enthusiastic about returning to his element, which typically brings him peace. The outcome of the hunt mattered less to him than the experience itself. Being in nature has a calming effect, slowing down his thoughts and quieting the usual busyness in his mind.

Archery season began in mid-September, and Logan had already embarked on one hunting trip. After celebrating my birthday, he was eagerly anticipating his second excursion. Throughout the week, he had been working diligently to wrap up all his projects, ensuring nothing was left unfinished before his departure.

Before moving to Minnesota, hunting was a completely foreign concept to me, unlike Logan, who had grown up with the backwoods of

Minnesota always within reach. He was a seasoned and passionate hunter, and our annual September hunting trips became a tradition after we started dating. These trips provided us with moments of adventure and connection in the heart of nature. Under Logan's guidance, I learned how to use a compound bow and recurve bow, picking up these skills was surprisingly natural, almost as if I had acquired them in a past life and was simply reawakening them.

This year, Logan expressed a desire to accompany a friend he had known for over fifteen years, someone with whom he often bonded over car discussions and repairs whenever he took his car to his friend's shop for service.

Initially, I felt a twinge of disappointment because I enjoyed our woodland escapades, not particularly for hunting but for the serene embrace of nature's element. Yet, I understood Logan's yearning to venture with a male friend, freeing himself from concerns about my safety in the woods, a sentiment he had frequently voiced. Despite my capability to be self-sufficient, it was just his protective nature.

In our usual routine, Logan and I were inseparable, turning even mundane errands like a visit to the gas station into a trip for two. While I treasured every moment together, I recognized the value of his time with friends and have encouraged it.

It was the evening after my birthday when Logan called me out onto our enclosed porch. As soon as I stepped outside, he said in a frustrated yet teasing tone, "I had been calling you. Why didn't you hear me?"

"I'm sorry, I was still doing dishes and didn't hear you," I explained.

"You don't love me like you used to," he joked, his tone slightly serious.

I chuckled and responded, "I love you so much more. Why would you say that?"

"It used to be that all I had to do was think of your name, and you'd appear. Now, even when I'm yelling your name at the top of my lungs, you don't hear me," he said sarcastically.

I laughed empathetically and said, "I'm so sorry, Baby," then walked over to sit on his lap. I wrapped my arms tightly around him and kissed him firmly to show just how much I loved him and how deeply sorry I was that he had to call me so many times before I stepped out.

The night was dark and quiet as usual, as we settled into our end-of-day routine, relishing each other's company and engaging in conversations about whatever came to mind. Logan had been eagerly planning his hunting trip all week.

"I've never hunted black bears before, but Frank has done it several times, so I'm really looking forward to going with him," Logan said with enthusiasm. He seemed genuinely excited about the prospect of trying something new.

Logan has always been an avid bow hunter, clearly favoring bows over guns and strictly limiting his hunting to bow season. So, when the topic of black bears came up, I couldn't help but feel concerned. I wasn't entirely sure what they looked like; in my mind, I pictured massive brown bears, more familiar to me from growing up in California. I knew they could be staggering in size—an adult bear standing six to eight feet tall and weighing between 800 to 1,500 pounds. With a worried expression, I turned to Logan and asked, "Are you serious? Do you think your arrow will be effective enough to take down a bear efficiently with just one shot?"

To reassure me, Logan calmly explained that black bears were generally similar in size and weight to a large buck, perhaps slightly larger but not significantly so. "Besides," he added confidently, "there are two of us, and I've navigated this area before. I know the terrain and what to expect."

His reassurances prompted my next question, "I've joined you on your hunting trips before and haven't seen any bears. Where exactly will you be hunting this time?"

As Logan shared the location—a reserve north of Hinckley, just along the Wisconsin border—an eerie feeling crept over me. Although I had never been there before, I suddenly envisioned the forest in my mind, and a sense of unease settled in. I voiced my concern, "Honey, something feels off about that area. I feel like you shouldn't go there." The feeling of unease lingered, refusing to dissipate.

Logan then shared a memory from his last visit to that area. "It's been twenty years since I've been there," he reflected, delving into the details of that particular trip. "I was dating Michelle at the time, and I went hunting with her and her two brothers, Ethan and Noah. It was broad daylight, and being accustomed to the forest, I thought little of it when we spread out in different directions to find spots for our deer stands. But soon after I started trekking, I felt disoriented."

As Logan recounted his experience, I interjected, "But you never get lost. I've followed you through dense forests in the dark, and you always seem to have an instinctual sense of direction. How did you manage to get lost?"

"I don't know," he admitted. "It was bizarre. Once I realized I was lost, setting up a deer stand became secondary. All I wanted was to find my way back."

Logan continued narrating his struggle to retrace his steps, but every part of the forest seemed identical, leaving him feeling trapped in a loop. "After a few hours, I came to a river and contemplated whether I should cross it to reach the other side."

I gasped, growing more concerned. "Honey, why would you think you needed to cross it when you hadn't crossed a river to get to where you were lost? It doesn't make sense," I said, bewildered by his story.

"I suppose after being lost for hours, desperation clouded my judgment, and I just wanted to find anyone who could point me in the right direction," Logan explained. "But just as I was about to cross, I heard Noah's voice somewhere behind me. I turned back, following his voice. I yelled loudly, hoping he'd hear me, but he didn't respond. I also heard Ethan and Michelle chatting and laughing nearby."

I listened intently, then remarked, "If you could hear them and were yelling, Michelle should've heard you and helped."

Logan shook his head. "She had a toxic attitude. The more I yelled, the more she found it amusing. Eventually, I managed to calm down and followed their voices. When I reached the car, I was drained, and my face was pale from my traumatizing experience. I just wanted to head home after that."

I took a deep breath, steadying myself against the frustration and disappointment stemming from an irresponsible person he dated decades ago. "I'm relieved you're okay, but that's all the more reason to avoid that forest," I said. Logan assured me that experience had taught him valuable lessons. He now trusted his instincts and was prepared for any situation, adding that he would be going with a reliable companion who would have his back. Knowing Logan, he doesn't trust people easily, and if he feels confident, I have to trust Logan's judgment too, but I was still worried.

With a deep breath, I exhaled slowly, summoning a faint smile. "Just promise me you'll be extra careful," I pleaded, my concern evident. It was a small plea, but a silent prayer for his safety.

The next morning,[36] we rose early to explore the house that held the promise of becoming our forever home. Our offer had been accepted, and it felt like a dream unfolding. Situated on a sprawling six-acre lot with its own private fishing pond, it appeared to be a piece of paradise waiting for us to claim as our own.

As we strolled the grounds for the second time, Logan's eyes lit up with excitement as he gestured toward the open area beside the house and painted a vivid picture of his vision. "This is where we'll build a

---

[36] Saturday, September 23, 2013

massive deck," he said, his voice filled with enthusiasm. "It'll extend all the way out onto a floating dock, bridging over to the gazebo that'll sit atop the water."

My eyes followed his directions but shifted to the worn-out dock nearby, a clear indication of the improvements needed, though an easy feat for Logan. "The deck will then branch into two levels next to the house, creating cozy seating areas. And see that staircase? It'll wind its way up to the flat roof, which I plan to transform into a rooftop patio with a stunning view of the entire lake."

I watched in awe as Logan described each detail with passion in every word. Then, his gesture pointed to another part of the property just behind the house, a spacious area nestled before the trees. "Here, we'll have seven studio suites and a gym room," he continued, his voice filled with excitement. "Each fully equipped with private bathrooms and kitchenettes, perfect for our kids, their families, your family, or our friends when they come to visit."

A smile tugged at my lips, touched by his thoughtfulness and generosity. He had a heart as vast as his vision for our future home, which didn't only include us but also those he cared about.

Next, he pointed to a spot between the house and the garden. "Right here, I'll build a larger studio suite for my brother Scott," Logan said. "I want him to live with us without worrying about the cost. He was the only person there for me before you came into my life, and I want to repay that kindness."

I turned to Logan, "Baby, I'm grateful for every person who has played a part in making your life beautiful. Your compassion is what sets you apart."

"One more thing," Logan continued, gesturing towards the street, "just to the right of the dirt road before you turn onto our driveway, we can partition that area into another lot and build a duplex as our income property. It's far enough from the house that we'll still have our privacy.

Each duplex will have its private patio and deck overlooking the lake." I looked at him in admiration; he had everything planned out.

As I took one more look around, I could envision our life unfolding in this picturesque setting. It was more than just a house. It was a place where our dreams would take shape, where family and friends would gather, and where every corner held the promise of cherished moments. I imagined our dogs running freely, our children and grandchildren fishing off the dock, and summers filled with laughter and love. It was a scene straight out of our dreams, waiting to become our reality.

Leaving the house, we headed over to have lunch at our favorite Thai restaurant on Rice Street. In our opinion, they served the best curry in town. As our food arrived, Logan's excitement for our new home was still radiating. He couldn't stop smiling. He continued to share his plans between bites, his eyes sparkling with anticipation.

"My hope is for us to move in by Christmas," he mentioned between sips of water. Seeing this side of him, so full of joy, warms my heart every time. In the years since I've known Logan, he has confided in me about never having a true home. Even in childhood, belonging eluded him, often feeling like the outcast. As an adult, he roamed, never settling into a conventional life. My love for him runs deep, driven by a desire to see him truly happy, which fills my heart to the brim with contentment.

"As soon as the snow clears, I'll start working on that large deck because it'll set the scale for everything else. Imagine having our cultural wedding there, inviting all our family and friends to see our new home," he mused.

"I would love that, Honey. It would be absolutely beautiful," I replied, envisioning the celebration that would bring our families together.

Although we had been legally married for a year in an intimate ceremony, we decided to wait until we were in our forever home to have our cultural wedding. It felt more meaningful that way, inviting our family into the warmth of our new home, making the occasion even more special. Our cultural wedding would be a traditional Hmong ceremony, bringing both sides of our family together in a ceremonial feast that symbolizes unity. In Hmong culture, marriage isn't just about a man and a woman; it's about the union of two families.

"In this home, I will build the sunroom you've always wanted, with plenty of light for your plants and a reading nook. Off to the side, I'll build a platform for the grand piano so I can serenade you whenever you're sitting in there," Logan happily exclaimed. I love how he never forgets the things I've shared—my wants and desires. He always keeps me in mind in all his planning.

When we moved into our current home towards the end of summer in 2020, I bought a used upright piano. Having played since grade school, the piano has always been a source of therapeutic joy for me. Logan, who had never played before, was quite excited about it. His eagerness to learn was palpable, and for two entire years, I dedicated myself to teaching him almost every day, especially during our evening conversations. Logan's dedication was unwavering; he learned to play by ear and began composing his own songs, which he would play for me with a shy yet proud smile.

Recently, we gave away our piano in anticipation of purchasing a new baby grand for our new house. Logan worried that by the time we moved, he might forget how to play. I reassured him, "You're a natural talent on the piano. You won't forget. I know you'll pick up right where you left off."

I cherished every moment when Logan played for me. Often, I would sit in the living room, captivated by the melodies he created. Sometimes, I'd slide onto the piano bench next to him, resting my head on his shoulder as his fingers danced across the keys. Those moments were intimate and meaningful, deepening our connection through our shared love for music and each other. There were times when his playing moved me to tears because he played with such deep compassion. I'd wrap my arm around his waist and treasure that moment. The anticipation of hearing him play on the new baby grand piano filled me with happiness and made me look forward to our move even more.

As we enjoyed our meal, Logan's expression shifted when he suddenly remembered something important. "I almost forgot about Keith's car," he said. "It's still in the shop for some final touches. He's 16 now and needs a reliable vehicle." We had been talking about getting Keith a car for some time, but it was Logan who took the initiative to make sure Keith had one. His thoughtfulness always tugs at my heartstrings. Despite not being my children's biological father, his love for them knows no bounds.

"It should be ready next weekend when I return from my trip," he assured me with anticipation. "We'll pick it up together." I couldn't help but smile as I reached for his hand across the table. "I love you," I said. He playfully blew me an air kiss and joked, "I know. I'm perfect." I chuckled and squeezed his hand affectionately, replying, "You truly are."

It was two nights before his departure, and we were getting ready for bed. I reached into my dresser and retrieved a beige pouch made of material reminiscent of an old-fashioned flour bag. Logan had just finished showering and stepped into the bedroom with a bath towel wrapped around his waist, water droplets glistening on his broad shoulders and sculpted chest. Even after four and a half years, the sight of his bare chest never failed to leave me breathless and speechless. I paused, my eyes lingering on him, my breath catching in my throat. Noticing my reaction, he smiled and gave me a kiss, breaking my gaze. Recollecting myself, I handed him the pouch. His eyes widened with surprise and curiosity, knowing I had something special for him.

"What's this?" he asked, pleasantly surprised.

"It's for you. Open it," I replied with a smile.

Undoing the strings, he revealed a compass nestled within the pouch. A look of appreciation crossed his face as he turned it over in his hand, feeling its solid weight.

"This is really nice. It feels durable and has a nice weight to it," he remarked.

"It's a military-grade compass, nearly indestructible," I explained, noting the olive-green color, aluminum frame for endurance, and the phosphorescent pigment for low-light navigation.

The glass face made it waterproof, a detail Logan appreciated as he examined it carefully. Having served in the U.S. Army, he was well-versed in the importance of a reliable compass.

After admiring and inspecting every detail, he carefully placed the compass back in its pouch. Leaning in, he kissed me tenderly. "Thank you, Baby," he said with gratitude. "I love it."

The thought of Logan encountering any harm or difficulty always stirs strong emotions within me. At times, I tell myself that I'm just over-worrying, but I cannot help it. I feel a deep-seated need to ensure his well-being at all times.

Pulling out my phone, I opened the map app and showed him a blue dot hovering over our house, representing his current location on the map. "Always keep your phone with you," I instructed, my voice a blend of concern and determination. "I'll be tracking you every step of the way while you're out there. I'll mark your campsite, deer stand, and every trail you take. I've also downloaded the entire reserve and surrounding area onto your phone's map app, so you'll still have access to your location offline even if there's no service. And if you ever find yourself lost, trust your compass to guide you back home to me, because I am your North, and you are mine."

As I spoke, my words trembled, and I struggled to keep my voice from cracking. Tears welled up in my eyes, and the weight of my words became evident. Seeing my emotions, Logan gently wiped away my tears and kissed me again.

"Thank you for loving me so much. I'll only be gone for a few days," he murmured, his voice filled with appreciation and gratitude.

"One more thing," I said as I handed him a bright orange whistle securely fastened to a sturdy carabiner. "This is so you won't have to shout," I explained, telling him to affix it to the belt loop of his pants and not his gear, a simple yet crucial reminder if he were to become separated from his gear.

The unsettling feeling about that particular forest reserve he was venturing into still lingered, but I had to tell myself, *with thorough preparation, everything will be okay, and this isn't his first hunting trip, nor will it be his last.*

CHAPTER 25

ONLY A FEW DAYS

TUESDAY MORNING ARRIVED,[37] and Logan was busy preparing for his imminent trip, ready to head out at any moment. I sat in my office, the morning sun piercing through the branches of the giant maple tree in our backyard. Light filtered in from all three sides of my fully windowed room, where a variety of pothos and arrowhead plants hung, and a collection of Logan's bonsais were aesthetically placed throughout. Immersed in my usual work rhythm, I could hear the faint sounds of Logan's boots walking on the wooden floor downstairs as he gathered his gear, the steady rhythm echoing through the house.

Not long after, I heard Logan's distinct footsteps approaching from behind me. He entered our bedroom, dressed casually in dark blue jeans, a simple black V-neck T-shirt, and a thick brown hooded zip-up sweater. The sturdy boots on his feet signaled that he had finished packing and was all set to leave.

---

[37] Tuesday, September 26, 2023

"I'm ready to head out, Baby," he announced, his voice carrying a mix of readiness and a hint of wistfulness.

Our morning routine usually involved a quick exchange of affection: a kiss and a hug, followed by me watching him leave through the backyard gate from my upstairs office window. We'd wave to each other as I continued to watch him drive off. If he wasn't in a rush, we'd sit on our enclosed porch, enjoying the morning light, savoring a cup of creamy hot coffee while discussing our plans for the day before another exchange of affection as he set out.

But today was different. It was his hunting trip, and he'd be gone for a few days. Even a few days felt long, and I didn't want to miss the chance to properly see him off. Setting my work aside, I joined him in the bedroom. "I'm going to miss you, Honey," I murmured as I tiptoed to wrap my arms around him tightly. His response, "I miss you already," carried a weight that reflected the upcoming days without him.

As he embraced me, his gaze fell upon the half-finished scarf resting at the foot of our bed. We had chosen the yarn together at a craft store, selecting a plush and velvety material reminiscent of cashmere, featuring rich hues of maroon and navy. I had been diligently working on it for weeks, continuing our yearly tradition of crafting him a new scarf.

He had a unique taste for scarves—luxuriously oversized, with a length that allowed them to cascade down to his calves when wrapped loosely around his neck. Before meeting me, he had often struggled to find someone who could create such scarves for him. He was thrilled when he discovered my crochet skills, frequently telling me that I was his perfect match, as my strengths complemented his areas of interest and vice versa. His distinctive fashion sense was one of the many things I loved about him, and I cherished the fact that he appreciated wearing something handmade by me.

When he saw the scarf, he asked eagerly, "Do you think you'll have it finished by the time I return?"

Knowing he'd be back in a few days, I replied with a smile and determination, "I'll put in extra hours to make sure it's ready when you walk through that door."

He then gave me an extended kiss and said, "That would be perfect. I can't wait to wear it this winter." The excitement in his voice infused me with even more determination to finish it in time.

As we descended the stairs, I followed closely behind. We paused at the halfway landing of our L-shaped staircase, bathed in the soft morning light streaming through the window. He turned around, his eyes meeting mine with a mixture of affection and anticipation.

In that fleeting moment, he pulled me into one more tight embrace. I reciprocated with a firm squeeze, cherishing the warmth of his presence. Reluctant to part but trying to lighten the mood, I playfully quipped, "Make sure you don't have too much fun without me."

He responded with a playful grin, "Oh no, I never have fun without you," causing a smile to tug at my lips.

We continued down the familiar path through our living room and kitchen, heading toward the back of the house. The soft echo of our footsteps on the wooden floor was a comforting sound within the walls of our home. Logan's hunting gear lay neatly arranged on the floor of our back mudroom. As he carefully gathered each piece and slipped his outdoor backpack over his shoulder, I drew him close for one last embrace and kiss.

He bent down to nestle his head on my shoulder, his arms hanging by his side, cradling his gear. It was his silent way of hugging me when his hands were full. In that moment, there was a sense of unhurried calmness, as if we had all the time in the world. Slowly, I released my hold and opened the back door to let him out. Following closely, I helped him load his belongings into the car. Meanwhile, our boy Sabre, dashed about in excitement, his playful energy revealing his desire to join the adventure, unaware that he would be staying behind with me.

Once everything was loaded, Logan settled into the driver's seat. With the door ajar, I stood beside him, giving him one last lingering gaze. A heavy sigh escaped me, but his smile softened my expression. "I love you. Let me know when you get there," I said with a mix of longing and reassurance.

Logan leaned forward and pressed his lips to mine in a final kiss before I stepped back to close the door.

"I love you, too." He replied.

I watched as he reversed through the gate of our backyard. As he reached the edge, he turned back, pursed his lips, and blew me an air kiss, then winked. "Lock the gate. I'll wait until I see you safely inside," he called out, his protective nature evident even in broad daylight. Smiling at him, feeling his love, I secured the gate and headed back into the house.

Before closing the back door, I stole a glance to see Logan still there, his warm smile a comforting sight. We exchanged one last wave before he drove off, leaving me with a mixture of emotions.

The day drifted by in its usual rhythm. Keith was at school, often staying late for rehearsals for the school play or academic clubs, and I knew I wouldn't see him until much later. The quietness of the house was amplified by their absence.

Around a quarter past one, still immersed in my work, Logan's call broke the silence. The familiar hum of the road in the background indicated his ongoing trip up north toward Hinckley. "I'm still en route, Baby," he reassured, knowing I often worry about his well-being.

"We just left Frank's place. My car's parked there, and we're cruising in his pickup truck since he's towing the camper. Plenty of room for both of us," he explained.

I told him I was happy to hear from him and wished him a wonderful and safe trip. I thanked him for checking in, and as always, before ending the call, "I love you," bridged the physical distance between us.

It was 8:35 pm when Logan called to check in, and a grateful smile spread across my face as I answered.

"We made it here just before 3:00 and got our deer stands set up. Now we're back at the campsite, enjoying the campfire before turning in for the night," Logan's deep, comforting voice resonated through the phone.

I shared that I had been tracking his progress on the map app, noting each of his locations: the campsite, his arrival time, the trail to his deer stand, the exact spot where he set it up, and how long he stayed there before returning to the campsite. Logan appreciated my thoroughness and then asked about my day and Keith's. I told him it was the usual, just very quiet and long without him.

"How's my boy?" he inquired. I assured him that Sabre was doing well, adding a comforting detail to our conversation.

As we continued our call, a new voice filtered through the background, distinct and unfamiliar. Curious, I asked Logan, "I thought it was just you and Frank? If you're talking to me, who's talking to Frank?"

Logan explained that Frank's brother, Dan, had spontaneously decided to join them for the night but wasn't there for the hunt. He had just arrived a few hours ago to hang out with them and would be leaving in the morning.

"That's good," I remarked, then added, "Safer by the number." As we ended our call, we exchanged the usual, "I love you," and "good night."

The next day unfolded with my usual routine of tracking Logan's locations.[38] Each blink of the blue dot on the map app felt like a small connection, a virtual tether to where he was. It brought a quiet comfort, a semblance of presence even in his absence. His experience in that forest two decades ago lingered in my mind, and I did not want him to go through that again.

That morning, I had an appointment with Dr. Laura. My shoulder had been bothering me for nearly a year, but it was only a month ago that I started seeing her because the pain had become so severe that I couldn't dress or bathe myself. Even the simplest tasks with my left arm caused excruciating pain, like a knife being jabbed into the socket of my shoulder with each slight movement. Despite undergoing several treatments and therapies, nothing was working. Finally, she said, "It appears that you have a torn rotator cuff. The only thing I can do for you is refer you to a specialist."

I didn't like the sound of that but agreed, responding, "Logan is on a hunting trip right now. When he gets back, we'll go together."

She smiled, nodded, and said, "Okay. I'll send your referral over to the specialist, and they'll reach out to you to schedule an appointment."

By 8:30 p.m., I was eagerly anticipating Logan's check-in call, but the phone remained silent. The evening felt too quiet, so I tried keeping myself busy by cleaning the living room, yet there was no word from him. Checking his location, I saw he was still stationed by his deer stand. Assuming he was engrossed in his hunt, I remained patient.

As 9:30 p.m. approached, a sense of unease crept in. Logan's absence from checking in was unusual. Throughout our years together, his calls had been a constant, a reassuring presence even in mundane moments. His thoughtfulness always shone through, whether I was away for a short errand or out for the day. His simple check-in calls, filled with warmth and concern, showed how much he cared about me. What

---

[38] Wednesday, September 27, 2023

someone might find a nuisance, I appreciated because it was a level of consideration and care I had not experienced before.

Feeling a growing concern, I refreshed Logan's location and saw that he had returned to the campsite. This eased my worry slightly, but the absence of his call nagged at my thoughts. I decided to dial his number, but it rang unanswered.

He must have caught something, I reassured myself, imagining him engrossed in cleaning and preparing whatever game he had hunted. *I'll give him a few more minutes,* I told myself, trying to quell the rising unease.

By 10:00 p.m., with still no call or text, anxiety settled in. I dialed again, only to be met with his voicemail. His location remained fixed at the campsite.

At 10:30 p.m., I made one last attempt to reach him, the phone ringing fruitlessly once more. Frustrated and worried, I resorted to sending a text: "Are you asleep yet?"

Minutes ticked by, each one stretching into an eternity of silence. With no reply, I texted another message: "You're probably asleep now. I hope you had a wonderful day. I miss you. I love you.[39]"

As the clock neared 11:30 p.m., still shrouded in silence, I reluctantly set the phone aside and settled to sit on my bed, restlessness settling over me like a heavy blanket. Unable to shake off the worry, I busied my hands in crocheting his scarf, hoping that the rhythmic motion would be a soothing balm to my troubled mind.

Just then, my phone rang. I felt a second of relief thinking it was him, but when I glanced at the screen, it was Val's name. *Why would Logan's sister call me this late?* I thought. She never calls me this late, especially not when her phone is typically set to "Do Not Disturb" around

---

[39] Text message was timestamped at 10:52 p.m.

this time.

My mind raced with possibilities, jumping to the worst-case scenario: *something must be wrong with Logan's mom*, and the timing couldn't be any worse because Logan is at least two hours away. His mom was older than my parents, and her health had been a concern lately.

Answering the call with a sense of urgency, I braced myself for the news. "Where are you?" Val's voice carried an edge of concern. Confusion set in as I assured her I was at home. "You're not with Logan?" she asked.

Upon hearing Logan's name, the flags in my head immediately went up, waving at high alert. Trying not to think too far ahead, I composed myself and answered, "No. He went hunting." I could feel my nerves suddenly surging, especially since I hadn't heard from him.

I then sensed an instant drop in Val's voice as she said, "Oh no. You don't even know."

Then came the words that shattered my world.

"The police just stopped by," Val's voice faltered, delivering the devastating blow. Apparently, Logan's address was still registered to their house in the system.

The weight of her words hit me like a ton of bricks, and my heart sank to the pit of my stomach. The arrival of a police officer at your doorstep is never a harbinger of good news.

With trembling hands and a tightening in my chest, I listened as Val continued, her words forming a blur of disbelief and despair. "The police said Logan passed away."

My place in this world immediately became disoriented around me as I struggled to process her words. "No... no... that's impossible," I struggled to get the words out, the denial thick in my throat. "He's away on his hunting trip, that's all," I explained, almost pleading with reality to align with my desperate hopes.

The solidity of Logan, my rock, I refused to let it crumble in an instant, and I clung to the belief that he was invincible, that this had to be a mistake. But as Val's words sank in, reality crashed over me like a tidal wave, drowning me in its violent reign. I crumbled, tears streaming down my face as the weight of it all engulfed me.

Desperate to know what happened, I asked Val, only to be met with confusion because she didn't know either. The police had only informed her, offering no further details. She expressed hope that when she called, I would be with Logan, as we were always together. It was a rarity to find Logan without me or me without Logan.

I inquired if the police had left any contact information for updates or any details at all. Val managed to provide me with a number left by the officers, which belonged to the lead investigator at the scene. She explained that they were still actively conducting their investigation. Moreover, due to the area's poor service coverage, we would have to wait until the officer was closer to town before expecting any substantial updates.

We ended the call, and I dialed the lead investigator's number without a second's delay, desperate for any information. Every fiber of my being was trembling as I pressed the phone to my ear, the ringing echoing in my mind, stretching on as I waited, hoping for a response on the other end. Denial tugged at one side of my consciousness, while urgency fueled the other, propelling me on a desperate quest for the truth.

Miraculously, someone picked up on the other end—it was the lead investigator. I introduced myself as Logan's wife and conveyed that I had been informed of the gravity of the situation. I needed to know what was going on. He expressed his condolences, but I did not want to hear it. Despite his reluctance to divulge details, he promised to keep me informed as the investigation progressed.

Refusing to end the call empty-handed, I asked, "Can I ask you just one more thing?" With a hesitant agreement from the investigator, he responded, "I will do my best to answer." I pressed on, needing to know the exact time of my husband's passing. His response, "About 7:30 p.m., ma'am," hit me like a sledgehammer.

The reality of the situation crashed down with each passing second as countless scenarios ran through my mind about how this could possibly have happened and how I had not known. I had been anxiously awaiting Logan's call all evening. It was unlike him not to reach out, and that fact alone should have been enough for me to realize something serious had happened. For more than a week, I had sensed something was off about him venturing into that forest. Why had I allowed him to go? Why hadn't I heeded my instincts? Countless questions raced through my mind, each one a dagger of regret.

In a desperate attempt to ground myself in reality, I summoned the courage to initiate a group video call with all three of my daughters. Through tear-filled eyes and a trembling voice, I delivered the devastating news. It was the first time they witnessed my unraveling to such depths, my pain laid bare before them like never before. In a state of disbelief and heartbreak, they wept alongside me over the phone.

Besides their father, Logan had become the only other father figure they knew after my divorce. They cherished him deeply for the incredible ways he had breathed new life into me, and Logan reciprocated that love by treating all my children as his own. My daughters echoed my questions, each of us grasping for answers in our shared confusion and disbelief.

Suddenly, a realization hit me like a lightning bolt—Frank! He had been there with Logan; surely, he knew what had transpired. I swiftly informed my daughters that I would call them back and ended the call. However, I realized I didn't have Frank's number.

Frank was Logan's old friend, but we had never been formally introduced. It wasn't until a couple of weeks before Logan's trip that

Frank appeared, involved in a remodeling project they were collaborating on. I had only glimpsed Frank from my office window as he and Logan were busy loading and unloading tools into Logan's work van before heading out to the job site. My knowledge of Frank was limited to what I had heard from Logan's anecdotes, but Logan's trust in people was very selective. He wouldn't have included Frank on this hunting trip if there wasn't a significant amount of trust between them.

Frantically searching for a lifeline of information, I remembered they were connected on Facebook. With trembling fingers, I logged into Logan's Facebook Messenger and called Frank through the app. It was just after 2:00 a.m., and my heart pounded with anxiety and anticipation, unsure if Frank would answer. When he picked up, a wave of relief momentarily washed over me, but it was quickly replaced by disappointment and anger as a thought crossed my mind: "How is it that I can hear your voice but not my husband's?"

Then I reminded myself that, regardless of how I was feeling at that moment, I needed answers. I composed myself and listened. In the background, I could discern the familiar sounds of travel on the road, and I imagined he was returning from the hunting area. Without delay, I introduced myself as Logan's wife, urgency tinging my tone as I sought the answers that had eluded me.

He apologized repeatedly as he recounted the details of what had happened to the best of his memory. Ignoring his apologies, I focused solely on extracting the facts. I made it clear that I did not want him to skim over anything. Closing my eyes, I meticulously filtered through every word and description, painting vivid mental images of each scene as it unfolded.

It was as though decades of practice and conditioning, gained from working under intense pressure in highly regulated environments to untangle chaos across countless projects, were now at the forefront, and my husband was depending on me not to get it wrong. I approached the situation with a critical eye, carefully piecing together every fragment to form a coherent whole, while desperately trying to hold back my tears.

In the aftermath of the call, the grim truth unfolded, and I took only the facts:

- Logan had been shot.
- Old revolver – no safety.
- Gun dropped while Logan was handling his gears.
- Gun struck the ground releasing cocked hammer.
- Fatal shot.
- Impact was swift - Logan drop on impact.
- No pulse when emergency responders arrived.

CHAPTER 26

IN DREAMS

*I*T WAS SUPPOSED TO BE ONLY A FEW DAYS, and now my husband will never be coming home. Just yesterday morning, I held him in my arms, and now he's gone. Frank had no more useful information to offer. He reached the point where he could only keep apologizing for not being able to do anything. I realized that no matter what he said, it wouldn't be what I desperately wanted to hear—that this was all a terrible mistake, and Logan was safe and on his way back home to me.

It was now the middle of the night. Stepping into my office, darkness surrounded me, broken only by the faint glow of string lights from the neighboring yard. With trembling hands, I lit a tall white candle for Logan and placed it on the windowsill. The flickering flame served as a silent witness to my sorrow and despair, and as a beacon of hope to guide Logan home. He took his last breath in that forest, and I couldn't bear the thought of him remaining lost there, as he had twenty years ago. Tears streamed down my cheeks as I whispered a silent prayer, urging him to come home, to follow his compass, to head north. For I will always be his North, waiting for him.

My heart weighed heavy with the burden of an uncertain future, one that I no longer wanted to face because my person, my Logan, would not be in it.

I had spent the entire night immersed in tears, my mind engulfed in a thick fog of despair, and my heart felt like it was beating just enough to barely keep me alive. The moment I learned of Logan's passing, it felt as if a brick had lodged itself in my heart, making every breath difficult. Sleep was a distant echo amid the turbulent emotions swirling within me.

As the first light of dawn began to creep over the horizon, while the sky was still cloaked in darkness, I called Shye. I didn't know who else to turn to so early in the morning and was relieved to hear her pick up. "Logan passed away," I said, struggling to find the words. Shye and Logan had known each other since childhood. Their families had been part of the same church community for years. She had become an integral part of my life ever since I was introduced to her during our inaugural event four and a half years ago.

As soon as the weight of my words reached her ears, Shye didn't hesitate to inquire about details. Her response was immediate and resolute. "I'll be right over." Within minutes, her car pulled up in front of our house. As soon as I opened the door, Shye wrapped her arms around me. I let out a deep, soulful cry, as if I had been holding back that one cathartic release all night long. We sat down on the enclosed porch, Shye patiently waiting for me to regain my composure as I struggled to steady my breath.

Just as I began recounting the events to Shye, another car

pulled up and parked in front of the house. It was Jessica. She stepped out of the car and walked towards the porch. I hadn't informed anyone other than my daughters and Shye, and I wondered how she had come to know.

Jessica walked through the porch door and reached for me with a compassionate embrace. Through my tears, I managed to ask, "How did you know?"

She replied, "Val told me to check in on you and filled me in a little about what happened." Gratitude swelled within me for Val's thoughtfulness, even amid her own grief. I leaned into Jessica's embrace, finding strength in the support of those who cared for Logan and me.

I continued to cry, overwhelmed by the immense love Logan and I shared and the profound weight of our loss. We had lived each day fully, sharing everything and never leaving any words unsaid. There were no regrets, no "I should have said this or that." We knew the depth of our love for each other and only longed for more—more time together, more memories to create.

After Shye and Jessica left, I faced the daunting task of breaking the news to Keith. Unsure whether sitting him down would help, I approached his room and did my best to gently tell him that Logan had passed away. From the time he was old enough to talk, Keith had never shown tears to anyone, not even when his grandma passed. He had always been a happy kid, mature in how he processed his emotions. But upon hearing about Logan, he wept, revealing a depth of emotion I hadn't seen before.

Meanwhile, my daughter Charlotte and son-in-law Kenneth had relocated to Wisconsin at the beginning of summer. They wasted no time, arriving at my house just before noon. On the same day, my twins from Colorado boarded the earliest flight they could find, landing at our doorstep by evening. Logan's love for all my children was profound, and in their eyes, they had lost a father figure. Despite his non-biological status and the relatively short time he had been in their lives, his impact was deeply felt.

The following days blurred together, and sleep remained elusive as my thoughts were consumed by the longing to see my husband. Every time someone referred to him as "his body," it felt like a blade slicing through my heart. To help ease my restless nights, Shye sought out remedies. Knowing my fragile state, she was concerned I might rely too heavily on sleep aids to cope, so she opted for natural alternatives—gentle yet effective in their calming effects.

Logan passed away on Wednesday night, and by Friday, I still hadn't seen him. The coroner's office explained that their facility didn't allow visitors. In order for me to see him, I had to arrange for the funeral home to transfer him to their morgue. The words— funeral, morgue, coroner's office, body—swirled in my mind, challenging my comprehension.

Every step I took was instinctual, driven by an innate need to ensure my husband's dignity, to make sure he wasn't just left in a freezer without respect. Shye, a close friend of a funeral director, often provided funeral draping services and floral arrangements for his clients. She quickly reached out to him, and together we made arrangements for Logan's transfer. However, the earliest I could see him would be on Monday.

My heart sank with each passing moment, praying fervently for his well-being. I clung to the hope that he couldn't truly be gone, while my mind struggled to accept the harsh reality and make sense of it all. I constantly reminded myself, "Stay strong. Keep your mind clear. Logan still needs you."

I informed my relatives the day before about my devastating loss, only to be met with the reaction I had feared. Because Logan and I had not been married in a traditional Hmong wedding ceremony, our legal marriage was considered irrelevant according to Hmong cultural norms, deeming us merely engaged or unmarried.

My dad lamented that, in the absence of a cultural marriage, there were no familial ties between my side and Logan's. Therefore, my family was considered outsiders to the circumstances of Logan's funeral and wouldn't even have a place at the proverbial table to discuss it, as it was the sole responsibility of his family and relatives.

Adhering strictly to these cultural beliefs, my parents forbade me from making any contributions to my husband's funeral, except for just being there, adding another layer of heartbreak to my already overwhelming grief.

I shed tears but collected my emotions and said, "He is my husband, whether they consider our marriage valid or not. I intend to give my husband a proper funeral worthy of his honor, even if I have to do it alone."

Friday afternoon,[40] I was asked to go over to Logan's brother Steve's house to discuss the aftermath and plans for his funeral. Surrounded by his family, I was physically present, but my mind drifted, and the conversation seemed distant. Everything felt

---

[40] September 29, 2023

surreal, and I couldn't shake the overwhelming sense of disbelief. Every part of me fought hard, denying that we were here in this moment to talk about my husband's death and funeral. Tears welled up constantly, unable to contain the weight of this new reality that I desperately wished to escape.

Being there without support from the elders on my side of the family, I anticipated that his relatives would voice the same objections about our marriage. Nevertheless, I was determined to do everything in my capacity as his wife. As expected, Logan's relatives shared the same consensus. However, I hoped for more hands-on support from them in planning and arranging his funeral and was ready to shoulder all the funeral expenses.

As we started discussing the funeral arrangements, his brother reluctantly revealed that he had an insurance policy for Logan. This was news to me, as Logan and I had discussed all our finances when we got married, and neither of us knew such a policy existed. Hearing this brought me brief comfort, which quickly dissipated when his brother said, "As Logan's legal wife, it is your responsibility to take care of all the financial expenses. Go ask anyone."

As I sat there and listened to what was coming from his mouth, I felt an intense emotion of anger emanating from my right. I couldn't help but turn my attention to look, only to see that there was nothing visibly there. But in my mind's eye, I could see my husband standing next to me, emotionally enraged and in pain, eyes glistening, pointing directly at his brother, yelling at the top of his lungs, "In my entire life, you never gave me anything. You were supposed to be my big brother. Instead, you kicked me out of your home when I was old enough. You're the only one with an insurance policy on my life that I did not even know about. Now that I'm dead, you're making my wife pay for everything when we were just starting out our life together?"

I continued to stare at the empty space, unsure what to make of why I was feeling his emotions so intensely. My heart was hurting for him. I did not want him to feel this way. A silent rage began to brew inside me. He was my entire sky, my person, and my home. No amount of money in the world could ever replace the irreplaceable person he was to me. I desperately needed both sides of the family to understand that we had lost a very important person.

I refused to let my husband's memory be tainted by bitter bickering over money, so I met his gaze and said, "I am not questioning you about your money; I am questioning you about your love for your brother." My words hung in the air, heavy with emotion. Reluctantly, he agreed to help, but his assistance would be minimal, despite the substantial sum he would receive from my husband's death.

I thanked him for his contribution. Turning to Logan's mom, composed myself, and gathered my courage to tell her, "Whether I was married to your son for a day or fifty years, whether our wedding was recognized legally in the eyes of the law or culturally within our families, he is my husband through and through because I married him in front of God, a handful of good friends, and our children. As his wife, I will honor him no less."

With that said, and without hesitation, I informed his family that I will shoulder the bulk of his funeral expenses because just as his dreams were my dreams, and his hopes were my hopes, his loss was my greatest loss of all, and my marriage to him was not conditional on a wedding. It was because I love him more than my own life.

By Saturday night, I was mentally and emotionally drained. In the four days since Logan's passing, tears had been a constant companion, with sleep eluding me, giving me no more than a few hours. My body seemed to crash out of sheer exhaustion, only to jolt awake at the slightest sound, plunging me back into the relentless battle against reality and succumbing to tears.

Understanding my body's desperate need for rest, I turned to the sleep aid Shye had provided. For the first time in days, I drifted off into a deep slumber. I had been sleeping on Logan's side of the bed ever since he left for his trip. Due to my shoulder pain, I had been curling up to sleep only on my right side for about a year now, facing away from the door and the edge of the bed.

That night, somewhere between sleep and wakefulness, I felt a gentle warm pressure on my shoulder, filling me with a sense of love and comfort I hadn't felt in days. Uncertain if I was dreaming or awake, thoughts of Logan flooded my mind, and I heard his voice in an ethereal whisper, "I'm going to take it away. You have a heavy journey ahead of you, and this is one less thing to suffer because I'm not there to help." I then felt a warm kiss on my cheek, and I let out a soft whisper, "I love you, Logan," and drifted back into sleep.

The next morning, as I gradually awoke from my slumber, the familiar rush of emptiness washed over me, just as it had every single day since Logan passed. No matter the length of my sleep, the routine of loss weighed heavily, and I couldn't fathom how I would endure this for the rest of my life. An ocean of tears was released as I remained in bed, consumed by grief.

Amidst my tears, memories of my dream resurfaced. *Was it merely a dream?* I wondered, the experience feeling incredibly real. But reality swiftly intruded—Logan wasn't here. I was still me, without him. I rose from bed to immerse myself in a hot shower, hoping to wash away both the tiredness and the harsh reality. Tears continued to stream and mingled with the hot water, a silent testament to my pain.

Logan's smiling face materialized before me every time I closed my eyes. It was agonizing yet comforting. His face was the only one I yearned to see, and I couldn't bear to open my eyes unless he appeared before me. The stark reality of never seeing his beautiful face and my favorite smile again weighed heavily on me, crushing my heart with a physical pain that seemed impossible to endure.

I wanted to cry out in rage and hurl myself into whatever wreckage was within reach, but I barely had the strength. Anger seethed within me, directed at God and every circumstance that had led to this moment, robbing Logan and me of the happiness we had so beautifully built together. I stayed in the shower, crying for as long as I could, until the water began to turn cold.

I knew I needed to compose myself. Logan's gentle voice echoed in my head, "Get it together, Baby. I know it hurts, but you have to get it together." Hearing his words made me want to cry even more, but for Logan, I had to hold it together.

In moments when the tears were too much and my head began to ache, I would hear Logan's voice, "Don't cry, I'm still here," a gentle yet firm plea for me to hold back the tears.

Somehow, his voice, even if it was just in my imagination, brought a sense of warmth and calmness over me. I could feel it in my heart and around my neck, steadying my breathing and quelling my tears.

I rummaged through my closet and dresser, still wrapped in my bath towel, trying to find something to wear. Each breath felt heavy and laborious, weighed down by grief. Logan's soft voice echoed in my mind once more, "I'm sorry, Baby. I made a mistake," he said. Hearing those words filled me with an immense sorrow that seemed apart from my own. I wondered if it was only because I was grieving. I had never grieved this deeply before, having never lost someone I loved so much.

I then began a mental dialogue with Logan, "Don't be sorry. You have nothing to apologize for. I'm not hurt by you; I'm hurt by the circumstances, by whatever force took you from me. It wasn't your doing because I know you would never choose to leave me." My heart and soul ached for him. I allowed myself to immerse in that feeling for a moment before collecting my thoughts and telling myself, *Steph, you're grieving. You're just grieving. You're not really hearing Logan. He is gone.*

I collapsed on the floor of my bedroom, tears streaming down my face in an uncontrollable wave of sorrow. I cried until the tears subsided, then forced myself to get dressed. Making my way downstairs, I waited silently in the living room for Keith, who was still getting ready. It was our Saturday morning routine to gather groceries for the week ahead, a routine that often included Logan. Despite my lack of appetite, I tried to focus on ensuring Keith had what he needed.

"I'm ready, Mom," Keith's voice echoed through the quiet

house as he descended the stairs. I met his gaze with a faint smile, masking the heaviness weighing on my heart. Keeping our routines as normal as possible was my attempt to shield him from his own grief and from witnessing my breakdowns. I tried to only fall apart when I was alone in the sanctuary of the bedroom Logan and I had shared.

Keith smiled back. He could see the tiredness in my eyes and asked if I was okay. It was a simple question, but I didn't know how to answer. I knew I was not okay, but I didn't want him to worry, so I shrugged and said yes.

On the way to the store, Keith asked curiously, "Mom, were you on the phone last night?"

I glanced at Keith and said, "I talked to your sisters but knocked out early," recalling that I had taken some sleep aid. Keith was quiet for a moment, then asked again, "Are you sure you weren't talking to anyone really late?"

With my hands on the wheel and focused on the road, I said, "Only your sisters," feeling a little unsure why he would ask again. It's not like him to question me twice.

As we pulled up to the store, I shifted the car into park and looked over at Keith. He wore an expression that suggested he had something on his mind but wasn't sure how to voice it. "Is everything okay?" I asked, sensing his unease.

"Yeah, everything is okay," Keith replied hesitantly. I left it alone.

We got out of the car and went into the store to do our grocery run. On the way out, as we were walking towards the car, Keith spoke up. "I kept asking you if you were talking to someone because last night, around 3:00 a.m., I woke up to use the bathroom. I was wide awake when I walked past your room and heard voices coming from inside. At first, I thought you were on the phone because who else could be talking at that hour?"

My curiosity piqued, and I tilted my head slightly towards Keith, as if that would help me hear better. "That's very strange. I wasn't talking to anyone. What did you hear?" I asked.

Keith hesitated before cautiously saying, "I heard Logan talking."

I raised my brows, but surprisingly, I remained calm, which was unusual given the significance of what Keith was sharing. "Are you sure?" I questioned, trying to fully grasp the meaning of his words.

"Yeah, I know Logan's voice. I've heard you both talking numerous times from behind your closed door. I couldn't mistake it, and I know he's gone," Keith asserted confidently. "The other strange thing was, you were talking to him too. That's why I thought you might have been on the phone."

I sat back, digesting Keith's words. The idea of hearing Logan's voice again, even if it was just a figment of our imagination, stirred up a mixture of emotions within me. I instantly recalled my dream, remembering what Logan had said about taking away my shoulder pain. Just then, I cautiously rotated my shoulder. There was no pain. I realized that this morning, in the shower and while getting dressed, I was not in pain. I had been so consumed by my grief that I hadn't even noticed the absence of my shoulder pain. It was as if it had miraculously disappeared.

No, that's impossible, I thought to myself. *I must be in shock.*

My body is still in shock because I lost the love of my life, I tried to convinced myself.

I didn't tell Keith about my experience, but I said, "It's very interesting what you heard. I don't know how to explain it and I don't know what to say."

CHAPTER 27

THE LONGEST DAY

ONDAY MORNING FELT LIKE AN ETERNITY TO GET HERE.[41] We were scheduled to see Logan for the first time since the incident. I had no idea how I would react upon seeing him, only that I needed to be by his side.

His brothers, Scott and Steve, accompanied me as we met at the morgue. Stepping out of the car and approaching the building, my body trembled. I struggled to maintain my composure while grappling with this harsh reality. I wasn't prepared to see Logan in this state, and I knew deep down that I never would be, but I had to see him. Perhaps seeing him would convince me that this was the new reality. I needed to know that he was being treated with dignity.

Every step felt like wading through thick fog, my legs heavy with dread. The world seemed to slow down, each moment stretching into an eternity as we neared the entrance. The cold, sterile environment of the

---

[41] October 2, 2023 at 10:30 a.m.

morgue was a stark contrast to the warmth and vibrancy that Logan always exuded. The thought of him lying there, lifeless, was a reality I struggled with and did not want to accept.

The mortician greeted us at the front door and led us to a set of double doors. Scott and Steve stood behind me. As the doors opened, I immediately saw Logan—his legs positioned away from us, a white sheet covering him from the neck down. The moment I caught sight of his hair, I knew it was him, and my whole world crumbled once more. There was no waking up from this; it was the brutal truth. In that moment, it was real, and my entire world lay on that cold metal table.

As I approached him, it felt like the room stretched further away with each step, making the journey to his side seem endless. Nevertheless, I didn't stop; my tears flowed freely, each one marking the intense, raw pain coursing through me. When I finally reached him, I instinctively rested my head on his shoulder, letting my tears fall onto him.

"I am so sorry, my love," I whispered to him softly. "I am so sorry I couldn't save you." With my head resting on his shoulder, eyes closed, I reached up and gently laid my palm against his cheek. Every night from the start of our life together until the day he left for his trip, we would settle into bed for sleep. I nestled my head against his chest, listening intently to the steady rhythm of his heartbeat, while my hand rested on his cheek to feel his warmth. This ritual always filled me with a profound sense of completeness, affirming that my life was whole with him by my side. His heart's gentle rhythm would soothe me into sleep, safe in his embrace.

But this time, there was no heartbeat, no warmth, and no comforting embrace to assure me that everything would be okay. My entire world had become lifeless and dark, and I didn't know how—or if—I wanted to continue in this new reality where Logan wasn't a part of it.

After a moment, I raised my head from his shoulder to look at his face, the face I had loved so dearly and that had been so full of life just a week ago. I traced the lines of his face with my eyes, remembering every smile and every expression that had ever played across his features. Overcome with longing, I wished for the impossible—to return to the day before everything changed.

Circling to where his head rested, I ran my fingers through his hair, tears streaming endlessly. Placing my hands on either side of his face, I rested my forehead against his and whispered a silent prayer. I spoke to him about the candle I had kept lit since his passing, a small flame burning steadily in my office window. It serves as a beacon of light, hope, and love, guiding him home. Each time the candle burned low, I replaced it with a new one, never allowing the flame to die, and I promised to keep it lit until he was home. I asked God to watch over him and keep him safe. When I finished, I placed a tender kiss his head, letting him know that my love is greater than my pain.

His brothers spoke with the mortician, hoping for any insight into how Logan was shot. However, the mortician, bound by the ongoing investigation, was unable to share any details about Logan's passing. I quietly inquired about when his report would be ready but received a vague estimate of a week. My heart was heavy as I glanced one last time at Logan, wishing he could speak to me, even though I knew the cruel reality that he never would again. I didn't want to leave, but I had to force myself to. The weight of leaving without him was unbearable.

Sitting in my car, the world felt distant and detached, mirroring the numbness in my soul. I tried to make sense of everything, but this moment was so permanent. There was no room to negotiate or create a different outcome. It just was, and it was nothing I wanted. I felt lost.

I pulled out of the parking lot and headed home, my eyes dazedly fixed on the road as I drove on autopilot. The music playing softly in the background was nothing but a hollow echo, lost in the vastness of my grief. I had hoped that seeing Logan would somehow make his absence real, but the ache in my heart persisted, refusing to be soothed by mere sight.

I pulled up in front of my house and shifted into park. At that very moment, "You Are the Reason" by Calum Scott began to play. It was Logan's ringtone, but this rendition of the song was new to me—an acoustic version that filled the car with a slow, melancholic tune, instantly piercing through my heart and shattering it even more on impact. Tears flowed freely as I listened, a gut-wrenching cry escaping my lips—a raw expression of the sorrow that consumed me. I cried harder than I ever had before in my life, as if I were dying in that moment.

Then, amidst my anguish, I heard Logan's voice—a soft ethereal whisper in my mind. "I didn't want you to see that. Please don't cry. I'm still here," he said. His words seeped through the darkness, deepening my sorrow. Instinctively, I looked over to the passenger seat, feeling an intense presence as if he were there—an invisible aura of warmth trying to comfort my pain. Yet, I told myself it was impossible. He wasn't there, and I was left alone in a world that felt infinitely dark and cold without him.

I clung to the steering wheel, finding only emptiness. The song continued, each verse a painful reminder of what we had, the years together that were now no more, and his beautiful smiling face I can no longer touch. If my heart could stop beating, this would be the moment, as I'm weighed down by an unbearable sorrow threatening to consume me whole.

When the song finally ended, I forced myself to pull it together, wiped my tears, but the ache in my chest remained—a constant reminder of the void left by Logan's absence.

As I stepped inside the house, my phone rang, the caller ID flashing the name of the Orthopedic Shoulder Specialist office. A young woman's voice came through, explaining they had received a referral from my doctor and wished to schedule an exam. I had completely forgotten about the referral and was taken by surprise. I raised my left arm, cautiously rotating my shoulder—no evidence of pain.

"I actually don't need it anymore," I said, my voice laced with uncertainty, puzzled by the sudden change.

"Thank you for letting us know. I will inform the doctor," she replied before we ended the call.

After hanging up, I raised my left arm again, extending it freely. It was a surreal moment. Just a week prior, dressing myself was almost impossible; the pain in my shoulder was unbearable. Now, it was as though that agony had never existed, leaving me both amazed and bewildered.

The logical and analytical part of me delved deep into dissecting the events that might explain why my shoulder no longer ached after Logan's passing. Was it simply the numbing effect of the traumatic shock from losing my husband, as suggested by the haunting memory of Val's call? Or could it be something more ethereal, like that night when I dreamt of Logan by my side? It felt too vivid, too real to be just a dream. Not to mention, how Keith heard Logan's voice from our bedroom that same night too.

I couldn't help but wonder, *was Logan really there? Did he truly take my pain away as he said he would? I know his love for me is undeniable, but could this transcend into something miraculous?*

These questions lingered in my mind, weaving a tapestry of hope and uncertainty. With no definitive answer, I decided to put the thought to rest and reassured myself, *let's give it some time and observe if the pain returns.*

It was Wednesday,[42] a week since Logan had passed. Despite my initial decision to wait for his siblings to choose his final resting place together, the days since seeing him had altered my perspective. A part of me had died alongside him, and I realized that, like him, no matter how much I longed for that part of me back, it was impossible. I resolved to secure a double grave, marking a final act toward finding peace for both of us—a choice steeped in personal significance and intimacy. It was a decision I needed to make autonomously, free from the need for approval or external opinions.

I recall driving past Roselawn Cemetery several times since my move to Minnesota. It always struck me as a serene place with park-like features, filled with trees, lush foliage, and an array of colorful flowers. Every time I glanced at that cemetery and saw the name "Roselawn," a sense of gentle peace washed over me, like falling asleep to the soothing sound of a soft warm breeze. So, when I was searching for a final resting place, Roselawn Cemetery was the only location that came to mind.

I arrived at the cemetery and parked my car in front of the office. Stepping inside, I struggled to hold back tears, taking a deep breath to steady my nerves and contain my emotions. However, the moment the cemetery director approached, her comforting and sympathetic voice broke through, "How can I help you?" Tears welled up in my eyes as I replied with a huge lump in my throat, "I'm here to find a double grave."

She kindly smiled, understanding the emotions I was trying hard to conceal. Retrieving a map of the entire area from her desk, she went over the significance of each lot. I looked over the map carefully and my eyes rested on an area closer to the backwoods, away from the noise of the street.

We drove out to the area together so I could see it for myself. Stepping out of the car, I strolled along the lawn lined with marble

---

[42] October 4, 2023

headstones, taking my time to absorb the surroundings. Though the sky was slightly overcast, I knew the area would be bathed in sunlight whenever the clouds parted, something I knew Logan would appreciate.

I walked until I came to a spot that resonated with me. Standing there, I took in the panoramic view from all directions. It sat atop a slope, offering a clear view of the trees lining the edge of the forest to the north. Our headstones would face east, where the slope descended toward more trees in the distance. I imagined a brilliant sunrise greeting me and Logan every morning.

As I gazed in the direction of the sunrise, I closed my eyes for a moment and a gentle breeze caressed my face. I released a peaceful sigh, knowing in my soul that this place, this spot, was exactly the place I had been searching for. The cemetery Director marked the location of the double grave on her map, and we headed back to the office.

She asked me to take a seat in her office and handed me a catalog filled with headstones of all sizes, shapes, designs, and materials. Initially, I had planned not to engrave my name on the headstone until after I passed, leaving the task for my children. All my life, I had feared seeing my name on a headstone. However, since Logan's passing, I no longer feared death.

As I sat in that solemn office, sifting through the catalog, the thought of seeing only Logan's name etched in stone felt profoundly melancholic and lonely. A wave of loneliness washed over me, and I couldn't bear the idea of his name standing alone. He had been alone his whole life, and my love for him couldn't let him feel alone in his final resting place too. I decided to have my name and date of birth engraved as well, reserving only the date of my passing for a later time. It was my silent promise that I didn't marry him until death do us part—I married him until my heart beats for the last time.

I chose a large headstone with two tall black marble slabs standing side by side, joined by a heart-shaped, lighter-shaded marble piece where we could place our photo. The photo I chose was one we took on our wedding day just a year ago. Each slab would have our names engraved, adorned by two doves symbolic of peace and love. The slabs would sit on a base that is four feet wide with two tiers. On the second tier, I had the engravings done:

> Meet me **where the end begins**, in echoes,
> Where your world is me, and my world is you.

As I completed the form for the headstone, I decided to text my daughters to let them know that I was at the cemetery and had chosen to have my name engraved on the headstone too. Just as I opened the Messages app, I saw three dots hovering over Logan's message avatar, as if he were composing a text message to me in real-time. Since the time we had been together, I had pinned his message avatar to the top of my screen. Seeing those dots, knowing that Logan was no longer here and that his phone's battery had been completely drained for five days, I couldn't believe it. *How was it possible that he was trying to send me a message?*

I quickly took a screenshot to ensure I wasn't imagining things,[43] then I waited eagerly to see what message would come through, my heart racing. Just then, I heard Logan's voice in a soft echo, "Don't engrave your name. By doing that, it's like you're sentencing yourself to a life of loneliness, and I don't want that for you. I want you to carry on with your life and be happy." My heart sank.

Immediately, I thought, *Am I wrong for doing this? Is Logan disappointed by my decision?* As soon as those questions sank in, I silently snapped back at Logan, "No. This is my decision. I've decided, and you don't get to tell me this anymore because you're not here."

---

[43] Screenshot was saved at 12:10 p.m. on Wednesday, October 4, 2023.

As soon as I said that, a sense of calmness washed over me, and I heard Logan's voice again, "You're stubborn, but that's why I love you." I continued to stare at my phone's screen, waiting for a message, but then the dots disappeared, and no message ever came through.

Was someone messing with his phone? It's still in the possession of the investigator. I've continued tracking his phone since he passed because seeing him on the map made me feel like he was still here. The last data I had showed that it turned off on Friday after the battery ran out.

"Perhaps the investigator is looking into his phone for evidence," I thought. "That has to be it," I assured myself. The voice I'm hearing must just be a normal part of grieving.

My friends Shye and Jessica organized a candlelight vigil for Logan on the rooftop of Lou's apartment complex. [44] It was a spot that overlooked a serene view of the lake below—a place Logan and I had frequented, drawn to its ambiance and the warmth of gatherings around the fire pit. For the vigil, Charlotte took on the role of photographer, capturing the poignant moments of the evening. We invited our closest friends to join us, each bringing a piece of Logan's life through their memories.

As the evening unfolded, we enjoyed food and drinks while subtle laughter and soft conversations mingled with tears around the glowing fire pit. Despite the chill from the occasional gust of wind, the fire provided a comforting warmth. Each friend was given a white candle cradled in a small, clear vase, symbolizing the light Logan had brought

---

[44] Candlelight vigil held on Saturday, October 7th, 2023.

into our lives. As we encircled the fire pit, the candles flickered against the twilight, casting gentle shadows on everyone's faces.

One by one, our friends shared their anecdotes and reflections about Logan, painting a picture of a man whose spirit was too large to be confined by the mortal world. Not everyone was able to speak—grief was a heavy cloak—but their presence spoke volumes. I held back no tears as I recounted tales of the life we had shared, each memory a bittersweet shard of our heartbreakingly short time together.

Everyone who gathered agreed, Logan was a force of nature—a man who lived with gusto, cherished his friendships profoundly, and always standing by his promises. Remarkably, for a man who wasn't the typical revelries of drinks and parties, Logan was the mastermind behind the grandest event in town, creating spectacles of joy that brought the community together.

After the last story had been shared, a few of our friends stayed behind to help with the cleanup. I remained seated by the fire pit, mesmerized by the dance of the flames, my mind and heart still battling to accept this new reality. As the night air grew brisker and the gathering dwindled, only Shye, Jessica, and Lou stayed behind. In the quiet of the nearly empty rooftop, their presence felt like a gentle anchor, holding me steady in the sea of my grief.

Each of them embraced me, their hugs a silent promise of enduring support. As it became colder, we bid each other goodnight. Then, Charlotte, my pillar of strength, drove us back home. Sitting in the passenger seat, I gazed out the window, watching the city lights blur past into the night.

That evening, as I quietly settled and prepared for bed, my phone lit up with a message from my friend Sherrie. She and her son Bruce had attended the candlelight vigil. Her text read: "I didn't want to say this earlier, but I just wanted to let you know that Logan was there." A deep stillness came over me as I processed her words.

Then she sent another text: "I saw him standing opposite you, and I managed to capture his essence on my phone. He was admiring you with so much love. When you became emotional, he drew closer, as if to embrace you. It overwhelmed me too, and I forgot to capture that moment." She attached the photo she took. It showed many of us gathered around the fire pit. Just off to the side, where I had been sitting, there was an unmistakable green aura—a spectral presence.

I wasn't startled; deep down, I had sensed his presence all along but had dismissed these feelings as mere echoes of my grief. Sherrie's message and photo only confirmed what I had been reluctant to accept— that Logan's spirit lingered close by, a silent guardian in my moments of sorrow. This realization bridged the gap between my denial and acceptance, offering a bittersweet comfort.

The following week, my youngest brother, Henry, texted me, inquiring about the details of Logan's funeral so he and his wife could make travel arrangements from Colorado. I informed him that the date was not yet finalized, as some aspects were still pending due to Logan's ongoing investigation. Logan's family and I hadn't reached a consensus on the funeral date. This uncertainty loomed over us, adding to the weight of our grief.

After sending the text, I returned to the main message screen, only to see three dots hovering over Logan's avatar again. My heart quickened, a mix of hope and anxiety flooding my chest. Would something finally come through this time? Or was it merely the investigator delving into Logan's phone once more, possibly combing through our shared conversations? The latter seemed improbable. Combing through alone couldn't have caused the dots to appear. Driven by my tendency to document everything that might someday hold significant meaning, I took a screenshot.[45]

As I contemplated these puzzling thoughts, Logan's voice echoed in my mind once more, repeating the words, "It was my fault. I made a mistake." Just like when I first heard those words over a week ago, a wave of intense sorrow washed over me. Then, he added, "I was stupid. I wasn't careful." His self-deprecation shattered my heart. I couldn't bear to hear him speak of himself that way, even if it was just my imagination. Feeling compelled, I decided to call the investigator to inquire about any progress made.

He informed me, "At this time, we are leaning towards an accident but have sent the gun to our labs for testing. The process can take months." Hearing that the investigation was leaning towards an accident alleviated some of my initial concerns, and it made me reflect on Logan's whispers, saying it was his fault. I was still trying to make sense of it. But the prospect of waiting months for closure was disheartening. Logan's family was adamant about not holding the funeral until the case was resolved. The thought of my husband lingering in a freezer for months with nothing but a sheet, especially with winter approaching and considering his past struggles with the cold, was unbearable. I knew Logan better than anyone, and subjecting him to such a fate felt cruel and selfish. Regardless of his condition, he was still my Logan.

Before ending the call, I had to ask the investigator, "I was wondering, have you checked his phone and text messages recently?" My heart raced as I awaited his response. Part of me hoped he would say no, allowing me to cling to the hope that Logan was reaching out to me. The other part hoped for a yes, seeking a logical explanation, as I couldn't grasp how Logan could be messaging me from beyond if it were indeed him.

The investigator's answer came swiftly, but the seconds felt like an

---

[45] Screenshot was saved at 11:04 a.m. on Thursday, October 12, 2023.

eternity. "We have not looked into his phone. All his personal items were placed into a secure locker at the coroner's office and have not been touched since the day they were brought in with him. I am the only one with access," he said.

I let out a sigh of relief, but then he questioned, "Is there a reason you think we should look into his phone and text messages?" I hadn't fully thought through my question before asking and was caught off guard by his inquiry. Quickly, I responded, "No reason. It's just that strange occurrences have been happening on my phone. It feels like Logan is trying to text me, but nothing comes through."

There was a moment of silence, indicating the investigator's perplexity, and then he replied, "Yeah, we have not touched his phone, and that is beyond the scope of our investigation." I now felt somewhat foolish for asking and even more foolish for explaining my reason, but I needed to know.

We were scheduled to meet at Steve's house again on Saturday to continue our discussions about planning Logan's funeral.[46] It had been two and a half weeks since he passed. I informed everyone that I had gone ahead and purchased his final resting place and explained my reasons. I also shared that the investigator is leaning towards an accident, but it will take months for the lab results on the gun. Scott chimed in, saying, "I spoke with the investigator too, and he said the same thing to me."

I then proposed that we shouldn't keep Logan in a freezer for an extended period, especially with winter approaching. I didn't want to have his funeral in the snow, as I know he would not want that. Waiting for the case to be closed before laying him to rest will only provide a temporary balm for our grief, but it doesn't do any justice to my husband. The investigator can continue their investigation since the autopsy has

---

[46] October 14, 2023

already been concluded.

I pleaded with his family, expressing how cruel it felt to make him wait in a freezer when he had been waiting his whole life for everything. Tears streamed down my face as I spoke, "I love Logan with all my heart. We had plans to move into our forever home, and he was so happy about that. For the first time in his life, he would finally have a physical place he could call his own. As his wife, it tears me apart that the home I would end up getting for him would be a wooden casket placed in a lot that is arms wide and six feet deep. This isn't how it was supposed to be."

His family was reluctant but agreed.

CHAPTER 28

DUST TO DUST

HE FUNERAL DATE HAD BEEN SET,[47] marking one month since Logan passed away. With less than two weeks until the funeral, I grappled with conflicting emotions. I wanted to honor Logan with dignity and avoid prolonging his time in a freezer, but the approaching day filled me with dread and despair—knowing it would be the last time I would see his face and hold his hand.

Each day, I immersed myself in the somber tasks of organizing Logan's funeral, my cheeks constantly wet with tears. Night after night, I poured my heart into completing the scarf I had started for him, determined to have it ready in time. With every stitch, my sorrow wove itself into the yarn, a silent testament to the depths of my pain.

When I finally tied off the last thread and carefully folded the completed scarf, a flood of emotions washed over me. Placing it on our bed, I couldn't help but bury my face in its soft warmth, feeling the

---

[47] Thursday, October 26, 2023

echoes of our love intertwined in every loop and twist. The weight of grief pressed down on me as the realization settled in: this would be the last tangible creation I made for Logan. It was a bittersweet farewell to a cherished tradition, a final act of love in the face of loss.

I had some leftover yarn, so I decided to make myself an identical scarf, albeit smaller to fit me. This way, we could each have a scarf, a tangible connection to keep us linked despite our physical separation. It was a way to keep him comforted with all my devotion, knowing that a piece of me would be laid to rest with him.

I wanted Logan's suit to complement the colors of his scarf, so I chose a dark navy blue suit that I knew he would love. However, the fact that it was on sale left me feeling unsettled, as if I hadn't given him the reverence he deserved. I decided to hold onto it and hung it up in his closet. Then, I went to the mall to purchase another suit of the same color, this time opting for a high-end designer brand without any sale signs. The absence of discounts somehow reassured me, aligning with Logan's penchant for looking his best. I also selected an elegant and sophisticated maroon button-up shirt, envisioning how dashing he would look in it.

As the sales rep tallied up the purchase at the cashier, I was astonished to find that the price was exactly the same as the previous suit, differing by only a mere cent. Immediately, a tinge of frustration crept in, and I silently asked Logan, "Are you doing this to me?"

I then headed over to Logan's favorite shoe store within Hmong Village.[48] He adored elegant dress shoes and took immense pride in each pair he owned, all of which were exclusively from a particular vendor who imported them from Asia. While I had accompanied him on every shoe-buying excursion, the precise location of the vendor within Hmong

---

[48] An indoor Hmong shopping mall in Saint Paul.

Village eluded me. Logan always took the lead during our visits, and I seldom paid attention to my surroundings whenever he was with me.

Upon arriving at Hmong Village, my plan was to comb through every aisle until I found the vendor, confident I would recognize it when I saw it. However, the moment I entered the glass double doors of Hmong Village, it was as if Logan intuitively guided me through the bustling maze of vendors without making any wrong turns, flawlessly navigating me to the shoe vendor. I was amazed at how effortless it took me to find it.

As soon as I spotted the vendor, I composed myself and said, "My husband often purchased shoes from you, exclusively from your store. Unfortunately, today, I'm here to buy his last pair." The vendor looked at me, surprised, and inquired why it would be the last. I explained that my husband had passed away. He paused, processing the news, then realized who my husband was and asked, "Is your husband the tall brother who spends hours trying on shoes in my store every time he visits?" I nodded, a mixture of sadness and warmth flooding my heart as he remembered Logan.

The vendor rose from his seat, retrieving a box from the top shelf, and shared, "I've held onto these shoes just for your husband, knowing he would come by to get them. They are the ones I know he would have wanted."

As he opened the box, I felt an instant connection. I knew the style and design that Logan loved, and these were perfect for him. But my heart sank when I saw they were size eight and a half, the only pair in that design. I feared they might be too small, but the vendor said confidently, "In this particular style, it's the perfect size for your husband. I promise you." I hesitated for a moment but given his familiarity with both his shoes and my husband, I trusted his judgment and took the shoes. As I made my way out of the store, I thought, "This had to be fate, and Logan had to be behind this."

Later, when I returned home, my phone rang. It was Chase. His voice, usually so calm, carried a weight as he said, "We'll all be there for Logan's service, but unfortunately, Dad won't be. He says that since you two didn't host a cultural ceremony for your marriage, he cannot attend the funeral as the father-in-law." My eyes were dry when Chase relayed the message; instead, a surge of disappointment and anger washed over me. "If he couldn't attend as the father-in-law to my husband, he could have at least shown up as my father. Yet, he chose rigid cultural norms over supporting his own daughter on the darkest day of my life."

Chase offered an apology on Dad's behalf, but his words fell on deaf ears. I replied, a bitter edge to my tone, "We had planned to hold a cultural ceremony after we settled into our new place, which would have been in just a few months, but we were robbed of that opportunity. Now, Logan lies silent, deprived of his voice and choice, yet Dad still has both, and this—this is what he chose. I'm grateful to have you and my other brothers' support through this, but I cannot accept your apologies on Dad's behalf. Nor can I forgive him for this."

Chase agreed that Dad's decision was poorly made, adding that he had expressed the same concerns to Dad, but his decision remained unchanged. Before we hung up, he shared that he, his wife, and my other brothers, along with their wives, would arrive the morning of Logan's funeral. I thanked him for their unwavering love and support.

Our friend Nate, who handled all the videography and editing during our big event, was tasked with putting together Logan's tribute video. I reached out to Logan's family and friends, asking them to send any photos they had of him. Unfortunately, there were few, as Logan wasn't fond of taking pictures. In family photos, he rarely smiled. The only times he smiled were in candid shots when he wasn't aware.

I selected two songs for his video: "Please Remember Me" by Tim McGraw to accompany his photos from childhood and with his family, and "You Are the Reason" by Calum Scott as a tribute to our life together from the time we met.

As I sifted through more than a thousand photos and videos of Logan that I had captured over the last four and a half years, memories flooded back—our first beach outing, thrilling zip-lining adventures, serene fishing trips, exhilarating hikes, trips we've taken, and countless cherished moments. Despite this treasure trove of memories, it felt like there weren't enough. Tears welled up as I realized there would be no more new memories to create with him, a painful truth that weighed heavily on my heart.

Charlotte arrived a week early to help navigate the somber task of finalizing the details for Logan's services. We sat cross-legged on my bed, the soft murmur of my grandson's play forming a bittersweet backdrop to our conversation. As we reminisced, I shared my loving memories of Logan, clutching them close as they were my last tangible link to him.

I found myself compulsively looking at my phone, pulling up the last text message I had sent Logan. I read it again for the umpteenth time, my heart sinking with each word. I had sent it at 10:29 p.m., unaware that he had passed away around 7:30 p.m. that evening. The message was simple, wishing him a good day and expressing my love and how much I missed him—an echo of normalcy in the face of the irreversible. As I shared my regret with Charlotte, fixated on the screen, the three dots that signaled he was composing a message suddenly appeared over his avatar again for the third time. It was as if Logan was still part of our world, communicating with me. I knew this time that his messages weren't because of the investigation.

Surprised, I turned the phone to show Charlotte. "Are you seeing this too?" Her eyes widened as she confirmed, "Yeah, I'm seeing it too. That is crazy!" I quickly took a screenshot to document another message from Logan.[49] At that moment, Logan's voice, a comforting whisper echoed: "I saw the message, Baby. That's why I've been trying to message you. I miss you and love you too."

Tears streamed down my face as I absorbed the words, finding a small solace in the vast emptiness his departure had left. "I don't know why, but I've been hearing Logan," I confessed, my voice thick with emotion. Charlotte placed her hand on my knee and patted it gently, her voice soft with understanding. "Maybe you are, Mom. It's just like Logan to make sure you're okay, even now." Her words, meant to soothe, only highlighted the profound depth of his absence, weaving a thread of the supernatural into our grief-laden reality.

The day before Logan's memorial service,[50] I made the decision to go alone to the morgue to dress my husband for the last time. His half-sister kindly offered to come with me; she didn't want me to face it alone. However, I insisted I needed this final, solitary moment with him. Our conversations had been ceaseless every day since our fateful night at Mystic Lake, and with every word exchanged, it had only been us in a world we created for ourselves. I longed for one more moment alone with my husband, to share our last words together. Even if he couldn't respond, I believed that his soul would hear me, and that thought would provide a glimmer of reassurance for my shattered heart.

I carefully packed the suit and button-up shirt I had personally chosen for him, along with his cherished shoes from the vendor he frequented. The scarf, a labor of love crocheted with every fiber of my being, and a soft white blanket, a final token of affection from Scott symbolizing their brotherly bond, were also included.

The mortician allowed me a moment of privacy with Logan. I gazed

---

[49] Screenshot was saved at 7:52 p.m. on Thursday, October 19, 2023.

[50] Wednesday, October 25, 2023 at 10:00 a.m.

tenderly at his beautiful face, noticing that he hadn't changed much since the last time I saw him. Tears streamed down my cheeks as I engaged in my final conversation with him. "Fate is cruel," I whispered, "showing me the happiest years of my life with you, only to rip them away." There were so many things I had wanted to say to him on my way to see him, but now that I was here, all I could do was cry in the silence of that moment, hoping that wherever he was, the sun would shine down warmly on him and that he wasn't lost.

I took a cloth that I had brought from home and dampened it in warm water to tenderly wipe his face one last time, an act of love I performed daily when he returned home from work. We would sit on our enclosed porch as he decompressed and removed his boots. His face was marked with sweat, sawdust, and dirt from long hours in the sun, working in construction. In those quiet moments, as I cleaned away the traces of his labor, I would often whisper to him, "Every time I wash your face, I fall deeper in love with you." Tears streamed down my face with every tender motion as I gently brushed the cloth around his eyes and cheeks, not forgetting behind his ears. I recalled what I had playfully said to him once before, "Only someone who truly loves you will remember to clean behind your ears."

Moments later, two large men as tall and brawny as Logan entered the room to help me dress him, as his size made it impossible for me to do it alone. I provided them with the clothes and watched as they respectfully dressed him in his final attire. Just as the shoe vendor had promised, the shoes were a perfect fit, bringing a wave of relief.

Once he was dressed, the casket was brought out, and Scott's blanket was spread across its interior. Logan was gently lifted into the casket, and as more tears poured out, I painfully struggled to accept this fate.

After ensuring he was laid comfortably and positioned just right, I draped his beloved scarf around his neck and spread the rest of it over him, letting it extend down to his calves just as he liked. It was surreal to watch him lying silently in the casket. Every action felt forced against my will, but my love for him was so profound that I wanted to ensure he would always be taken care of, no matter the circumstance and no matter how painful it was.

I rested my hand over his heart and, in a soft whisper, said, "I'll see you tomorrow, my love," then forced my unwilling feet to lead me home.

I had shared my vision for setting up the funeral home with Shye a few weeks ago and placed a rushed order for navy blue chiffon drapes. I envisioned a serene setting with all-white draping complemented by navy blue accents and a subtle touch of silver. Meanwhile, Shye dedicated herself to crafting intricate floral arrangements, meticulously ensuring that every detail reflected our love for Logan, including those ordered by our friends and family.

The night before Logan's memorial service, my daughters and I gathered in the living room to assemble delicate white boutonnieres, wrapping them in navy blue ribbons with Logan's name intricately inscribed in silver glitter. We also carefully selected some of his most memorable photos, encasing them in elegant frames, ready to adorn the memory table as a reflection of his life. As we worked through the night, we shed tears and shared stories about what we cherished most and what we would miss most about Logan. We continued until all the boutonnieres were finished and neatly placed in a box for the next day.

The day dawned early at the funeral home, shrouded in an air heavy with anticipation. Outside, a chilly overcast mirrored the somber mood, casting a gray gloom over the day. Shye's meticulous efforts through the night transformed the place into a scene of absolute perfection. She thoughtfully set up the tables covered in navy-blue silk for the memory table, a focal point of evocative remembrance. With delicate care, my daughters joined in, arranging the photos, florals, and candle accents, each element adding to the solemn beauty of the display. It stood as a testament to our love and loss, a poignant tribute to Logan's life.

By 9:00 a.m., the hearse carrying my world had arrived and was parked just outside the funeral home door. I cradled the large framed photo I had printed, intending it to be placed next to his casket. Standing by the door, peering out at the hearse, I could see the mahogany casket I had selected for Logan. The weight of reality was sinking in; the end was drawing near. Holding his photo tightly, tears streamed down my face as though I were weeping into his chest, reminiscing about all those moments when I was falling apart and he was there to console me. Yet this time, it was just his photo, unable to embrace me in return.

Logan's brothers, nephews, cousins, and my son Keith stood together, a solemn presence, as his casket was carefully pulled out of the hearse and placed on a rolling platform adorned with a white skirt. My tears flowed inconsolably; my heart weighed down by the unbearable pain. It was surreal, a day that I never imagined would arrive until we were old and gray.

As I turned to lead the way towards the front of the chapel, each of the men reverently took hold of Logan's casket and followed closely behind me. Tears streamed down my face, mingling with the overwhelming pain in my heart. I closed my eyes, seeking consolation amidst the sorrow, and pressed onward, guided by the steady presence of my daughter Cassie with her arm gently wrapped around mine.

Logan's memorial was confined to a single day, a reflection of his wishes not to have the extended ceremonies typical of traditional Hmong funerals. Standing there, amidst a sea of somber faces, I grasped for the first time the true purpose of these prolonged farewells. They weren't for the silent ones who have departed; they were for us, the living, grappling painfully with the threads of letting go—a process far more arduous than I had ever imagined.

The service commenced with a solemn morning prayer led by the family's church pastor, giving way to an extended viewing. I remained steadfast by his casket throughout; those final hours were sacred, and I was determined to cherish every last moment. Friends from as far away as California and Washington State converged to offer their final respects. One by one, as they approached, they recounted memories—moments filled with love for Logan. Even the lighter anecdotes brought tears to my eyes, a poignant reminder of all the joy he had brought into our lives.

I stood beside Logan, clutching his hand, whispering through my tears, "I will miss these hands every day for the rest of my life." Suddenly, a brash voice shattered the solemnity. A man behind me was loudly questioning how Logan had passed, morbidly curious about whether photos from the autopsy or the scene of the incident, detailing his wounds, were on display. When some of the elder women told him no such images existed, he scoffed, "That's too bad. Those pictures are the most interesting part; they should be shown to everyone."

My heart raced with indignation, and I spun around to face the intruder—an older man, no taller than myself, clad in a somber gray suit. I locked eyes with him, my voice firm and unwavering, "If you cannot show respect for our most cherished and beloved person, then you must excuse yourself right now and leave. I don't know you and I don't care who you are. I don't welcome you here. This is a place of mourning, not morbid curiosity." He held my gaze for a moment, perhaps seeing the resolve in my eyes, then turned and exited the room without another word. I would later learn he was regarded as a "Hmong community leader," a title his behavior belied.

Some guests approached, attempting to take photos with Logan in his open casket, and I immediately stopped them. Despite the surge of uneasiness, I held my emotions in check and respectfully told them that was not allowed. Instead, I suggested an alternative that honored his spirit. I directed them towards the memory table, a vibrant collection of photographs capturing Logan's cherished moments. "Please, take your photos there," I urged them. "That's what he would have preferred."

Others sought to capture moments with me, and although I graciously complied, I detested the ritual of posing for photos at funerals. Each smile was a mask, a forced facade that contradicted the turmoil churning within. It felt as though I was forced to smile while dying inside.

Towards late afternoon, everyone gathered again in the chapel, pouring in from the doors where people had been hanging out in the hallways and dining hall. As the room hushed, it was time for the family tribute to Logan to begin.

I sat in the second aisle, first seat from the center, with my children alongside me. The room darkened, and then his tribute video began to play, featuring a cascade of photos from his life, accompanied by the somber sound of the two songs I had selected, mingling with the subtle cries and sniffles of our friends and family in the room.

When the video concluded, the lights returned, and Scott was the first to approach the podium. His voice trembled slightly as he conjured images of a shared childhood with Logan, with subtle laughter echoing through their recollections. The tone shifted as he delved into more poignant memories that marked their passage into adulthood. He paused, gathering strength before recounting a particularly tender moment—the day Logan and Steve helped move him into his college dorm. At their parting, Logan turned towards him, his eyes gleaming with unshed tears, and said, "I love you, bro." Scott, choked by unspoken norms of masculinity, had remained silent. That silence had haunted him. As he continued, he spoke of how Logan always wore his heart on his sleeve, his compassion and love for those closest to him ever evident.

With each memory, Scott's voice grew heavier, burdened by the weight of all the unspoken "I love you's" that lingered in the air like ghosts. He admitted to himself and to the hushed room that he always thought there would be more time. Now, with Logan's absence a stark, unyielding truth, regret gnawed at him fiercely. He closed his eyes briefly, then, with a resolve born of grief, he looked toward the heavens and whispered, his voice cracking, "I love you, brother. Mus zoo koj os.51" Not a dry eye was in the room.

Next, our dear friends Susan and Nic approached the podium. With warmth and sincerity, they shared heartfelt stories that illuminated Logan's character, beginning with the memorable day they first met him on an inaugural camping trip. Nic recalled the immediate rapport he felt with Logan, a bond that quickly deepened through numerous hunting and fishing excursions. Meanwhile, Susan emphasized Logan's remarkable generosity and bravery. She spoke with fervor about his aspirations, his unwavering determination, and his extraordinary success in orchestrating the grandest event our town—and particularly our Hmong community—had ever seen, setting a new standard of excellence.

Susan then called on everyone in the room who had played a role in bringing Hmong Nouveau to life—from the models and volunteers to the designers—to join her. Together, they formed a unified front by Susan's side, a testament to their collective gratitude for Logan's enduring legacy and the significant void he left behind. The front of the chapel transformed into a tapestry of familiar faces, each one a reminder of the deep connections forged. My heart swelled with love and compassion as the profound sense of loss we shared palpably filled the air.

Susan then beckoned me to join them as she unveiled a striking

---

51 Mus zoo koj os (pronounced: moo zong ko o) means "safe journey."

sculpture—a tall pillar of white marble crowned with a silver Hmong lock, 52 symbolizing hope, peace, and devotion, in honor of Logan's extraordinary life and accomplishments.

Gently, she passed the sculpture to me to accept on Logan's behalf. Its weight was substantial in my arms, but I held it close to my heart. Overcome with emotion, tears streamed down my face, profoundly touched by the depth of their love and remembrance. Through my grief, each person at the front of the chapel stepped forward to embrace me, offering their comfort and solidarity in our shared sorrow.

In the quiet hours of the past few evenings, my children had diligently crafted and rehearsed their speeches, each a tender tribute to the man who had become so much more than just a figure in their lives. Together, they walked to the front, their speeches carefully written in the notes on their phones. With eyes glistening, they stood side by side, drawing strength from one another.

They spoke in order of age, from the eldest to the youngest, with Charlotte stepping up to the podium first. Her voice wavered slightly as she recounted her initial wariness upon meeting Logan. As the eldest, a fierce protective streak was her nature, she was initially guarded. However, Logan's sincere kindness and warmth soon dissolved her doubts, revealing his deep affection for both me and her siblings.

Next, Kayla shared stories of Logan's immense generosity and the subtle ways he showed kindness that deeply resonated. Whether it was sneaking off to settle a restaurant bill or quietly slipping her some extra money—even when unnecessary—his actions consistently affirmed his role as a paternal figure in her life.

Cassie's turn brought a lighter moment as she recounted her first fond encounter with Logan, struggling with acrylic nails in the kitchen.

---

[52] Also known as xauv (pronounced: so), a specific Hmong design that resembles a decorative padlock, usually made of silver.

Without much hesitation, he had whisked her, her sister, and me off for an impromptu pampering session. It was a simple gesture, but for Cassie, it was a meaningful acknowledgment of his understanding and care.

Keith stepped forward, pausing briefly to compose himself amidst the rush of emotions. He lowered his head, taking a moment to find his voice as he glanced at the speech on his phone. He began recounting his experiences under Logan's patient guidance—from learning archery to the family outings, fishing trips, and driving lessons. Keith also reminisced about the times he joined Logan at work, learning to wield power tools and work with wood. These memories painted a vivid picture of Logan as not only a mentor who imparted practical skills but also as someone who taught profound life lessons through their shared experiences.

As each spoke through tears and trembles, the depth of their love and the ache of their loss filled the room—an evocative reminder of Logan's indelible impact on our family.

As the family tributes concluded, it was my turn to address the gathering. This was undoubtedly the most daunting speech I had ever faced—not only because of the sharp pain gripping my heart, but also the thick lump in my throat that threatened to choke my words. I held a seven-page speech in my hands, painstakingly prepared, yet it felt insufficient to encapsulate the essence of Logan—the extraordinary man and husband he was to me and the father figure he had become to my children.

I began with a trembling voice, "This must be a mistake to be standing here today. This isn't supposed to be my husband's funeral." My voice faltered as I struggled to continue. "I never envisioned myself speaking here so soon, certainly not before we were grey and old, surrounded by our children and grandchildren, sharing the countless cherished moments and stories from the beautiful life we built together, the places we discovered, and the joy that filled our days."

I shared how Logan was not merely the love of my life; he was my best friend, the man of my dreams, and unquestionably the most difficult person to ever let go. As I spoke, my raw emotions cascaded over each word, each syllable slicing through my heart like a blade. It was vital for me to depict Logan through my eyes—his profound generosity, his willingness to make sacrifices, his inclination to go above and beyond for those he loved.

To conclude my tribute, I recited a poem by an unknown author, "When God was Making Husbands." The words resonated deeply, reflecting Logan's golden heart and how perfectly he complemented my soul. The poem beautifully summed up all that Logan meant to me, concluding with the lines:

Next time when we meet,
will be at Heaven's door.
When I see you standing there,
I won't cry anymore.

I will put my arms around you,
and kiss your smiling face.
Then the pieces of my broken heart,
will fall back into place.

By the time I finished, my vision was blurred by tears, rendering the faces before me indistinct—unable to discern who among them was weeping with me.

I had just settled into my seat amid the quiet murmur of the gathering when Dr. Laura approached from behind. She tapped my shoulder gently, her face marked by a somber expression as she extended her condolences. Logan had built a deck for her the previous year, a project through which she had come to know him as a kind and meticulous man. After we exchanged a few words, she asked with a tone rich in kindness and concern, "How is your shoulder? Were you able to see the specialist?"

I shook my head. "They called, but I never made the appointment. Strangely, the pain vanished right after Logan passed. I thought it might be the shock, the trauma of losing him. But it's been a month now, and the pain hasn't returned at all."

Her eyes widened, a mix of astonishment and professional curiosity lighting them up. "That's quite remarkable," she murmured, clearly intrigued by the unexpected turn of events. At a loss for words, she reached out and placed a comforting hand on my shoulder. "Well, I'm just relieved to hear you're feeling better, and that the pain has disappeared," she said, her voice warm and genuinely relieved, reflecting the peculiar serendipity of my sudden recovery.

As the day began with a solemn prayer, it similarly concluded. One by one, the mourners departed, arms linked with their loved ones, leaving the chapel for the warmth of their homes. Yet, I remained, my heart anchored steadfastly to Logan, the thought of leaving him alone in the vast, quiet chapel—or leaving without him altogether—unbearable. I lingered to hold his hand once more, whispering into the stillness, questioning if he was pleased with the memorial we had crafted in his honor, and expressing my hope that he could sense the depth of love that enveloped him; his absence had created a void far deeper than the silence around me could ever suggest.

The gentle voice of the funeral director interrupted my thoughts. "I am sorry, but it is time to close now," he said, his hand gently resting on Logan's casket as he began to seal it for the night. Tears streamed down my face as my children, my pillars of strength, gently guided me toward the car. Each step away felt like I was parting from my own soul.

As dawn broke, we gathered again in the solemn quiet of the chapel for a morning prayer, steeling ourselves for the journey ahead to the cemetery where Logan would be laid to rest. With each step toward his final resting place, my heart recoiled, grasping at the last fleeting moments together, yearning for more time with him that would never come.

For one final time, the funeral director opened Logan's casket, granting those gathered a last opportunity to say farewell. Given the biting cold and dampness of the winter air, it was decided that the casket would remain sealed once we reached the cemetery. A wave of panic washed over me as the stark reality of our final parting loomed ever closer.

Around my neck, I wore the matching scarf I had crafted for us both. Leaning over Logan, I placed one hand over his heart and gently grasped his other hand, savoring the painful privilege of this final touch. I stroked his hair—lush and full, a source of his quiet pride—and whispered a promise through my tears, "There is no goodbye. Our separation is merely a pause until we see each other again."

The tears that fell were like crystals, softly landing on the scarf I had crocheted for him. Each tear was a testament to the years we never said "goodbye." We always parted with "See you later," or "See you soon"—because "goodbye" was a word too final for our forever.

As the funeral, director carefully closed the casket for the last time, my gaze remained fixed on Logan, capturing the last sliver of his face before it vanished from my sight. My heart shattered further, scattering its fragments like cosmic dust across the universe. A guttural cry broke from my lips—a sound of deep anguish, as if something vital within me was tearing apart and a part of my very soul had extinguished as the lid shut tight.

My son stood solemnly among the group of men, all ready to carry Logan with reverence to the hearse. Beside me, my friends gathered, their voices soft and soothing, attempting to break through the shroud of my grief. Yet, my world was constricted to a single, unbearable truth: Logan was gone. The thought of never seeing him again sliced through me, tearing at the very fabric of my existence.

As they secured Logan's casket within the hearse and softly closed the door with a gentle thud, a hollow silence fell. The hearse began its slow procession, carefully navigating out of the funeral home's parking lot. I followed closely behind in my car. On any other day, the route from the funeral home to the cemetery seemed to stretch endlessly, but today, it felt cruelly brief. Tears blurred my vision as I peered through the tinted glass at the hearse ahead, catching fleeting glimpses of Logan's casket. Memories flooded my mind—the first magnetic glance from Logan's deep, soulful eyes, our first unexpected kiss in the "best place in the world," the shared thrill of our first adventure, the heart-stirring moment he sang his proposal, and the joyous day we pledged our lives to each other. Each memory, a treasured chapter of our life together, now felt painfully unfinished.

As I looked in the rearview mirror, a line of cars trailed behind, carrying those who loved us and whom we loved in return. My children, quiet in their grief, accompanied me as we made our way to the cemetery. When we arrived at Logan's final resting place, I saw that many of our family and friends were already there, their faces etched with profound sorrow.

Keith and the men arranged themselves into two orderly rows, prepared to escort Logan to his final earthly sanctuary. At the graveside, the pastor's voice carried a solemn reverence as he recited Psalm 23:1-6, his words weaving a blanket of comfort over those assembled. He concluded with a heartfelt prayer, his voice fading just as Logan's casket was gently lowered into the vault amid the freshly turned earth.

My legs trembled, barely supporting the weight of my sorrow as I stood rooted to the spot, overwhelmed by grief. Clutching the scarf around my neck, I felt a tenuous connection to Logan. Envisioning him peacefully wrapped in his own scarf, I silently prayed for his peace in heaven.

The vault's lid was carefully secured, shielding his precious essence from the world. Friends and family approached one by one, each participating in the poignant tradition of casting a handful or a shovelful of earth into his grave as a final act of homage. However, when my turn came, my heart seized. The act of tossing soil onto his casket—burying the love of my life—was a step for which I found myself wholly unprepared, and I couldn't proceed with it.

My daughters gently gathered a selection of flowers brought over from Logan's service—white and blue roses, symbolizing the purity and depth of our bond, fragrant lilies representing the restoration of innocence after death, pure white carnations, and the delicate wisps of baby's breath. They shared their intention to press these blossoms into a frame as a lasting tribute. This gesture, they explained, would serve as a perpetual memorial to the enduring love between Logan and me, a love that neither time nor fate could ever diminish, fervently lasting until our very last day.

Before we left the cemetery, I sent one last text message to my husband: "I love you more.[53]" Not to say I loved him more than he loved me, but that I loved him "more" than all the sad days to come, more than the tears that will keep falling, and more than the heartaches I will carry until my last breath. He was everything to me, and I needed him to know that I would continue to cherish and honor his memory, despite the pain.

---

[53] Text message timestamped at 12:18 p.m. on Friday, October 27, 2023.

CHAPTER 29

HEAVEN

Y HUSBAND WAS LAID TO REST THIS MORNING. As the day unfolded, the somber farewells gradually gave way to departing guests. Some hurried to catch their flights, while others departed quietly, each returning to the comfort of their homes, carrying with them memories of the day's poignant moments.

Meanwhile, a lunch gathering was arranged at Steve's house, serving as a tentative bridge between my family and Logan's following the service. As voices mingled and the sound of dishes being arranged filled the air, I found myself drifting into a detached daze, enveloped in a bubble of grief, somewhat removed from the surrounding activity.

Despite the animated discussions and the occasional subtle laughter that filled the room, an undeniable void lingered—a stark, noticeable absence that echoed the warmth and laughter Logan always brought to every gathering. His laughter, once the heartbeat of our shared moments, now left a heartbreakingly silent space that nothing could fill.

In that moment, all I craved was solitude—to retreat to the sanctuary of our shared bed, to curl up amidst the lingering traces of his presence, and allow my tears to be absorbed by my pillow. Perhaps in the embrace of sleep, I might find a fleeting reunion with him, a whisper of his laughter echoing in my dreams, a glimpse of his loving presence that once filled every corner of our lives.

After everyone had departed, leaving only Logan's brothers, a few close family members, myself, and my children, his brother Steve unexpectedly broke my daze. He turned to me and spoke in a firm tone, "Just because you're Logan's legal wife doesn't mean you're entitled to any of his insurance money."

Steve's words caught me completely off guard and left me stunned. My husband had just been laid to rest, and not once had I mentioned or asked for any part of his insurance money. For him to bring this up at such a time was utterly incomprehensible to me.

I quickly composed myself and responded to Steve in a clear, firm tone, ensuring there was no room for misunderstanding. "I want to make this absolutely clear, once and for all, so you never have to worry again, and let everyone here bear witness to my words: I do not want any of that insurance money. When I asked you how you could help, it wasn't your money I was seeking but your love for your brother. After you indicated that your ability to help was limited, I never raised the subject again," I said, my heart rate accelerating as I met his gaze with a resolute expression.

"We have laid Logan to rest, and as for the money, even if you were to force it upon me, I don't want it. It will always be a bitter reminder that it exists solely because my husband is no longer here. No amount of money can compensate for the loss of his life and everything we shared," I said, my voice steady but filled with disappointment and dismay. I couldn't believe that in the wake of losing my husband and the future we had envisioned together, his concern was about the money. Taking a deep breath, I focused on maintaining composure in both my tone and breathing.

Just then, Scott spoke up, interrupting the tension. "I need to mention something about his headstone," he said, walking over to the living room and sitting opposite me. "I want you to hold off on placing the order for it," he continued. His request took me by surprise, leaving me perplexed. I paused, trying to digest his words. "The investigation is still ongoing. The investigator said it was an accident, but not everything has been finalized yet," he explained.

As I processed Scott's words, a heavy realization began to sink in. "Why would the outcome of Logan's case affect his headstone? It won't change his name, the day he was born, or the day he passed," I questioned, seeking clarity without jumping to conclusions.

Scott took a moment to gather his thoughts before responding, his words hanging heavily in the air. "I just want to be sure that no one else had a hand in his death—not just you, but everyone around him," he confessed.

My previous conversation with his family regarding the headstone instantly resurfaced. I had shared with them that I had acquired a double headstone and grave because a part of me died with my husband. The only practical reason Scott would suggest otherwise is if he believed I had a role in Logan's death. After all, "everyone around him" has no influence or connection to Logan's grave or headstone, nor would they be laid to rest next to him. This wasn't a trivial assumption I could lightly brush off as if he had accidentally spilled water. This was a grave insinuation that I had a hand in ending my husband's life. The weight of his words left me hurt beyond measure, a wound much deeper than mere disappointment.

Despite the turmoil inside, I remained composed as I spoke. "I know you love Logan, and from the bottom of my heart, I appreciate you for that," I said. "As his brother, you have every right to question everything because that is your love for him. You are your brother's keeper, and he loves you too, so I will not hold that against you," I added, striving to convey understanding. "But I cannot pretend that your insinuation doesn't hurt me. Every day since his passing, I have been crying and trying with all my will to keep myself together."

Scott tightened his lips, as if to prevent himself from saying any more. These were Logan's only brothers, and their words cut through me, eroding my hope of maintaining a familial connection with them—a bond I had hoped to preserve as one of my last links to my husband. I considered that they might be speaking from a place of grief, but some things are far too painful to bear. I couldn't pretend otherwise, especially when I had just lost my entire world. I did not expect them to understand that pain, nor would I ever wish it upon them.

Logan always looked out for me because I tend to see the best in everyone, often making excuses for their lack of basic etiquette or courtesy. He would tell me, "Don't be naive. When someone tells you something, take it at face value." *He never wanted me to trade my self-respect for someone else's comfort.* Now that he's gone, his words are permanently etched into my resolve. I am determined to become someone he wouldn't have to worry about and someone he could be proud of.

I solemnly pardoned myself and left with my children.

As the night drew to a close, I found myself alone in the silence of my bedroom. With weary steps, I made my way to my office, where the faint glow of Logan's white candle still flickered on the windowsill—a small flame I had kept burning since the harrowing night I learned of his passing. Tonight, with a heavy heart, I approached the candle, my hand hesitating slightly before extinguishing the lone sentinel that had pierced the darkness for the past thirty days. As the smoke spiraled upwards, carrying the last wisp of light with it, I whispered a silent prayer into the stillness: may Logan be safely sheltered in his eternal home, untouched by the chill that lingers in the air outside.

The next morning, my children, my son-in-law, and I drove to Stillwater and sat on the same stone steps where Logan and I had sat four and a half years ago. We all took a selfie to capture the moment, just as he and I had done, knowing that one day this single moment would hold significant meaning for me. And indeed, it did. He changed my life. I sat there, gazing deeply into the water, wondering if he knew I was there too. My eyes welled up with tears until my vision blurred.

We then walked to the water's edge, and each of us released a white dove balloon into the air as we said a silent prayer. My son Keith was the only one who voiced his prayer aloud, and when he finished, he said, "I'll miss you, Dad."

We watched the dove-shaped balloons ascend higher into the overcast sky. As they drew nearer to the clouds, they looked like angels dancing above. I breathed a soft whisper, "Heaven is lucky to have you."

In the days that followed, I carefully gathered all of Logan's shoes, arranging them with reverence in a display case. Each pair, a cherished artifact of his life, represented his unique style and passions. As I handled them, memories surged vividly—Logan in those very shoes, each moment a snapshot of joy and life. With a heavy heart, I then turned to his wardrobe. I collected his clothes and washed them one last time. I lingered over the task, tears blending with the rhythmic churn of the washing machine, mourning the finality of it all. Once dried and folded, I placed his garments back in our closet, aligning them with precision and care, resigning myself to the fact that they would remain undisturbed, a silent homage to his enduring presence in my life.

As I moved through the house and sifted through his car, I discovered lighter after lighter, each one a tiny artifact of his presence. I collected them in a tin box, which soon overflowed with these small, yet significant, remnants of his daily life. I added to the collection two unopened packets of cigarettes that Logan had left on our enclosed porch, where he often sat to smoke at the end of his day. Each item, a tangible echo of his routines, felt too precious and too infused with his essence to simply discard.

As I continued to rummage through his car, my hand brushed against his glasses, hidden in the corner of the dashboard—a pair he only wore at night. Tears welled up as a cherished memory from the early days of our relationship surfaced. I recalled a conversation with my friend Finn, who was back in California. He had immediately noticed the joy in my voice and asked, "Why do you sound so happy?" Initially hesitant, as I usually guard my privacy in new relationships, my happiness won out and I confessed, "He's incredible. More intelligent than he gives himself credit for, and that's what makes him so interesting. He's funny, tall, and devastatingly handsome."

I had enthusiastically listed all the qualities I adored in Logan and then playfully added, "You know how I have a weakness for men in glasses. If only Logan wore glasses, he'd be perfect." I chuckled at the thought, not expecting reality to align so serendipitously. Yet, just a few weeks later, during a night drive, Logan reached for something in the corner of his dashboard. As he unfolded the glasses and placed them on, a perfect fit, my heart leapt. Watching him navigate the dimly lit streets, the soft glow of the headlights and passing city lights illuminated his focused expression behind the lenses. I whispered to myself with a smile, *he is perfect*.

The memory was a poignant reminder of the early sparks of our love, now treasures of my heart as I held his glasses, heavy with the weight of his absence.

Amid the clutter of his workspace, I unearthed scattered notes he had hastily scribbled, his old tablet—the one I gifted him when he decided to transition his construction business to a paperless model—and drawings of ambitious projects he had dreamed of tackling one day. Each item, a fragment of his daily life, felt sacred in my hands. I couldn't bring myself to discard any of these relics. By preserving these seemingly mundane objects, I felt I was clutching onto the remaining traces of his presence, each one a precious link to the man I so dearly miss and love.

I had become what some might call a sentimental hoarder, carefully collecting all the objects of his that I stumbled upon around our home and placing them in a cherished chest alongside other mementos of our life together.

This collection held the faded movie tickets from our first cinema date, the little black umbrella from the first time he sheltered me from the rain on University Avenue, and the ring he had meticulously crafted for my first birthday celebration with him—too precious and delicate to wear for fear of damaging it. There was also a little straw hat we had found on a breezy summer day, which I had exclaimed over for its cuteness. Ever thoughtful, he had transformed it into a keychain for me. Additionally, there was the two-dollar bill he had artfully folded into an origami heart, whispering that it was a charm for luck.

Alongside these tokens, I placed the shoebox where he kept photographs capturing the spectrum of his life's moments, and the last few dollar bills his mom had given him, folded in half, too precious for him to spend. In preserving these meaningful items he had loved, I was keeping his spirit intertwined with mine, honoring a shared past that I held dear. What he cherished, I too cherished.

Almost two weeks after he was laid to rest, it was his 49th birthday. I picked up his favorite cake, a raspberry tres leches from Café Latte on Grand Avenue, along with a golden wax candle. I spread a red blanket over the grass where he lay and carefully placed the cake on a small stool in the center. Nestling the candle into the middle, I lit it and began to sing his birthday song, my voice wavering in the chill autumn air.

When I finished, I closed my eyes and whispered into the gentle wind, asking him to make a wish. The world seemed to hold its breath; then, softly, his voice echoed in my mind's ear, "I only wish for you to be happy." Tears streamed down my face at his words, a sweet sorrow filling me. The tender echo of his voice tugged at my heart, shattering it again because he was no longer here with me and had spent his birthday wish on my happiness.

I had been visiting him every day, sitting and having conversations with him, clinging to a tradition that bound us from the very start—a ritual now painfully difficult to let go. On one particularly arduous day, after the burdens had piled high, I found myself yearning for the comfort and warmth of his shoulder to lean on. After a draining final meeting, I got up from my desk and drove to see him, tears streaming down my face with each mile of the drive.

Upon arrival, I settled beside his grave, my knees pressing into the grass as tears streamed down my face. Inconsolable, I released all my sorrow and whispered to Logan, "Heaven must be so breathtakingly beautiful that you probably don't miss me as deeply as I miss you." Tears cascaded nonstop, each drop tracing a scorching path swiftly cooled by the biting wind. My eyes remained tightly shut. Although the sky was overcast, behind my closed lids, I perceived a radiant glow—a light that seemed to hover above me before descending to meet my gaze.

My eyes remained closed, engulfed in grief and struggling for breath, when an unexpected warmth grazed the corner of my lips—gentle as a kiss, unmistakably Logan's. In that moment, serenity washed over me, steadying my breathing and halting my tears. My heart, broken and fragile from my loss, now felt warm and gentle, filled with an immense sense of love.

I remained still, basking in a profound peace, a calm I hadn't known since Logan passed. Once my heart felt full and comforted, I inhaled deeply, a renewed sense of connection anchoring me. Slowly, I got to my feet and made my way home, carrying with me the comforting presence of his love.

That very night, I was swept into a dream. Logan and I were on our enclosed porch, basking in the warmth of a perfect summer day. Sunlight spilled across the space, and a gentle breeze whispered through the window screen, carrying the faint scent of blooming flowers and fresh leaves. We settled into our favorite chairs, where we had spent countless evenings lost in conversation. Logan's expression was serene, his smile radiant, igniting an irrepressible joy within me as I smiled back at him.

Then he spoke, his voice as clear as if he were right beside me in the waking world, "Heaven is beautiful. The sun shines every day. But I still miss you. You were the best thing in my life and the hardest part I had to leave behind. You are the only person I would choose to experience it with all over again." A tear escaped my eye as his words washed over me. Driven by a mixture of sorrow and curiosity, I asked, "What do you do in heaven?"

Logan's smile never wavered as he replied, "There's so much to do here, and I am learning all the time. My soul is constantly developing." Intrigued, I probed further, "Do you sleep?" He shook his head and explained, "No, sleep is for the living. It's only required because you have a heart and brain that need rest. Here, our souls aren't bound by bodily organs, and we never feel the need for sleep."

Afraid that he may have been in pain when he took his last breath, I had to ask, "How did it feel to die?"

He smiled gently and placed his hand on mine. "I didn't die. I'm still here. It was only my physical body that couldn't continue anymore because of my injuries. I did not feel pain. There was a moment of darkness where I couldn't breathe, and then suddenly, from the top of my head, my light dispersed in every direction of the forest before gathering together again. I found myself standing outside my body."

As he spoke, I felt a wave of his experience wash over me. It was as if I were emerging from a deep ocean, taking a breath of life for the first time—not through my lungs, but through every inch of my being. The sensation was profound, filling me with an overwhelming sense of peace and understanding.

"Were you scared?" I asked further.

"I was confused at first, but I was not scared. My dad was there to greet me," he explained.

I was surprised when he shared that, knowing how distant they were in life. Logan continued, "He is not the same person he was in life, burdened by stress, regretful decisions, and the anxiety of earthly existence. He gained new insights and perspectives, seeing and understanding things revealed to him during his life review. We all go through that, experiencing the pain and remorse we inflicted on others as if it were our own. It's all to gain a deeper understanding of the lessons in our journey. The things we used to worry about in life mean little the moment we take our last breath. My dad and I had a long conversation and reached a mutual understanding of forgiveness. He found peace, and so did I."

Hearing Logan share that, I was touched to know that he was not alone and that any emotional pain he and his dad carried on earth did not transpire into the spirit realm.

"We also feel the love we received from others—that's how I know you loved me the most," he said. "I knew you loved me, but I never knew how deep your love was until now."

Before more could be said, I awakened from the dream. Its vividness left me feeling perplexed by how strange yet remarkable it was to have such a lengthy conversation with Logan. It felt so real that I couldn't disregard it, and the coincidence of it happening right after I had questioned him about heaven was uncanny.

A feeling began to sink in, convincing me that the warmth of light I felt at his place of rest had to be him. I remembered every word as if it had been part of a real conversation just moments ago. I lay in bed, pondering the dream, wondering if the strength and depth of our love were enough to bridge the gap between our worlds.

To fill my sense of loss and emptiness, I drove around the streets of Saint Paul and Minneapolis. Every street Logan and I had driven on reminded me of him, as if each one recorded every conversation we had, playing them back like a record as I passed through. My only introduction to this state was through him, having met him just four days after moving here. He was the one who anchored me to this place. Perhaps if I hadn't met him, I would have moved on already, just as I had done every other year for the last twenty years before coming here. But because he was my home, I stayed. Now that he is gone, I don't know what to do with the rest of my days, and I don't want to go anywhere else. Any place without traces of Logan would feel even more empty.

The house we had planned to be our forever home no longer appealed to me. It now felt too big and too empty. Since we hadn't closed on it, my realtor suggested showing me another house that was smaller. As I walked through this new house, I noticed a huge window in the open kitchen overlooking a serene lake. The lot was less than half an acre, and the lake was shared with other surrounding neighbors. It had all the features I wanted and required no upgrades. It was perfect as it was, yet it only made me sadder because Logan wasn't there. It marked the first house I had to explore without him by my side. I told my realtor I'd think about it and drove home.

On the way home, I cried, the road before me blurring, and I spoke aloud to Logan. "I feel so lost doing this without you. We were supposed to do this together. All our dreams were for us." I couldn't stop crying as I continued driving. Five minutes from my house, I said, "Don't stop being a part of my life. I can't do this without you. I'll take anything. Don't stop sending me messages."

I pulled up to the house and was about to text Keith to come out to the car so we could go to dinner together when the three dots hovered over Logan's avatar again. My heart fluttered. *He heard me*, I said to myself. *It had to be him. What are the odds that I was just asking him not to stop messaging me, and now, here he is, messaging me!* I quickly sent a message to Keith to come out while I sat waiting to see if any messages would come through.

A minute later, Keith walked out of the house and got into the passenger seat. The dots were still hovering, so I turned the phone to Keith and asked, "You're seeing this too, right?" just to make sure. He nodded and said, "Yes." To capture this moment, I took a screenshot, adding to my collection of unexplainable events that this moment was real.[54] As we both kept looking at the screen, the three dots disappeared, and I heard another gentle echo, "I'm not going anywhere, Baby. Still here."

I took a breath, feeling a little lighter, and put the car into drive, taking Keith and me to dinner.

The next day, pondering the recurring messages from Logan that never seemed to arrive, I picked up my phone and looked at our exchanged messages, reviewing the last one I sent him. I then noticed a peculiar detail in our conversation history. It appeared that he had responded to my text, 'I love you more,' with a message that was

---

[54] Screenshot was saved at 7:01 p.m. on Wednesday, November 15, 2023.

completely blank but had a timestamp with a date. This discovery left me even more bewildered, particularly because the date indicated was far from recent; it was dated 4/11/1994, with a timestamp of 6:47 p.m., a time long before text messaging on cell phones was even conceivable.

"How could this be?" I asked myself, my mind racing through possible explanations and my in-depth knowledge of technology.

To delve deeper into this mystery, I brought up my calendar to scrutinize the significance of that particular date. It suddenly dawned on me—this date aligned precisely two weeks before I married my ex-husband.

In that moment, Logan softly whispered, "I should had married you first." His words stirred a deep well of emotion within me, and tears began to stream down my cheeks. This sentiment wasn't new; Logan had often expressed his longing to have married me first, to have loved me sooner, and to have shielded me from years of abuse and scars.

Though I was overwhelmed, I couldn't fathom how this was possible. The timestamp, so profoundly significant, felt like a bridge between the past and present, a poignant reminder of Logan's enduring love and regret. The blank message, seemingly sent from beyond the veil of time, carried more weight and meaning than any words could.

As I sat there, tears continuing to flow, I felt an inexplicable connection to Logan, as if he was reaching out to me across the years, his love transcending the boundaries of life and death. It was a moment of profound realization that love, in its truest form, knows no limits, no end, and no final goodbyes.

CHAPTER 30

SEVEN LANTERNS

*I*T WAS THE FIRST WEEK OF NOVEMBER. My friend Mai called to see how I was holding up. I confessed to her that I was living moment by moment, still lost in a sea of grief. Tears were my constant companions, blurring days into nights, and I found myself at his resting place every day. Even though I knew his soul was no longer there, just a few feet from me were the hands I had held a thousand times, the face I had kissed goodnight, and the love of my life I had embraced so tightly.

Then I shared with Mai, "What's strange is that when I'm at my weakest moment, crying so much my head throbs with pain, that's when I hear Logan's voice, like a soft echo, telling me, 'Don't cry. I'm still just right here.' I don't know if it's grief playing tricks on me, or if it really is Logan trying to comfort me from wherever he is in the ether."

Mai listened with a deep, empathetic silence before expressing her sorrow for the anguish engulfing me. As the conversation unfolded, I found myself delving deeper into the unexplainable events that had surfaced since Logan's passing.

His voice, an enigmatic whisper, seemed as if only I could hear it, except for Keith, who heard him too when he woke up in the middle of the night. Logan's presence, though invisible, pressed upon me with such vivid intensity that it was impossible to deny. It was a sensation I couldn't see but felt with piercing clarity.

I confessed to Mai, with absolute certainty, that it was indeed Logan. I don't know how I know; it's just an innate feeling. Our connection in life had always skirted the edges of telepathy, which we often joked about. There have been multiple occasions when Logan would sit contemplatively on our enclosed porch, and a sudden, inexplicable pull would draw me to him from whatever task I was doing. In my mind, I would hear him say my name, and I'd step outside, questioning if he had called me. Each time, he would say, "No, but I was thinking about it." We would share a knowing chuckle, dismissing it as mere coincidence, never really considering it a real possibility.

Mai continued to listen with compassion, free from judgment. After a moment, she shared that she had encountered others who had similar experiences, then added, "I have a friend who may be able to shed some light."

Curious, I asked who this friend was. She replied, "Her name is Kylie. She's a psychic medium, well-versed in these matters. You might consider speaking with her." The idea of consulting a psychic medium had surfaced before. My daughter, Charlotte, had suggested it too, as I had been sharing every encounter and experience with her. Yet, I had not given it serious thought, knowing I was still grieving and afraid of being disappointed if I were told it was all mere imagination.

Despite my concerns, Mai's suggestion lingered in the air, a possibility wrapped in the unknown. I paused for a moment, then replied, "Connect me with your friend," feeling a mix of reluctance and intrigue.

Mai arranged an introduction for Kylie and me through social media, and to my surprise, I recognized her from mutual professional gatherings. However, I had never known that Kylie possessed gifts in psychic mediumship.

Kylie mentioned that her schedule was full until December. I assured her patiently that there was no hurry; I could wait. She penciled me in for Sunday, December 10th, a month away.

Afterward, I called Charlotte to share the news that I had booked a session with a psychic medium. Admitting this felt almost surreal, but no more surreal than the persistent echoes of Logan's voice that I kept hearing. Uncertain of what to expect, I asked if she would come with me. I confessed my apprehension about the unknowns of the session and my reluctance to face them alone. Thankfully, since the appointment fell on a weekend, Charlotte agreed to make the drive from Wisconsin to join me.

A few nights later, as I was settling into bed, I reached for the framed photo of Logan and me that rested on my nightstand. My fingers gently traced the contours of his face, and my eyes lingered on the curve of his smile—a perfect smile I painfully yearned to see again.

From the day we first met, Logan and I were inseparable, except for the rare occasions when he ventured into the woods to hunt without me or the time he flew to Southern California for a funeral while I had to attend a wedding in Northern California. We split up our time to make it work, but even so, our separations were brief, never spanning more than a few days. Now, with more than two months having passed without him, each day felt like an eternity. The absence was a heavy cloak draped over my every moment, turning minutes into hours, and hours into days.

I continued to gaze at his face, still feeling my grief deeply as I spoke to him as if he were right beside me. In a voice softened to a whisper, tender and fragile, I confessed, "I don't know if you're reaching out to me, but I feel like this wasn't our first life together. It would be comforting to know."

Gently, I lifted his picture to my lips, pressing a kiss filled with longing against the cool glass, and murmured into the quiet of the night, "Goodnight, my love. I love you forever." I then placed the frame back onto my nightstand. Glancing at the time, I saw it was just after midnight. Taking a somber sigh, I turned off my bedside lamp.

No sooner had I closed my eyes than I was swept into slumber, my consciousness whisked me into a vivid dream. I found myself standing in an ethereal place resembling a Greek garden on a large flat chunk of rock and dirt the size of a football field. This formation was suspended in celestial space. This garden was lavishly adorned with curling vines, stones sculpted into elegant forms, and a riot of roses and lilies bursting with color. Beneath my feet, the cobblestones were intricately laid, each stone a testament to celestial craftsmanship.

On the western horizon, the sunset illuminated the sky with hues of pink, purple, blue, orange, and gold, painting it with strokes of divine artistry I had never seen before, yet felt intensely familiar. As I turned to take in the view from every direction, it seemed to expand into a boundless celestial heaven. Stars twinkled like scattered diamonds, and distant galaxies swirled in silent majesty, each light whispering from the infinite.

As I wandered through the dreamscape, I entered an expansive clearing paved with cobblestones and surrounded by exquisite flowers in every shade of pastel. At the edge of this clearing stood a tall man with a dark, flowing beard and thick brows. He was dressed in a beige and green cloak and a hat, reminiscent of a wizard from the films I had seen. His gaze met mine with a gentle, friendly smile, as if he had been expecting me. Behind him stood a majestic altar, framed by two large white marble pillars. At the top of this altar was a frame adorned with intricate designs in gold.

I moved closer, drawn by an inexplicable curiosity about his identity. Before I could utter a word, he inclined his head slightly, his fingers thoughtfully caressing his beard, and he posed a question with a mysterious smile that halted my steps. "So, you wish to explore your past life with your husband?" His voice was both a whisper and an echo, filling the space around us.

Startled yet intrigued, and fully aware of the surreal nature of this dream, having just inquired that question while looking at my husband's photo, I nodded and said, "Yes, I do." At my consent, he extended his arms with a graceful flourish, and seven ethereal lanterns rose into the air, hovering just above me. Each lantern was uniform in size and color, all beige and aged, yet distinct in form, adorned with arcane symbols whose meanings eluded me.

He gestured towards the first lantern with a subtle wave of his hand, and as if responding to an unspoken command, it gently came to life with a soft, ethereal glow. My eyes locked onto the radiant light, and I felt an irresistible pull, as though gravity itself had been redirected. With a gentle lurch, I found myself transported into a house that stirred vague memories, its familiarity both enigmatic and inviting. I knew I had been here before, but I couldn't remember how or when.

As I oriented myself, a handsome man emerged from the kitchen, dressed in a red flannel plaid button-up shirt and dark denim jeans. His presence was immediately compelling. He had a warm smile on his face and my heart was drawn to him with familiarity. Though his features were subtly altered, the essence of his being—the unique energy that I would recognize anywhere—confirmed that he was my Logan.

His appearance was leaner, and he wasn't as tall as Logan; his expression carried an air of youthfulness and mischief. He flashed a playful smile that seemed to light up the room. Drawn by an overpowering sense of connection, I swiftly moved into his arms for a warm, heartfelt hug. "It's you," I said, hugging him tightly. "I missed you so much," I added, feeling his arms tighten around me. "I miss you, too, baby," he replied, his voice filled with happiness and satisfaction.

Turning to gaze through the kitchen window, I was enchanted by the sight of a vast vineyard stretching across rolling hills. The vibrant green vines sprawled gracefully under a sky painted with the gentle hues of dusk, each row leading toward a horizon that disappeared beyond the slopes, resembling paths to infinite possibilities. To the side, a tranquil pond teemed with playful ducklings, while splendid weeping willow trees lined its banks, their graceful branches cascading toward the water's edge, creating a serene and picturesque scene.

Logan gently wrapped his arms around my waist from behind and asked if I was hungry, his voice a familiar and comforting undertone of home. I smiled, a soft murmur escaping my lips, "You're always feeding me, no matter what lifetime we're in." A light chuckle followed, "It's no wonder I can't seem to shed any weight."

He turned me around to face him, and with tender affection, he squeezed me in his arms once more, pulling me into an embrace as warm as the sun. Then, he planted a gentle kiss on my head, right where my hairline met my forehead, a tender gesture he had always bestowed with loving precision. I rested my head just above his chest, nestling into the warmth of his neck. Oh, how I've missed this feeling of wholeness. Feeling him in my arms, my heart felt full. Logan held me tighter and said, "You're beautiful no matter what lifetime."

We settled at a round wooden kitchen table, surrounded by the serene glow streaming through the windows and large white French doors halfway ajar. A gentle breeze wafted in, carrying the faint, intoxicating aroma of vine-ripened grapes. As I turned to Logan, my heart filled with a deep sense of contentment. His hand reached out to hold mine. I smiled at him and asked, "What have you been doing here?" Logan returned my smile and said, "What I do every day, taking care of the farm." He gave me a playful wink as if I should already know that this was our daily routine.

Peering out through the French doors, I could see a stable with horses and baby goats hopping and playing in the field. A feeling of recognition began to set in, as if this were our life from another time. But before much more could be said, a celestial flash enveloped me, whisking me away to another reality.

I wasn't ready to leave yet. I still wanted to be with him longer, but suddenly I found myself in the second lantern. I was standing in a sunlit yard filled with laughter, the smell of freshly watered grass in the air. The sky suggested it was no later than noon. Two boys, about seven and ten, chased a ball with youthful exuberance, while a little girl dressed in pink pedaled her tricycle in joyful circles. The garage door was open, revealing a man engrossed in repairing a car as he leaned over the open hood. An innate sense of connection told me these were my children. I was happy to see them.

The man glanced up, his face breaking into a warm, welcoming grin. He quickly wiped his hands on a rag before tossing it aside and immediately approached me with open arms. Though his features were slightly different, the essence of his spirit was unmistakable. He was my Logan too, his soul undeniably familiar.

I wrapped my arms around Logan's shoulders, and he responded with a tender kiss. As my eyes scanned our surroundings, I took in the inviting look of our suburban home we lived in, nestled on a lush corner lot. Its exterior had a sage vinyl with stone accent and white trim. However, the tranquility was marred by the semi-busy street that was unsettlingly close. I turned to Logan and said in a concerned tone as I pointed to the street, "I really don't like living this close to such heavy traffic."

Suddenly, my heart seized with familiar dread as I spotted my daughter pedaling her tricycle toward the dangerous road. It felt like a premonition unfolding. I knew the horror that was about to happen. Like a bad déjà vu, I had seen this before. Desperation fueled my legs as I sprinted toward her, screaming for Logan to intervene. But it was too late. She had already reached the street. Out of nowhere, a large truck appeared, hauling produce in its open bed, striking her with devastating impact right before my eyes. The debris of her shattered tricycle was scattered everywhere on the ground, mingled with the spilled produce.

I let out a cry of sheer terror as Logan and I rushed to her side in frantic panic, tears pouring down my cheeks. I tried to find her among the wreckage, my heart trembling as my hands cleared a path to her. When I finally reached her, I cradled her lifeless form. She was only four, so small, so delicate. Holding her tightly, I wept deeply, mourning the daughter I would never see grow up. Logan cradled us both as he cried in anguish.

In the midst of my sorrow, just as before, I was whisked away to another reality—the third lantern. This time, I materialized in a cozy, warmly lit living room, alive with the sound of laughter and play. Five children—two girls and three boys—darted about, their energy filling the space with radiant life. I knew they were my children too.

At the sight of me, they halted in their play, their faces lighting up with recognition and joy. With excitement, they charged toward me, their small arms wrapping around me in a flurry of hugs. "Mom, you're home!" they cried out, their voices brimming with happiness, suggesting I had been away for a while.

With tears still wetting my cheeks, one of my daughters asked, "Why are you crying, Mom?" I smiled at her and responded, "I'm just happy to see you all."

I looked at them with a big smile and asked them to sit so I could study their faces carefully and talk to them. They were all familiar to me, and I felt a strong fascination, wanting to get to know them more since I had missed out on so much while I was away.

They arranged themselves in a neat row across a large beige sofa in our expansive living room. My youngest, a very active boy of about seven, sat squarely in the middle, his small legs joyfully kicking back and forth. My eldest, a tall, handsome boy on the cusp of 14, sat on the far left, leaning into my youngest daughter, who was possibly 10, with big eyes and an enchanting smile. They all looked at me cheerfully, their faces glowing with happiness and love.

"Where is your dad?" I asked, eager to see him.

"Dad is upstairs," my 11-year-old daughter chimed in happily. She had a delicate face and a beautiful twinkle in her eyes.

Beside her, my middle son, eight years old, shy and not as talkative, but he seemed anxious and happy to see me as if he was patiently awaiting his turn to talk.

At that moment, a tall man descended the large spiraling staircase that ended in the living room, his presence commanding yet familiar. "Hey, baby, you made it home," he announced, approaching with a charming smile. He settled beside me, wrapping his arm around my waist and giving me a kiss on the cheek.

I couldn't help but smile at the sight of him—this version of Logan, whose charm and allure never failed to captivate me. His energy was still unmistakably his own. I turned back to our children, allowing my gaze to drift slowly across each beloved little face. My heart swelled with joy at their lively presence. My youngest, in particular, caught my attention—an uncanny mirror image of his father, bearing the same radiant smile that could light up the darkest room.

Sparked by curiosity, he inquired with a big grin, "Where did you go, Mom?" I replied, "I had important tasks to attend to, and they took me very far from here." Unabated, he pressed, "What is it that you do?" I smiled and answered, "I'm a time traveler. I travel through different eras, realms, and universes."

His eyes widened with wonder as he exclaimed, "That is so cool, Mom. In these other realms and universes, am I there with you too?" I nodded, a smile spreading across my face. "Yes, you are. You're my son there too."

Before I could say another word, the scene shifted abruptly, sweeping me into the next realm, the fourth lantern. In this life, I found myself in a dimly lit bedroom, the walls unfamiliar and oppressive. I heard a man's voice yelling from the living room, harsh and unsettling. My heart pounded with anxiety as I slowly made my way towards the noise to see who was shouting.

"What took you so long to get out here?" the man demanded harshly.

I stared at him, bewildered. "I'm sorry, who are you?"

"What are you, stupid now too? Did you forget we're getting married in a week?" he snapped, clearly offended by my confusion. Disoriented and increasingly anxious, I backed away from the living room and retreated to the bedroom. He followed, his anger apparent.

Suddenly, he yanked my hair, dragging me back into the living room. "You walk away when I tell you you can," he yelled.

I grabbed hold of my hair and tried to push him away, but he was stronger than me. He shoved me to the floor and demanded I kneel. Fearing for my life, I complied. *How did I get here? Why was I in this life?* As fear gripped me, memories started to settle in. I realized I had been here before, and I knew Logan was somewhere in this lifetime. I could feel his energy beyond the confines of these walls.

It felt like hours or days had passed by. I managed to sneak out and went for a drive, ending up in front of a door. Unsure of what to expect, I knocked. It didn't take long before I heard footsteps approaching. As soon as the door opened and I saw who it was, I burst into tears.

Logan immediately held me in his arms. "What happened?" he asked. I cried, not from fear or pain, but from the relief of seeing him. He gently held my chin, noticing the bruise on my face, then looked at the bruises on my arms.

"Stay here," he demanded, grabbing his jacket and keys.

"Where are you going?" I asked, but he kept walking towards his car. I realized exactly what he intended to do. I grabbed his hand and pulled him into my arms. "Don't go. You don't need to go. Stay here with me. I'm never going back," I pleaded.

"I just want to smash his face in. No one should be hurting you like this," Logan fumed, his chest heaving with anger.

I held him tightly. "Stay with me," I asked again. Gradually, his anger began to subside. He stayed, his rage giving way to calm.

I looked up at Logan and kissed him, knowing in that moment he was my forever. I took his arm and led him back into the house. Just as I closed the door behind us, a glimmer of light flashed before me, and the scene vanished.

The light of the fifth lantern illuminated and began to flicker brighter, my vision becoming clearer. My eyes scanned the room where I had awoken. It was a luxurious bedroom, its walls constructed from dark stone, grand and imposing. The large bricks made the room feel both ancient and eternal, humming with a mysterious energy as if they held secrets from eons past. Intricate tapestries depicting celestial scenes lined the walls, adding to the room's ethereal ambiance.

To the left of my bed was a large open window. I got off the bed and moved toward it, marveling at the sight of other stone castles in the distance. Their rooftops were bustling with winged beings gracefully taking flight and landing. The view was mesmerizing, a testament to the enchanting world I had found myself in.

The window offered a breathtaking view of the endless ocean, its waves crashing far below. It was at least a 50-foot drop to the water, emphasizing the lofty position in this sky-bound world. The air was filled with the soft rustle of wings and the gentle hum of celestial activity. I took a deep breath, expecting the familiar scent of salt, but instead, I was greeted by the sweet, floral fragrance of lilies.

Think, Steph, think. My mind raced with questions. *What do you know of this life?* I asked myself. Suddenly, a silhouette appeared in the doorway. A tall man with broad shoulders and majestic wings stepped into the room. I felt his energy—it was Logan. As he approached, I saw him clearly. He wore a white cloth wrapped around his waist and leather sandals; his chiseled chest bare. He exuded a strength and serenity that instantly calmed me. It dawned on me that I had dreamt of Logan in this form before, but at the time, it had seemed like just another dream. Now, it felt so real.

"I'm glad you're awake," he said softly, his voice filled with love. He walked over to me, wrapping one arm around my waist and placing his other hand on my neck, just under my ear. He pulled me in for a kiss. As I hugged him, I felt my wings embracing him too.

"I have wings!" I exclaimed, surprised by the realization.

Logan chuckled. "Who doesn't?"

The wings on my back felt so natural, like extensions of my own arms, that I initially didn't notice they were there.

As he turned to walk back towards the door, he reached out his hand, wiggling his fingers in his usual gesture for me to take it. Gladly, I grasped his hand, and together we walked out the door and up a spiraling stone staircase that led to the rooftop.

Standing on the rooftop, I was amazed by the sight of other winged beings soaring through the sky. The sense of freedom and exhilaration was overwhelming. I turned to Logan, my eyes wide with astonishment. "We can fly!" I exclaimed. The instant I thought about flying, my wings expanded, lifting me off the ground as if gravity no longer applied. It felt so natural; I had no fear.

I turned towards the sky and took off into the clouds, flying high above the ocean. There was no land in sight, just the endless expanse of water and sky. I turned to look at Logan, and he was flying closely behind me, his wings gliding effortlessly through the air.

I remember this life, I thought to myself. As a child, I saw this world all the time in my dreams. Growing up, I often felt a strong urge to jump off cliffs with the yearning feeling that I could soar. I would dream of flying effortlessly over oceans and fields or living in stone structures surrounded by an endless ocean. Despite knowing I couldn't defy gravity, the impulse was always there. Here in this world and this life, I feel like I'm home, a place where our spirits truly belong. Here, the only emotions I feel are happiness and love.

Returning to the rooftop of our home, we descended the stairs into our bedroom room. I turned to Logan to admire how incredible he looked. Logan's eyes locked onto mine, filled with a depth of emotion that made my heart race. He reached out, his fingers gently tracing the outline of my face, from my forehead to my jawline. The touch was electrifying, sending shivers down my spine.

"You're so beautiful," he whispered, his voice husky with desire and affection. He leaned in, his breath warm against my skin, and our lips met in a tender, lingering kiss. The world outside ceased to exist; there was only the two of us, wrapped in each other's embrace.

I ran my fingers through his hair, pulling him closer, deepening the kiss. Our wings unfurled, brushing softly against each other, creating a cocoon of warmth and intimacy around us. Logan's hands roamed my back, sending sparks of sensation wherever they touched. He kissed along my jawline, trailing down my neck, each kiss igniting a fire within me.

"Logan," I whispered, my voice trembling with emotion. He paused, his eyes meeting mine once more. The love and longing in his gaze took my breath away.

"I'm here," he murmured, his lips finding mine again in a kiss that spoke of promises and forever.

I held him tightly, not wanting to let go. But as we kissed, I felt his lips and touch melt away. As the vision from the fifth lantern faded, I realized that the lanterns were not lighting up in chronological order. When I opened my eyes, I was somewhere else. For the first time, I cried having to leave a life behind. I wanted to go back but I couldn't. The life I had just left—that was our first life together.

With tear-filled eyes, I wiped them away to see what the light of the sixth lantern revealed. Another chapter of my intertwined destinies with Logan unfolded before me. This time, our life together was set in a small, picturesque village nestled in the mountains of Asia during the early 1800s.

In this life, I was a healer, known throughout the village for my gentle touch and knowledge of herbs and remedies. Logan was a blacksmith, strong and reliable, with a heart as warm as the forge he worked at. Our lives were simple but deeply fulfilling, surrounded by a community that valued and respected us both.

We lived in a modest cottage with our two children, a son and daughter, who were young adults. Our home was near a flowing river, surrounded by a garden where I grew medicinal plants. Logan had his forge nearby, and the rhythmic sound of his hammer on metal was a constant, comforting presence. The villagers often sought our aid, whether it was for a poultice to heal a wound or a sturdy tool crafted by Logan.

An illness had swept through the village, and I worked tirelessly to tend to the sick. Logan stood by my side, offering support and strength, crafting tools and contraptions to help care for the ailing. Our combined efforts saved many lives, but the toll on both of us was immense.

One night, as the lanterns flickered and the village was quiet, we sat together by the fire. Logan took my hand, his touch grounding me in the moment. "We make a good team," he said, his eyes reflecting the firelight.

"We always have," I replied, feeling the deep bond that transcended the multiple lives we've lived.

Suddenly, the vision from the sixth lantern faded, and I was whisked away into the seventh lantern. As the light returned, I found myself sitting only a few feet away from Logan. The cityscape with the setting sun behind him cast a warm glow, highlighting his deep, soulful eyes. *Oh my*, I thought. This was the first day we met. This is my current life. It dawned on me in that moment—these lifetimes within these lanterns were the stories behind his eyes that I had wanted to know since the day I met him. My eyes began to blur with tears as I continued to look at Logan, overwhelmed by a profound feeling of eternal love.

This time, instead of looking away to give his attention to his friend, he continued to look right at me, then winked and flashed my favorite smile.

I walked over to talk to him, my heart pounding. When I reached him, he stood up to embrace me. I held him tightly and said, "I've been wanting to come back to this day since you've been gone."

He looked into my eyes and said, "Don't forget our seven lifetimes together. There will be countless more because you are my half, and we complete each other."

With that, he gave me a deep, heartfelt kiss, sealing the promise of our timeless connection before everything vanished into darkness.

My eyes slowly opened, and this time, I finally stirred from my sleep, still entangled in a haze of drowsiness. I rolled over to Logan's side of the bed, eager to share the wild dreams I had. "Honey, I dreamt about you…" I murmured in a sleepy voice as I reached over to my left side to wake him, but my hand landed on his empty pillow. The silence that followed jarred me awake. Reality set in—Logan wasn't there anymore. A wave of sorrow washed over me, and I cried into my pillow.

It felt as though I had traveled lifetimes in my sleep, dreaming for days and weeks, losing track of how long I spent in each. Confused and disoriented, I glanced at the clock. It was only 3:28 a.m., just three hours since I had closed my eyes. How could such brief sleep hold such lengthy dreams? I lay there, gazing up at the dark ceiling, pondering the unfathomable depths of my dream.

As I lay in bed recounting the memories from each of our lifetimes together, one stood out—the third lantern. *Why did I tell my son I'm a time traveler through time and realms?* I internally asked myself, feeling puzzled and intrigued by such an odd dream and an even odder thing to say. His energy felt familiar, reminiscent of my son, Keith. Each scene and lifetime unfolded with clarity, and I felt an intense connection to every face that appeared before me. Each gaze seemed to echo through time, forging a link that transcended the boundaries of each vividly rendered world.

And then there was the second lantern. The image of my daughter passing away in my arms still ached in my heart, and I couldn't shake it off. I could still feel her weight, the warmth of her small body. The loss was excruciating, and I cried into my pillow. It was just a dream, but the emotion was so profound, as if it had just happened.

Logan had said not to forget our seven lives. It's so strange and so real that I don't know what to believe. *Was it even a dream, or did I somehow evoke it because I was thinking about our past lives before I slept?*

I tried to go back to sleep, but I couldn't. After more than an hour of tossing and turning, feeling frustrated, I gave up and went downstairs to sit in my kitchen. The house echoed with silence, and I felt empty. If Logan were here and I couldn't sleep, he would wake up too, either to accompany me or invite me back to sleep in the warmth of his embrace. He always knew how to soothe my bothersome mind.

I made myself some coffee and sat at the kitchen table to scroll through social media, seeing what others were up to—a reminder that life goes on. But it did not make me feel better. The way I saw it, there was life with Logan, and there was life without him, and I was stuck in the part where I am without him.

Suddenly, my phone rang, and I realized it was already 6:00 a.m. Kylie's name appeared on the caller ID. "How ironic," I thought, picking up the call. She asked how I was doing. "I'm okay, I just woke up," I replied in a soft, tired voice, even though I had been awake for a while.

"That's good," she said. "Are you available to come in today instead for your reading?" I was surprised by her sudden request. It was an intriguing feeling, especially after I had just experienced a bewildering dream. I cleared my throat and told her, "I could, but I already asked my daughter to join me, and she lives in Wisconsin. I don't think she can make it today. What happened to December?" I asked curiously, remembering she had mentioned being fully booked.

"Your spirit guides and your husband have been visiting me since we last talked, and they've been leaving me messages for you. You need to come see me so I can give them to you," she explained. I was speechless. Not knowing what to say next, I paused, feeling perplexed, then said, "Let me check with my daughter, and I'll get back to you." Kylie agreed, and we ended the call.

CHAPTER 31

MEDIUM & SPIRIT GUIDES

I WAITED UNTIL MID-MORNING, when the light filtered through my window, before calling Charlotte. I told her that Kylie had unexpectedly contacted me, urging us to move our scheduled reading forward. She claimed to have urgent messages from my spirit guides and Logan. A whirlwind of emotions swept over me—surprise mixed with excitement, underlined by a current of worry and anxiety. I was unsure of what could be so urgent that I had to know these messages immediately.

What could Kylie possibly have to tell me? And spirit guides—do I even have them? My thoughts raced as I considered the possibilities. My mom is a shaman, and she often speaks of her shaman guides. She had mentioned to me during a car ride together that one of her children would inherit a profound spiritual gift and as far as I know, neither my siblings nor I have shown any signs of shamanic abilities. Then again, I don't even know what those signs are. *Could spirit guides be the same as shaman guides?* I wondered anxiously, feeling the weight of the unknown bearing down on me.

After our conversation, Charlotte's voice was reassuring as she said, "If you feel comfortable going alone, then I think you should, Mom. She might offer the clarity and peace you've been searching for—answers that could finally quiet your troubled mind." I took a deep breath, clearing away the residue of my anxiety, and agreed to see Kylie to hear what messages she had for me.

With the winter season, nightfall arrived early. It was nearly 6:00 p.m., yet the streets were already shrouded in darkness. Being November, we should have received snow by now, but it felt more like a California winter in Minnesota. I playfully remarked to a circular-framed photo of Logan hanging on my rearview mirror, "You really don't want me to shovel snow, do you?"

Since my time in Minnesota, I've rarely had to shovel snow. Logan always insisted it was his job, telling me to just "sit and look pretty," a phrase that always made me roll my eyes, even as I appreciated his thoughtfulness. It was the gentleman in him, and I was just getting used to being loved that way.

He wouldn't even let me scrape the frost off my car windows. He would often take the snow scraper from my hand and tell me to sit in the warm car while he did it. Now, in my first winter without him, there was hardly any snow at all. Friends have told me that Minnesota hasn't seen this little snow in over a decade. A part of me wants to believe in the magic that Logan loved me so much that he somehow stopped the snow. It wouldn't be surprising, because that was just how my Logan was. It's bittersweet.

I made my way to Kylie's house, still feeling anxious but also tinged with curiosity and excitement. Walking to the front of her house, I rang the doorbell. I noticed a red cloth on the door. I don't know much about shamanism. I converted to Christianity as a teen and wasn't inclined to ask my mom about her shamanic practice. Seeing the red cloth, I wondered if it might be there to ward off negative energy or some form of protection.

Just then, Kylie opened a door on the side of the garage and greeted me. She explained that they don't use the front door. I didn't bother to ask why and followed her into her house. Once inside, Kylie guided me through the garage and into the house. We ascended a small flight of stairs to a spacious living room dominated by an overwhelming white altar. Towering nearly as high as the 12-foot ceiling, the altar was a breathtaking spectacle adorned with gold stars and intricately carved dragons painted in gold trims, seeming to dance in the flickering candlelight.

Her altar was divided into three distinct sections, with 12 compartments, each meticulously arranged. [55] Soft, flickering white candles rested in glass candle holders, and gold trays bearing offerings of rice, incense, and joss paper. Delicate white carnations in tall glass vases added a touch of serenity, their fragrance mingling with the aromatic incense, creating a sacred space that felt both ancient and alive.

She directed me where to leave my coat and belongings, then invited me to sit on a wooden chair next to her altar while she settled onto her wooden shaman bench, with joss paper lining the bottom of each foot.

In our initial phone conversation, Kylie had instructed me to bring a handful of incense and a stack of joss paper as offerings to her spirit guides. After settling into my chair, I handed her the offerings.

"Thank you," she said, taking them and placing them on her altar. She then sat back on her wooden bench and asked for my permission to read my energy. I nodded and said, "Yes." She mentioned she would

---

[55] The 12 compartments signify the 12th shamanic realm, representing the highest ranking shaman.

need a moment to channel me. I took a deep breath as I watched her close her eyes. Less than two breaths later, she opened them again and said in a gentle tone, "Your spirit guide is here. She has been watching over you, especially during this time of grieving."

Her words sparked my curiosity while also leaving me somewhat confused—I had no real understanding of what a spirit guide was. Then she continued, "Your mom is a shaman, but the shamanic path does not call to you as you don't have any shamanic guides. You are guided by celestial beings." The revelation surprised me; *how had she discerned that my mom is a shaman?* During our phone conversation, I had only mentioned that my husband had passed away, and I'm seeking guidance for my sorrow, nothing more.

She continued, "Trust the messages you've been receiving from your husband. He has been speaking to you and messing with your phone and electronics. You can hear him and feel his energy and emotion." My heart raced with intrigue and nervous anticipation. I was both fascinated by her insight and hopeful about what it might mean. Tentatively, I asked, "Is it because I'm grieving?" She shook her head and replied, "No, Hon. You're a medium. You've had this gift; you just didn't know it." Her words left me momentarily speechless. I struggled to process this insight. I remembered sensing and knowing certain things from a young age that others didn't seem to notice, but I had always dismissed these intuitions as mere observation or common sense.

Kylie's voice brought me back from my thoughts, "Your guides have been vigilantly watching over you since you were young. But this particular guide, she draws near whenever you're sad and has been guiding you in those moments." I searched my mind to understand. There have been times when I've been at my lowest point throughout my life and I've felt whispers, but I had always considered them my own thoughts.

Kylie added, "She isn't alone in your journey; there are more—

celestial guides and other guides from different realms accompanying you as well. They're all here to help you through your spiritual path." Stunned, I paused to absorb the gravity of her words. My mind swirled with questions. Gathering myself, I finally managed to ask, "What exactly does that mean? I have not heard of celestial guides. How are they different from shaman guides?"

Kylie paused briefly before explaining, "There are 360 dimensions in existence, and shaman guides occupy the first 12 levels. These dimensions are closest to earth. Other guides occupy higher dimensions, while celestial guides, also referred to as angel guides occupy the highest dimensions in the heavenly realms."

I then remembered my mom mentioning something about 360 dimensions, [56] but as I was uninterested and unfamiliar with shamanism, I never paid much attention. I explained to Kylie that I found it overwhelming and didn't fully understand. However, I expressed openness to learning more about how the information she shared applies to me, especially given the new sensations I've been experiencing since Logan's passing.

"Remember, you've always had these gifts, but when Logan passed, the impact of your loss and your connection to him triggered an increase in your frequency that heightened all your ethereal senses. These senses allow you to perceive energies beyond the physical realm," Kylie explained. She then redirected the conversation to Logan. "Your husband is here too," she murmured, her voice catching as tears welled in her eyes. "He loves you so much." A tear spilled over her cheek as she continued, "His love for you is so powerful. I could feel it. Your love for each other is so beautiful. He had his flaws in this lifetime, but wherever those flaws were, you made up for them because you balance each other."

---

[56] In Hmong, it's referred to as 360 "tshooj ntuj", meaning levels or realms

Tears streamed down my face as I heard her words. The ache in my heart grew heavier, understanding the depth of what she was referring to. We completed each other's weaknesses, constantly filling each other's cups without hesitation. Together, we were stronger.

"Your husband wants you to know that he is so proud of you and how you handled everything with his funeral and his family. He knows it was not easy, but you did everything right," Kylie continued, revealing details about him and our life together that left me astounded; such intimate knowledge she couldn't possibly have unless she was truly in contact with him. We had always been very private about our life. My heart clung to every word as tears continued to flow.

Then, she revealed, "The bond you both shared in life and continue to share in death is profound because he is your twin soul, your twin flame. Your souls were born from the same celestial place and are not from this earth. That's why throughout both your lives, you never felt like you belonged anywhere else. Instead, you belong to each other and have journeyed through seven lifetimes together here on earth and in other realms too. He said he is sorry for leaving you so soon and wishes he knew earlier in this life how connected you both are, because he would do life all over again, with you and only you."

Overwhelmed, I paused—twin flames, twin souls, other realms, seven lifetimes—these thoughts swirled in my mind. The image of the seven lanterns, symbolizing our shared existence across varied realms, my dream that remained untold to anyone, not even my daughters— How could Kylie possibly know of these intricacies? It was an overwhelming flood of information I hadn't prepared for, stretching the bounds of my understanding beyond recognition. The only thing keeping me anchored to the possibility was that I had felt things, seen things, and heard things I could not explain, and this couldn't possibly be more fascinating or bewildering than that.

After Kylie finished unveiling details about our lives, she added,

"Your spirit guides are ready to assist you throughout your spiritual journey, and your husband will be here for you too. He has become one of your guardians. Did you know that his soul underwent extensive training?"

Tears welled up as I nodded. She continued, "He did that so he wouldn't have to continue his soul's journey to reincarnate. A soul cannot stay unless they are trained and have permission to remain here, to watch over and protect you for the remainder of your life until you are together again."

"It makes sense," I said, recalling my dream where Logan and I were sitting on the porch, and he mentioned developing his soul. At the time, it was a mystery to me, but now, it seemed to fall into place because in another dream, I saw him going through his transformation. He was wrapped in a golden glowing light in this celestial place.

As we concluded our session, Kylie imparted a final piece of guidance. "Your guides are eager to communicate with you, and they've shown me how to assist you." She explained that during my meditations, I should keep a bowl of water within reach. "This simple element," she elaborated, "acts as a conduit, enhancing your connection to your guides and making their presence more known."

She revealed another profound piece of information: "You are guided by an ascended master residing in a very high dimension. He is stern, possessing a sense of royalty and wisdom. He won't tell me his name, but he said that when you're ready, you will be able to travel to him yourself, and he'll personally tell you his name and teach you more about your spiritual abilities.

"In that dimension, you have a celestial chamber, a sacred space designed specifically for you," she continued with confidence. "Your guides and this sacred space are why, unlike your mom or a shaman, you do not require a physical altar or the need to chant to perform your spiritual work. Your celestial chamber is your altar. Your visions manifest naturally and quickly because your guides are always in connection with you."

I was still grappling with the flood of information that had just been shared, but a sense of relief began to sink in. It was reassuring to know that the messages I had received from Logan were genuine expressions from him and not merely creations of my grief. It was also comforting to realize that someone beyond my own mind understood what I was experiencing and that I wasn't losing my sanity. I expressed my gratitude to Kylie for her guidance and support.

Shortly after returning home that evening, I decided to follow the instructions from my spirit guides. Though nervous with anticipation, I carefully placed a bowl of water nearby, settled into my meditation space, and lit a candle to ground myself. I focused my mind and breathed deeply to cleanse my energy. For twenty minutes, I meditated in silence, hoping for a connection. However, the elusive sense of connection I sought didn't emerge. *I'm probably not doing it right*, I thought, wondering if there was more I needed to understand or feel.

That night, as I drifted into sleep, I was swept into the most extraordinary dream I've ever had. My mind's eye was filled with a spectacular tapestry of numbers and vibrant colors—light blue, gold, and white—each merging and morphing into intricate designs that danced like a mandala in the blue sky.

Amidst this visual symphony, a figure emerged—a woman clothed entirely in white. She stood tall and ethereal, her fair skin almost luminescent, and her fine white hair cascading like a waterfall of light. Yet, her features retained the softness of youth. Her presence exuded a gentle and nurturing aura.

With a serene smile, she spoke softly, "This is your awakening." One by one, my spirit guides from multiple realms surrounded me, greeting me. Though I couldn't make out their individual words, their collective presence felt overwhelmingly positive. There were at least twenty of them speaking simultaneously, as if eager to connect with me. Then, suddenly, I stirred from sleep, immersed in a strange but wonderous sense as I tried to decipher the profound messages I had been given.

November had come and gone, and we were now a week away from Christmas. Normally, by the time the last trick-or-treaters had vanished into the night, my Christmas tree would already be twinkling proudly in the living room. This annual ritual had always brought me joy, and I looked forward to it every year. However, this was my first Christmas without Logan, and the idea of celebrating felt empty and excruciating. While the world outside buzzed with festivities and cheer, the only comfort I found was in the quiet of our bedroom, wrapped under the covers, my tears drenching the pillow.

One quiet night, as I was lying in bed engulfed by grief, I heard Logan's whisper: "Put up the tree, Baby. Get out of bed. Go down to the basement and bring out all the decorations." His words were a soft echo in the silence. I lifted my head from under the covers and gazed up at the ceiling, listening to his voice. "I know how Christmas makes you happy. And it will make me happy too if you do that," he urged.

I sighed and forced myself out of bed. I wiped my tears and said in a somber tone, tinged with playfulness, "You're still telling me what to do." But hearing him warmed my heart. I made my way downstairs into the basement and pulled out all the decorations. My daughter Kayla was visiting for the holidays. She and Keith helped me put up the tree and the rest of the Christmas decorations. We even placed a festive wreath on the door.

When the weekend arrived, it brought with it an invitation to an intimate Christmas gathering at a friend's house. I had no desire to go, preferring the quietness of being home alone in my room. But Logan's gentle urging echoed in my mind, "Go to the party. Go hang out with your friends. Don't be alone. Live your life and enjoy it. Take Keith with you. I'll be there," he reassured in his soft, familiar whisper.

Reluctantly, I agreed and took Keith along. Logan was right; the smiling faces of all my friends at the party lifted my spirits. We played games, and I genuinely laughed—a kind of laughter I hadn't known in a while, though part of me ached for Logan to be there. We indulged in festive foods and danced around the kitchen island. For the first time in a long time, I found myself enjoying the moment, a distraction from the constant sadness.

Mid-dance, the music began to hiccup, skipping beats erratically. A smile graced my lips, and I knew it was Logan letting me know he was there. He often did that when I was listening to music—in my car, at home, or even while shopping—the music from the intercom would skip. His voice then caressed my ear, tender yet clear, "I told you I'd be here. I've been dancing with you. Keep smiling, Beautiful." His words were bittersweet, and though I smiled, tears began to pool in my eyes. Excusing myself, I retreated to the bathroom to wipe away the tears, feeling both his absence and his presence profoundly.

The weekend after, I was visiting my mom to help her with her shaman ritual to call in the new year.[57] An auntie I had never met before was there to help as well; she was also a shaman. After the ritual, the auntie needed a ride home, and I agreed to take her.

I drove her to her house and helped her carry her things inside. When I was about to leave, I gave her a hug. As she hugged me, she said,

---

[57] A Hmong term referred to as "hu plig xyoo tshiab" which means to call your spirits for the New Year. This is done for good health and fortune.

"Your husband is very talkative." I smiled at her and said, "Yes, he is." She then added, "He wants you to meet someone new and be happy." I took a deep breath and sigh, then replied, "Yes, I know, and I told him to say no more. I don't want to hear any of it." She smiled and said it's okay to be sad for a while. I nodded and left.

Every now and then, I would encounter gifted friends or individuals whom I've never met, yet they always seem to convey a message from my husband. He is always looking out for me somehow. If he is not whispering to me directly, he is doing it through someone else, whether in person or in a dream, to pass the message along. I feel like it was his way of ensuring I am not alone, that there are people I could talk to, beyond spending all my time in the quiet somber of our bedroom.

One early morning in January, during the quiet hours before dawn, I was jarringly awakened by a force gripping my arm and yanking me toward the edge of the bed. The room was still dark, and my eyes, bleary with sleep, barely made out a dark, shadowy figure darting back and forth from my bed to the floor beside me. I could hear its ethereal, winded scream echoing throughout my room as its bony fingers gripped tightly around my right wrist, pulling hard. A wave of panic washed over me as I used my other hand to push and pry its bony fingers off my wrist while pulling my arm back with all my strength to break free.

Just then, my panic was quickly quelled by the soothing voice of my spirit guide. I felt the gentle pressure of her hand on my right shoulder as she whispered, "Be calm. Your third eye is now completely open." Her words surrounded me like a soothing blanket, and instantly, the tension drained from my body; the shadowy figure loosened its hold and vanished into the ether.

Relieved and devoid of any lingering fear, I turned over and quietly murmured a request to Logan to soothe me back to sleep. Instantly, I was embraced by his warm presence and drifted back into a deep, undisturbed sleep.

I did not stir awake until sunlight had filled my room. Lying in bed, listening to the subtle quietness of the morning, I pondered what had happened before the sun came up. I examined my wrist, half-expecting to find marks, but the skin was unblemished. "My third eye is completely open," I whispered to myself, pondering its meaning.

Two months had passed since my session with Kylie. It was now January, and every day since that profound awakening dream, I've sensed an increase in my frequency that I hadn't recognized before.

I recalled many years ago, shortly after my divorce from my ex-husband, I would wake up with what I thought were panic attacks. I was clueless as to why, as there wasn't anything specific troubling me. Not sure what to call them, I assumed they were panic attacks because my heart rate would quicken, and I felt this warm and cool vibrating sensation all over my body. It always happened in the middle of the night and would jolt me awake from my sleep.

It wasn't until recently, as my frequency increased more rapidly and the feeling of nighttime panic resurfaced, that my spirit guide assured me it's only them increasing my frequency and to not be startled. In these moments, I call on Logan to comfort me, and he always does. His warming presence and embrace lulls me back to sleep, easing my usually busy mind and making my body completely at ease.

Whether I'm absorbed in work at my desk, deep in meditation, or navigating the bustle of daily errands, I would feel a constant, noticeable energy vibrating within and around me. It often starts as a subtle, cool or warm, tingly sensation at the back of my neck, then radiates forward in waves of vibration, arousing all my senses. This energy manifests in my arms, and at times, when standing, I experience the uncanny feeling of wading through water, though no water is present. It's an extraordinary sensation, entirely new and utterly transformative, suggesting realms and realities beyond my prior perceptions.

Talking to Kylie, she said, "It's a normal sensation because your guides are working to increase your frequency. As you grow stronger, more senses will develop. I can sense your energy growing. Your frequency is much higher than when I last saw you." Like Logan, I'm constantly developing too.

CHAPTER 32

UNTIL WE'RE HOME

AFTER LOGAN WAS LAID TO REST, I visited him every single day until daylight saving time ended and night fell earlier. By the time I finished work, darkness had descended, so I had to reduce my visits to once a week on my days off. Logan had also been gently nudging me not to spend every day at the cemetery because, being a medium, I appeared like a lighthouse in a sea of spirits. Like moths to a flame, they might hover around me, and depending on the spirit, he didn't want anything to attach themselves to me and follow me home. He reminds me that he is with me no matter where I am and to always be careful. I always felt his protective presence during the drive there and on the drive home, and my spirit guides are always watching over me, an ability that I've grown sensitive to discerning.

Every week, without fail, I visited him, always bringing a bouquet of red roses adorned with a delicate arrangement of baby's breath and fern. Rain or snow, it didn't matter; I made sure that the place where he rested was never without flowers, because he once mentioned that those he cared about most rarely showed up for him. I wanted to ensure that he knew, through my actions, that I would never forget and will always be there for him, no matter the circumstances.

In life, he always gave me flowers for every special occasion, and occasionally, for no occasion at all, I would do the same, expressing to him that "men should receive flowers too."

One day in February, after a winter with barely any snow, the weather began to warm up, and the sun lingered longer through the clouds. I wanted to get Logan flowers before leaving on my trip with a few of my best girlfriends, who felt a happy mini getaway was needed. Our flights were scheduled for the next day.

I went to the store to pick up my usual red rose bouquet for Logan. However, as soon as I saw this bouquet of yellow roses, tinted with a slight shade of red, I felt an instant happiness that seemed to appear out of nowhere. It was as if my heart had suddenly brightened at the sight of those flowers, so I decided to get that bouquet instead.

When I arrived at Logan's resting place, I said to him, "I don't know why, but when I saw this arrangement, I was instantly happy because it reminded me of the colors in the sunset we both love, your favorite drink made of pineapple and grenadine, and your favorite scarf—the first one I made you. We could use a bit of happiness right now."

I carefully arranged the flowers in a garden vase with a sturdy spike that anchored it to the ground and placed it on the lawn where he rests. I sat there with the sun's glow embracing us. Taking in the moment, I closed my eyes, feeling the gentle breeze caressing my face and hair.

Logan then softly whispered, "I was there, and I was happy too when I saw those flowers because they reminded me of the yellow bouquet you held on the day we got married." I had momentarily forgotten that my wedding bouquet had yellow flowers too. This month, two years ago, he proposed to me with his song. The anniversary of his proposal made me more emotional than usual, but his sweet reminder made me smile, and lightened my sorrow. With tears seeping through my closed eyes, I felt the warmth of his love in my heart.

March came along, and my daughter Charlotte, her husband Kenneth, and my grandson came to visit. She brought us a box of donuts, which I thought was a very sweet gesture. I placed the unopened box on top of the coffee table in the middle of our living room. After a moment of catching up and playing with my grandson, I had almost forgotten about the box of donuts and suggested that we have some.

Upon opening the box, I found an ultrasound picture affixed to the bottom of the lid. The moment I saw it, my eyes lit up, and I immediately looked at my daughter. She smiled at me, mirroring my happiness. Rising from my seat, I hugged her tightly, tears unexpectedly streaming down my face. Taking a step back and observing her, she was already barely showing. "How far along are you," I asked.

With a smile, she replied, "I'm 13 weeks now." Hearing that made my tears flow even more. "That means you're already approaching your second trimester," I remarked.

She chuckled and confirmed, adding that they had wanted to tell us sooner but waited to surprise us in person because of how special this baby was.

A few months ago, just before Christmas, I visited my family in Colorado for a weekend and had an extraordinary experience. On my first night there, I slept in my niece's bedroom. For some reason, I couldn't fall asleep. I tossed and turned until I suddenly remembered there was a crib in the room, and in it was a baby. I thought, maybe cuddling with the baby and feeling its warmth might help me fall asleep. I immediately got up from my bed, walked over to the crib, and picked up the baby, holding it in my arms.

The baby was dressed in a soft beige flannel bodysuit. It felt tiny in my arms as I walked back to my bed to sit down. Suddenly, it dawned on me: How did this baby get here? This must be a dream. But I don't remember falling asleep. I was tossing and turning, feeling frustrated, and then suddenly I'm here in this dreamscape. The experience was the most puzzling and surreal I had ever encountered.

Suddenly, Logan walked into the room and confirmed that this was indeed a dream. He said, "I brought you this baby to hold." Surprised, I replied, "Honey, it'd be a miracle if I were somehow pregnant after you've left." He chuckled and said, "This is Charlotte's baby. I wanted you to hold your grandchild first before I bring this baby to her." I looked down at the little baby, its legs kicking and arms waving, and felt an overwhelming surge of love.

Next, I awoke, and it was already morning. There was no crib in the room, and no baby. I shared my wild dream about Logan, the baby, and the crib with my sister-in-law, Yuri, who is my brother Henry's wife. Yuri then said, "Oh, that just gave me chills. Where was the crib located?" I told her it was at the foot of my bed, against the wall.

She then confirmed that when she and my brother were touring the house with their realtor, planning to purchase it, there was a crib in that exact spot. The room had been set up as a nursery. However, the family moved before the baby was born, so there was never a baby in that room. I thought it was such an interesting coincidence.

Upon returning to Minnesota, I shared my extraordinary dream with my daughter Charlotte. She responded, "I'm not surprised. I had been praying to Logan, asking him to watch over the souls of my future children before they come to me in this lifetime." Hearing that filled me with happiness. Knowing that she loves and trusts Logan enough to watch over her future children was a precious and endearing gift of knowledge, making my heart feel full.

I then asked her, "Are you two planning to have a second child?"

She replied that they have been trying but haven't been successful yet. I smiled and said, "Perhaps soon. I have a good feeling about Logan. He always comes through on his words." When they showed up at my home and announced that they were now expecting and had been for 13 weeks, it meant they conceived just a couple of weeks after my dream. I thanked Logan for his unwavering love and for always being there for me and my children.

One morning in April, my alarm did not go off as it normally did. It was set for 7:00 a.m. every weekday. However, I did not hear it at all. I had a very vivid dream that kept me from waking, and these dreams are usually so real that they seem to drain all my energy. By the time I woke up to look at the time, it was already after 9:00 a.m. I figured I was so engrossed in my dream that I didn't hear it. I got out of bed to get ready for the day.

Thankfully, I don't schedule early morning meetings, so there was no panic there. However, as I walked into the hallway, I noticed my son's bedroom door was closed. Normally, every morning, my son would wake up to catch the bus to school, which picks him up right in front of our house, and he would always leave his door open, letting me know that he had already left. Curious, I went to knock on his door. Surprisingly, he was still asleep. "Why didn't you get up to go to school?" I asked.

Still drowsy, he rubbed his eyes and looked at the time. "Oh shoot! I did not hear my alarm," he exclaimed in a sudden panic. "I had set four different alarms on different devices, and I didn't hear a single one," he continued to explain.

"It's ok, Keith. Don't worry about it. Strangely, I didn't hear my alarm either. Why don't you just stay home today? I have a video conference meeting at 10:00 a.m. and won't be able to take you to school and make it back on time."

After I was done getting myself ready, I settled at my desk for work. I thought about my dream and how real it was. It was one of those dreams with Logan where it felt like I was awake. It reminded me of the dream I had in Colorado last December when he brought me my grandchild to hold.

I was lying in bed, deep in sleep, when I was awoken by Logan standing at my bedside. The feeling was very strange, yet I knew I was still in a dreamscape. "Hey Baby, wake up," he said in his low, deep, comforting voice. "I have to get going now." I rose from my bed and saw him standing just a foot away, wearing a white T-shirt and gray cargo pants. I looked down towards his feet and noticed his work boots were already on, always an indication that he was ready to head out for work. He carried a duffle bag in his left hand that rested at his side, while his right hand held onto the strap of his backpack slung over his shoulder.

He then set his bags on the floor and said, "Give me a kiss and hug, Baby, before I go." Immediately, I got out of bed, my heart slightly panicked. "Where are you going?" I asked. "I have to get to work," he replied. Suddenly, my memory flashed back to that Tuesday morning when he was leaving for his hunting trip. I felt a sense of urgency not to let him go, yet a slight hesitation because I knew I couldn't force him to stay.

I tiptoed forward to wrap my arms around his shoulders and neck, pulling him into a close embrace as he encircled my waist, squeezing with the same affection he had shown that morning. I clung to him, feeling the solid breadth of his shoulders and the comforting warmth of his chest against mine. We lingered in that embrace, savoring the moment before reluctantly parting. He picked up his bag and walked out of our bedroom. I followed closely behind, longing to keep him with me, but the words to make him stay remained unspoken.

We walked through our hallway and down the short steps, stopping at the halfway landing by the window of our L-shaped stairs. He turned around to look at me one more time. I stood on the step just above the landing so that we were closer to eye level, with him still slightly taller. Forcing the words out, I said, "Don't go. I'm afraid if you go, I won't see you again." Tears streamed down my face. He placed his bags on the floor and gazed gently into my eyes with a tender expression. Softly wiping away my tears, he said, "I have things to do, things to take care of. But I won't be long, and I won't be far away."

I tried to contain my tears, but I couldn't. They helplessly continued to flow. "I don't want to be without you," I said through trembling words and tears. He slowly raised his right hand to my face, pulled me in for a soft kiss, and I could taste the salty tears on my lips. He then gently tucked my hair behind my left ear and said in a tender, loving tone, "I love you. I will always be around, checking in on you from time to time. You'll always know when I'm around."

He continued to wipe my tears and kissed me one more time, then said, "In the meantime, try to be happy, even if it's hard. Live your life in the most beautiful way you can. I want you to live out all the adventures we planned, and one day, when we're home again, we will have many stories to tell." I cried as my chest trembled with each breath and hugged him tightly again. "I love you, Honey. I love you forever," I said. He gave me one more tight squeeze, kissed the top of my forehead where my hairline begins, and picked up his bags.

He turned and continued walking down the stairs, opened our front door, stepped out onto the enclosed porch, and disappeared into the light. Then I woke up.

I finished my workday and was sitting down for dinner at our kitchen table with Keith. It was just after 6:00 p.m. when he placed his phone face down on the table, having just finished looking through some messages. He cautiously looked up at me and said in an unusual tone, "Mom, it's a good thing I didn't go to school today."

Feeling a bit alarmed, I asked, "Why is that?"

"Well, I just found out that a kid brought a gun to school," he answered. My eyes widened in shock at what I had just heard. Before I could say anything, Keith added, "Thankfully, the gun was confiscated by the school before anything happened."

Relieved, I said to Keith, "It was definitely a good thing you didn't go to school today." I paused for a moment, then added, "I had the strangest dream about Logan this morning, and that's why I didn't wake up; otherwise, I would have made sure you went to school." I felt deeply thankful, believing Logan had kept us safe once again.

Just then, Keith said, "That's weird, I had a dream about Logan too." I immediately leaned in and gave Keith my full attention. "What did you dream?" I asked.

"I dreamt that Logan knocked on the front door, and I answered," said Keith, furrowing his brow as he concentrated on the details of his dream. "He asked me to go for a drive with him. Without much thought, I walked out with him, and we got into his car. We drove for a while, not really saying much at first, and then he said, 'We're on our way to see your mom,' and I nodded. The rest of the way, Logan was talking and cracking jokes like he always does, but I don't remember exactly what he said. We kept driving until we came to a building where you were. We both got out of the car and saw you. We were all standing there by this building, talking for a moment. Then Logan turned to me and said he had work to do and had to get going. He told me to be good and look after you, then gave me a hug. He turned to you, gave you a hug too, saying that he loves you, and then he got back into his car and drove off. That's all I remember of my dream."

I had been listening intently, not wanting to miss a word. When Keith finished, I felt even more relieved and said, "Logan was definitely looking after both of us. Even if I hadn't heard my alarm and you had woken up to yours, you would have gotten ready for school and left on your own. He loves you as your dad and wouldn't want anything to happen to you. Logan knows the turmoil I'd be in if anything happened to you." My eyes welled with thankful tears as I smiled at Keith.

We continued to sit at our kitchen table, both feeling fortunate and loved by Logan, whose presence still embraced and protected us every single day.

A month later, while I was asleep and dreaming, my mind's eye kept alternating between the number 10 and Logan, but nothing else was revealed. Each time the number 10 appeared, a slightly intense vibration would run through my body, varying in temperature from cool to warm, and I felt as though I was entering a trance, though I tried to resist it. Logan would then appear, and the feeling would dissipate. This continued throughout the night.

By now, I had gained more control over my spiritual abilities and understood enough not to be afraid, though I was still learning. When I woke up in the morning, I was perplexed about why Logan would show me the number 10. He was very adamant that I pay attention to the number but would not explain why. Even when I asked, I didn't receive any usual whispers, feelings, or intuitive insights, which had been my strongest senses.

Feeling confused and intrigued, I called Kylie and told her about my dream, hoping she could shed some light. After explaining it to her, she said, "I'm not getting anything. I don't interpret dreams, and your spirit guides and Logan aren't telling me anything either. But pay attention to the day. That's all I have for you." We continued with a few exchanges about our mornings before hanging up the phone.

I looked at my calendar and saw it was Monday, May 6, 2024. I thought to myself, "Okay, the 10th. It's this Friday. I don't have anything significant planned except for a meeting I scheduled about a month ago. It's set for 6:00 p.m. at Unison Restaurant to discuss the plans for our next big event."

Before Logan's passing, he had meticulously put together the roadmap for our third Hmong Nouveau Fashion Show & Concert. After he passed, people approached me about continuing the event, but I informed them that I wouldn't be doing it anymore. The pain of losing him was too much, and I remembered all too well the amount of work and stress involved. The tears, the sleepless nights, and how Logan was always there to shoulder the burden and soothe my unraveling emotions made me doubt my ability to continue without him.

But then I kept dreaming of Logan making announcements about his big event, and I was reminded of his hopeful smiling face and his inspiring words about wanting to do something great. This was his brainchild and legacy. I couldn't let him down. So here we are, at it again, for the third time. Perhaps that is why he was so adamant that I pay attention to the 10th day of this month.

Friday came, and everything seemed normal leading up to it. I headed over to Unison with a red folder in hand, filled with the agenda and all the materials I needed to go over with my planning committee. I ordered food and appetizers for everyone, something that was always important to Logan, ensuring everyone was fed and taken care of. After more than an hour of discussions and sharing ideas, we adjourned the meeting at about 7:30 p.m., feeling inspired and excited as we looked forward to a year and a half of preparing and executing our next event.

I thanked everyone on Logan's behalf, sharing a few heartfelt words. Pausing as tears welled up in my eyes and a lump formed in my throat, I ended with, "This was Logan's vision, and it means the world to me to have everyone on board in continuing his legacy." Everyone smiled and expressed their happiness to do this all over again in his honor. Their support and commitment filled me with gratitude and a renewed sense of purpose.

As everyone got up to leave, a few stayed behind to chat and eat in the restaurant. Melanie, one of the planning committee members, came up to me and said, "I have to get going. My boyfriend and I have plans to see the northern lights tonight. I hear it's going to be extraordinary because a northern light show as big as tonight's only happens once every few years." I nodded, excited to learn about the northern lights display. When my friend Jessica asked if I wanted to join her and her boyfriend for the trip, I hesitated and said, "I think I'll just go home. I didn't make any plans to go that far north, so you guys go ahead."

I can only take so much being out in public before I start feeling overwhelmed by the energy around me. When that happens, all I want is to be home, sheltered in my room where I can rest, meditate, or cry, depending on how I'm feeling. More often than not, I end up feeling completely drained and tired.

On my drive home, I kept hearing "Stillwater," but it didn't make sense to me, so I continued driving. When I arrived, Keith and Cassie were there. Cassie had moved in with us a month earlier from Colorado. She made this decision after Logan passed away, wanting to be closer to me and Keith and to bring joy and warmth back into our home and family.

As soon as I walked through the door, Cassie said excitedly, "Mom, did you know the northern lights are happening tonight?" I nodded, acknowledging that I did. After putting my things down, I continued to hear a soft echo of "Stillwater" in my mind. Stillwater was where Logan and I had sat on those stone steps almost five years ago, the place where I knew I would love this man forever.

I then said to Cassie and Keith, "Let's go to Stillwater. I feel like

Logan wants us to go there." We quickly got into the car and headed out to Stillwater. It was already about 9:30 p.m., and I didn't want to be out too late. We drove all the way to Stillwater, arriving just a few minutes after 10:00 p.m. I pulled into the same parking lot where Logan and I had once parked, facing the St. Croix River.

It was dark as we stepped out of the car, and I said to my kids, "Remember when we came here to release dove-shaped balloons for Logan?" They each smiled and said, "Yes, we remember." We began our stroll toward the water's edge, the gentle rhythm of the water lapping against the banks growing clearer as we distanced ourselves from the parking lot and its lights. In the distance, the lively melody of music drifted from a nearby restaurant where people were enjoying their dinner.

Suddenly, Cassie's voice brimmed with excitement as she pointed to the northeastern sky, exclaiming, "Mom, look! It's so beautiful. I see it." Entranced by her enthusiasm, we all followed her gaze upward. The dark sky had transformed, bathed in a mesmerizing dance of purple and turquoise hues.

The week before Logan passed, we had eagerly anticipated driving up to Duluth together to witness the mesmerizing spectacle of the northern lights. However, he was engrossed in wrapping up a project before his upcoming hunting trip, and I respected how dedicated he was to finishing his tasks before leaving for any leisurely activities. This had always been a hallmark of his character. By the time he got home, making the three-hour drive seemed unfeasible.

Despite my understanding, Logan promised, "I'll make it up to you," aware of my longstanding desire to see the aurora borealis. Little did we know, he never returned home.

As I stood along the water's edge in Stillwater, taking in the breathtaking scene of the night's display, a realization dawned on me with poignant clarity: this was what Logan wanted me to see. He kept quiet until the moment was just right for me to take notice of his nudging. It was his dramatic way of surprising me still. This was the significance of his insistence on the tenth day and Stillwater, a place that meant so much to us. His last earthly promise to make it up to me, and he certainly did in so many magical ways.

I don't know if we sensed certain things before they unfolded, as if an unspoken knowledge hung between us, whispering that our time together would be heartbreakingly short, or if it was simply because we loved each other so deeply that the fear of loss was inherently part of that love. Yet, we cherished every day as if it were our last, with a depth of gratitude that only such foreknowledge could inspire.

There were moments, suspended in the stillness between us, when my husband would confess, "I always thought I would die young." My heart would seize, and I'd hastily reply, "Don't say things like that." But he would only shake his head, a wistful smile playing on his lips as he said, "It's just a feeling I've always carried with me. That's why I never bothered with retirement plans, accumulated any debt, or acquired grand possessions like a house. I've always believed life is fleeting, a brief dance of light before the dusk."

Often, I'd find myself pleading with him, my voice tinged with urgency, "Take good care of yourself when I'm not around, because I need you. You hear that? I NEED YOU. I just found you, and I can't bear the thought of losing you. I will ALWAYS need you." This visceral, gnawing fear would echo through my thoughts whenever he was out of sight.

Reflecting on these heartfelt confessions that we exchanged time and again, I remain uncertain if we truly grasped the depth of our premonitions. However, we understood one irrefutable truth: every day we shared was an invaluable gift, a fleeting miracle not to be taken for granted.

Even in our last moment together before he drove off, it was a joyful memory. We were smiling, wrapped up in our love, happy just to be together. The last words we spoke to each other on the phone were, "I love you." Those words, filled with so much warmth and sincerity, have become a cherished memory that I hold onto tightly.

Loving someone so deeply, more than your own life, and then having to live without them is a unique kind of pain. You don't just mourn the person; you mourn every conversation, every dream and plan you've ever made, every memory you've ever shared, and all the memories you'll never get to create. The grief is indescribable, and there are no words that can truly capture the depth of that pain.

Losing my husband was unimaginable; we were just getting to the best part of our lives. Yet amidst the torrents of tears, the piercing heartache, the ethereal whispers and echoes, and the messages from heaven, a profound truth emerged: our loved ones never truly depart from us. How fortunate I am to say I had the chance to have one more conversation with him, even after his earthly breath had ceased.

Death, I realized, is only an ascendance to a higher realm of existence, where a thin veil separates us from our loved ones' eternal presence. If we pay attention and are open to seeing the signs, we may just catch fleeting glimpses of them—in a dream, in the melody of a familiar song, in the discovery of random coins in unexpected places, or even in the gentle caress of a breeze. These moments serve as poignant reminders that they are still with us, watching over us from their place beyond.

Though our time together in this lifetime was fleeting, the imprint left by my husband resonates deeper than any other experience I've ever known. Despite my flaws, mistakes, or the days I felt unbeautiful, he never wavered in seeing me as the radiant soul he painted me to be, inside and out.

I've been dragged, beaten, and drenched in my own blood and tears, enduring trauma that took many years to forgive myself for allowing and to overcome. But Logan's unselfish love has sculpted and changed me eternally, rendering every scar, whether visible or hidden, nonexistent. His love transformed my perception of myself and my capacity for healing. My human experience has been made better because of his existence.

In his eyes, I found a reflection of my truest self. He often spoke of how I saved him, how my presence charted a course to a future he once deemed unattainable. Yet, it was he who saved me, unveiling my inner strength to stand up for myself and revealing a capacity for self-love that I never knew existed.

Even beyond physical death, amidst my grieving and sorrow, when surrender seemed tempting, his enduring love echoed with words that stirred me from despair, a constant reminder of his everlasting presence. These intangible treasures, priceless and enduring, will stay with me every day for the rest of my life.

Everything has not been the same since he left. Losing someone who meant the world to me—the security of his embrace that lulled me to sleep each night and the warm face I've kissed as many times as there are stars in the vast sky—has brought inevitable changes. But I'm learning to live with the grief of my physical loss while also embracing a spiritual rebirth, knowing that our story hasn't ended. *A new chapter has emerged,* and we'll take everything we still have and make it worthwhile, cherishing each moment and being thankful for the precious memories I will hold in my heart until I see and hold him in my arms again.

If I could, I'd do it all over again—every joy and sorrow, every mistake—all to end up with him again, even knowing our story would end the same. Because he was unequivocally worth it. After all, grief is the echo of love's enduring resonance.

My husband once said to me during a playful conversation, "If I were to find you in another life, I wouldn't hesitate. I would come up to you, look you in the eyes, and take your hand," he took my hand as he was telling me this, "and I would kiss your hand," placing a gentle kiss on the back of my hand, "and then I'd say, 'I'm sorry to have kept you waiting,' and you would just know that I am the person you had been longing for." I smiled at him and replied, "Well, I hope you'll do that so I would know it's you. But find me sooner so I can love you longer."

Among the seven billion people in the world, I consider myself the most fortunate to have been in the right place at the right time to meet my Logan, my twin flame—two halves of the same soul. I'll treasure every radiant memory from the nearly five years we spent together until my last breath. In another life, when I am reborn, these memories will weave into the soft clouds of my dreams, bringing gentle smiles to my lips as a newborn starts anew. And I will find Logan in another form. Our eyes may not recognize each other at first, but our souls will, just as they have for the seven lifetimes before.

Until we're home again.

Until the next chapter.

I miss you. I love you.

POSTSCRIPT

THROUGHOUT THE WRITING PROCESS OF MY MEMOIR, Logan often visited me in my dreams, where we discussed specific chapters and the details he wanted to ensure were included. His presence and influence became integral to the book, making the words on these pages as much his as they are mine. Writing this memoir turned into an extraordinary and deeply healing experience, one I had not initially anticipated or thought possible. I realized that Logan was still very much a part of my life, and our story did not end with his passing.

Initially, when I wrote *Seven Lanterns*, I only mentioned having a vivid dream of seven lanterns, which revealed that Logan and I had shared seven lifetimes together. I then described meeting Kylie for a soul reading session where she confirmed this. I did not delve into the details of each life I saw in the lanterns because I wasn't sure if I should share an experience I couldn't yet fully understand.

After I said I was done writing the book, Logan visited me in a dream and said, "You need to go back and write more about the seven lanterns and our seven lifetimes together. It's important that we always remember these lifetimes. Write about our children, our home, the life we lived, and how much we loved each other." As I was waking from this dream, I replied aloud in my half-awake state, "Okay, I'll do that." Immediately, I sat at my desk and began to write out the details of our seven lifetimes. When I finished, the emotion and process of recounting my dream in detail deepened my belief that this is only a momentary separation for my husband and me until the next chapter starts anew.

On the morning I declared my book finally finished, before I had the chance to tell anyone, I received a phone call from Kylie. "Did you finish your book?" she asked, her tone both surprising and inquisitive. I was equally surprised by her question but answered, "Yes, I just finished it this morning." She laughed and said, "That's good. Logan was just here, all excited and happy, telling me you had just finished your book." I smiled and laughed with her, warmth filling my heart, knowing that Logan shared my sentiment too.

I don't know why some people can recall their past lives while others don't. Take my son, for example. At two to three years old, he started telling stories that I thought were just his imagination, and I would often respond, "That's nice," not really taking his stories seriously. It wasn't until his stories became more detailed that he got my undivided attention.

One day, just before he turned three, we were sitting at our kitchen table. I had just made him lunch, and he was telling me stories as he always did. I usually perceived these tales as part of his active imagination and often responded with, "That's nice." However, this time he began talking about his best friend, who he said was blind. Immediately, I looked at him with a puzzled expression. At his age, I knew all his friends, who consisted of his older sisters and cousins, and none of them were blind. Moreover, we had never discussed blindness because we didn't know anyone who was vision impaired, so I was surprised that he even knew the word "blind."

He started his story, "My friend *long time ago* was blind. He didn't have any family and he passed away. My dad *long time ago* helped me dig a hole in the ground and we buried him. It was raining so much that day." Stunned by his words, the hair on my arms stood up. I began to ask him, "Did someone tell you this story? Did you see this somewhere?" The more questions I asked, the more frustrated he became, finally saying in an exasperated tone, "No, Mom. It happened *long time ago*."

In that moment, I realized that he often spoke of his dad from a long time ago. I had always assumed that "a long time ago" for him could have been that very morning or yesterday because children his age often don't understand the concept of time.

Curious, I pointed to his dad sitting on the couch and asked, "Do you mean your dad right there?" He shook his head. "No, Mom. A different dad. Long time ago."

Around the age of five, my son began to speak less and less about his memories from past lives, but through that experience, he showed me that past lives and life before our earthly birth do exist. Similarly, my husband's presence after his passing has shown me that life continues beyond our earthly existence. Our existence is a continuous cycle of profound lessons, soul connections, and transcendent development, moving from one plane of existence to the next.

Through my spiritual growth, I have come to realize that the decisions we make, the lives we touch, and the bonds we create truly matter. Beyond this earthly realm, we are more connected than we ever imagined. Each interaction and relationship we form contributes to our soul's journey, shaping us and those around us in ways that echo through time and space. This interconnectedness reminds us that our lives are part of a larger, eternal mosaic across multiple realms and universes, the Creator's perfect design of love, growth, and transformation. And we never truly lose those we love.

Looking back on these experiences, I realize that the universe is always speaking to us, if we are willing to listen. The dreams, the subtle signs, and the profound connections with our loved ones—these are all reminders that our souls are on a perpetual journey. Logan's guidance in my dreams, my son's vivid recollections of past lives, and the unending support from spirit guides have all reinforced the idea that our existence is far more expansive than we can comprehend.

The act of writing this memoir has been a transformative journey. It has helped me see the invisible threads that bind us to one another, transcending time and space. These threads are woven into a grand tapestry that tells the story of our souls—stories of love, loss, growth, and eternal connection.

As I close this chapter of my life and my memoir, I am filled with gratitude for the experiences and lessons that have shaped me. I did not anticipate that enlightenment would come as a result of completing this memoir, but I am forever thankful for the guidance and love from Logan, my spirit guides, and all the souls who have touched my life.

Thank you for joining me on this journey. May you find your own connections, your own lessons, and your own place in the everlasting canvas of existence.

ACKNOWLEDGMENTS

This memoir would not have been possible without the invaluable contributions of several individuals who supported me throughout this journey.

FIRST AND FOREMOST, I extend my deepest gratitude to my beloved husband, Logan, my twin flame. Your memories, unwavering love, and inspiration continue to guide me every day, reminding me of my strength and resilience. Thank you for instilling in me the profound gift of self-love, a beacon that shines even in the darkest moments. Your spirit emboldens me to pursue our dreams and adventures, carrying forward our shared vision. Until we're home again, our journey continues, and I cherish the countless stories we will share together.

I AM IMMENSELY BLESSED FOR MY FOUR CHILDREN, Caroline, Katelyn, Catheryn, and Kyle, who have been steadfast anchors during the most tumultuous chapters of my life. They are my lighthouse, continuously guiding me back to safe harbor with their love and propelling me forward toward my aspirations with their inspiring presence. Their unwavering support and joyful spirits have illuminated my path, urging me to chase dreams beyond my imagination and reinforcing the strength and resilience we embody as a family.

I EXPRESS HEARTFELT APPRECIATION to my spiritual coach, Kylie Yang, who has become a dear friend of mine through this process. Kylie's expertise and empathetic understanding have been instrumental in guiding me through the complex journey of spiritual development. Her insights not only facilitated my personal growth but also brought peace and alignment to my spiritual being amidst grief. Her unwavering support and intuitive guidance were pivotal during my most transformative phases. Furthermore, Kylie's spiritual counsel was crucial in helping me gain clarity and authenticity, enabling me to share my journey through the words that fill this book.

MY DEEPEST GRATITUDE AND APPRECIATION, to God and my spirit guides, for always being the light in my darkness. Even when it was hard for me to see the light in myself, I saw and felt you, and you reflected that light back to me. Thank you for always being there for me throughout my life and for being a significant part of my emotional and spiritual growth.

TO MY BETA READERS, whose feedback and insights helped shape the narrative, I extend my heartfelt gratitude. Your constructive criticism and encouragement were instrumental in refining this work.

I AM DEEPLY GRATEFUL TO MY PROOFREADERS for their meticulous attention to detail and dedication to ensuring the accuracy and clarity of every word. Your commitment to excellence has elevated the quality of this memoir.

A SPECIAL THANK YOU GOES TO MY EDITORS for their expertise, guidance, and unwavering support. Your keen editorial eye and invaluable suggestions have transformed this manuscript into its best possible version.

Each of these remarkable individuals has left an indelible mark on both my life and the pages of this book, enriching my journey, and imbuing my writing with deeper meaning and purpose. Thank you for your light, love, and belief in my visions.

ABOUT THE AUTHOR

Stephanie C. Vang is a dynamic entrepreneur, author, and visionary based in Saint Paul, Minnesota. Armed with a solid background in Information Technology and Management, she founded and now presides over Initiate Concept Inc., a consultancy specializing in Management, Technology, Startups, E-commerce, Marketing, and Branding.

Stephanie's literary contributions are growing, with upcoming projects including the co-authored memoir, "This Soul Was Not Meant to Be Born Silent," and a compelling trilogy titled "Feng, Soul Assassin." Her writing style—raw, honest, and introspective—draws readers into profound emotional journeys of resilience, love, spirituality, and self-discovery.

A devoted mother of four, Stephanie is deeply involved in philanthropy. She founded the Hue Logan Foundation, named in honor of her late husband, which supports students in art, music, and fashion through grants and provides essential items like shoes and coats to disadvantaged children. **All proceeds from her memoir, "Where the End Begins," benefit the Hue Logan Foundation.**

As an ardent advocate for cultural preservation, Stephanie C. Vang continues to inspire and impact with her creativity, resilience, and unwavering commitment to making a positive difference in the world.

Upcoming Books

This Soul Was Not Born to be Silent
A Memoir
by Kylie Yang
with Stephanie C Vang
Release date: December 1, 2024

Generations of Grace
A Collection Memoir of Three Generations
By Daisy Thao-Bjork
with Stephanie C Vang
Release date: February 1, 2025

Feng: Soul Assassin
A Trilogy
By Stephanie C Vang
Release date: To be announced, 2025

Follow/bookmark us for latest information and release

https://www.windgardenbooks.com
Facebook: https://www.facebook.com/windgardenbooks
Instagram: https://www.instagram.com/windgardenbooks